D1283450

Critical Studies of Education

Volume 4

We live in an era where forms of education designed to win the consent of students, teachers, and the public to the inevitability of a neo-liberal, market-driven process of globalization are being developed around the world. In these hegemonic modes of pedagogy questions about issues of race, class, gender, sexuality, colonialism, religion, and other social dynamics are simply not asked. Indeed, questions about the social spaces where pedagogy takes place—in schools, media, corporate think tanks, etc.—are not raised. When these concerns are connected with queries such as the following, we begin to move into a serious study of pedagogy: What knowledge is of the most worth? Whose knowledge should be taught? What role does power play in the educational process? How are new media re-shaping as well as perpetuating what happens in education? How is knowledge produced in a corporatized politics of knowledge? What socio-political role do schools play in the twenty-first century? What is an educated person? What is intelligence? How important are socio-cultural contextual factors in shaping what goes on in education? Can schools be more than a tool of the new American (and its Western allies') twenty-first century empire? How do we educate well-informed, creative teachers? What roles should schools play in a democratic society? What roles should media play in a democratic society? Is education in a democratic society different than in a totalitarian society? What is a democratic society? How is globalization affecting education? How does our view of mind shape the way we think of education? How does affect and emotion shape the educational process? What are the forces that shape educational purpose in different societies? These, of course, are just a few examples of the questions that need to be asked in relation to our exploration of educational purpose. This series of books can help establish a renewed interest in such questions and their centrality in the larger study of education and the preparation of teachers and other educational professionals.

More information about this series at http://www.springer.com/series/13431

George J. Sefa Dei

Reframing Blackness and Black Solidarities through Anti-colonial and Decolonial Prisms

 Springer

George J. Sefa Dei
Ontario Institute for Studies in Education
University of Toronto
Toronto, ON, Canada

Critical Studies of Education
ISBN 978-3-319-53078-9   ISBN 978-3-319-53079-6   (eBook)
DOI 10.1007/978-3-319-53079-6

Library of Congress Control Number: 2017933840

Printed on acid-free paper

This Springer imprint is published by Springer Nature
The registered company is Springer International Publishing AG
The registered company address is: Gewerbestrasse 11, 6330 Cham, Switzerland

I dedicate this book to my close family who have been the intellectual pillar for my academic journey so far and any claims I make to knowledge.

Foreword

In my opinion George Sefa Dei is the leading antiracist educator of this era. There is no intellectual more capable of taking on the issue of re-theorizing Blackness in the context of contemporary society. I have known George Sefa Dei for nearly 30 years and know how skillfully he has walked the treacherous path of defining and nuancing the notions of Blackness and Whiteness. There is something amiss with discourses on race and racism that continue to use terminology that is mired in the denotations of patriarchy, hegemony, and inequality. Dei is the defiant scholar picking to pieces the debris that covers the issues of Blackness and Whiteness. Rescuing the language from the dichotomies of race-baiters and people haters takes more than changing the words; one must also re-think, that is, re-theorize the meaning of the words.

The trope of Blackness has been heavily laden with negations, but the reframing of Blackness seeks to arrest the negations and reset the idea of anti-Blackness in the arena of human relationships. One cannot begin the process of re-theorizing with an appreciation of the literature and actions in the field of race studies. Of course, Dei understands that knowledge requires understanding in order to seduce wisdom from our racial condition. I am convinced that anticolonial and decolonial are key dimensions of this re-theorizing as Dei explains in *Reframing Blackness and Black Solidarities through Anti-colonial and Decolonial Prisms.*

Given his keen observation of the modalities introduced by the Black Lives Matter Movement and the commodification of Blackness, Dei thrusts ideas of citizenship, Black becoming, post-Blackness, and authenticity as dimensions of *Reframing Blackness and Black Solidarities through Anti-colonial and Decolonial Prisms.*

Dei reminds me of the late eminent Senegalese scholar Cheikh Anta Diop who was once asked why he used the expression "Black African" since most people assumed that Africans have always been Black. Diop lifted himself up to his full six feet two frame and said to the questioner, "To say Black is a political as well as a historical fact." In a similar vein George Sefa Dei has taken on the idea that Blackness is itself a word that has meaning in the context of our social and cultural contexts as defined by the encounter with Europeans. Of course, what he is contending is that the "hypervisibility" of Whiteness blurs the social reality of modern Western societies. Indeed we are choked with "racialized dichotomies" that strangle the normal relations between humans distorting our ability to see clearly that we are truly in this together.

While Dei sees that much of the confusion and cloudiness that surrounds the terminology can be attributed to "colonial continuity" I am more apt to see that the notions of Blackness and Whiteness experienced in contemporary society may have had life during the era of Europeanization of international trade, especially with the concomitant systems and institutions of the West that had an impact on the way people viewed themselves. Whites assumed during the fifteenth through the nineteenth centuries that they were a different species than Blacks. Societies were victims of racial polarities or racial thinking even before the first European nations took colonies in Africa. The period of the enslavement of Africans, however, must be credited with being the laboratory of the most disdainful thinking about Blackness. Dei understands all of this and therefore writes his book-length essay as an African who is an antiracist scholar but also one who has been racialized because of his Black body. He admits that those of us who occupy these Black bodies are complicit "in the domination" of the Lands of the Native Peoples while living on the ancestral Turtle Island that was occupied for thousands of years prior to the transatlantic invasions. Of course, African complicity is not the same as that of the invaders who also forced Africans on this Land. Yet it is clear that transposing Blackness onto the multidimensional canvas of the American Land further dismembers our bodies and our sibling relationships with other people.

No wonder Dei appreciates the fact that our Black presence had been constantly under a European gaze. This is not an ancient but a current fact. In 2016, more than 20 years after the independence of South Africa from apartheid, one of the biggest stories in the newspapers in South Africa was the sacking of White administrators who had held onto the idea that Black girls, at the Pretoria Girl's School, had to "straighten" their hair so that it would not look like a bird's nest. These White teachers in South Africa were doomed and trapped by their imposition of Whiteness on the Black girls. With tears and cries of shame the South African students protested the school's rule against Black hairstyles after several of the girls had been asked to leave the school because of their natural styles. As Dei say, "our experiences can be invalidated, our knowledge base can be questioned." Yet the defeat of racial impertinence is necessary everywhere. However, Dei knows that the Black scholar or critic or writer will usually find more accommodation in the academy if he or she is a postcolonial scholar rather than an anticolonial scholar. I have always been an anticolonial educator because, while progress is being made, the vestiges of colonialism are still present in the institutions of the West.

How does Dei view the "Declarations of Whiteness" or the "politics of declarations" where Whites believe that just the mere fact of their declaration that something is bad should be considered good behavior? Bad practice is not made good just because the culprit makes an announcement that he has been engaging in racism. Why should we applaud an admission of bad practice after such a long reign of psychological and physical terror? Only through education can good people, those who seek the expansion of freedoms, de-colonize themselves and others. There is a political and social yearning for the demise of special gazes and other privileges usually associated with Whiteness; in a real sense only the re-theorizing of Blackness can bring this idea to life because it shapes the terminology for a new generation of students.

Dei is brilliant in isolating the encapsulating problems of Homi Bhabha's post-colonial theorizing about the questions of power, culture, and identity. This preoccupation with the "subjectivity of the interstitial space" needs to be tempered by discourses of structure, materiality, and politics. In fact, as Dei recognizes, the anti-essentialist critique of Bhabha ends up being itself essentialist. Dei understands that the anti-essentialist is "unable to escape" from what he wants to critique. Furthermore the ideas of hybridity, in-betweenness, and the liminal space are important in textuality, but they may trap us in a White supremacist context so that even the critic is a victim of the conceptual prison.

The postcolonial and feminist "standpoint" sounds awfully close to the Afrocentric "perspective," "location," and "place" although bell hooks and others have not admitted the origin of the concept. This is not Dei's battle and he does not need to take it on yet in the struggle to understand subjectivity, identity, and agency; the Afrocentrists are perhaps more in line with Dei's appreciation of the perspective of an energized Blackness.

Dei's work in *Reframing Blackness and Black Solidarities through Anti-colonial and Decolonial Prisms* narrates the future of what writers like hooks, Stuart Hall, and Bhabha started and what Dei himself has written about in many of his previous works. To be sure these are contributions but what is radically different in this volume is the re-theorization of Blackness as a way to reschedule the coins of racist regimes. Dei does not elide the significance of race because he is not simply a cultural critic but a historian of race and by virtue of what he knows an antiracist. There is no post-Blackness and post-racialism as claimed by some of the cultural critics. No wonder Dei is concerned about "infuriating subtleties" and "racelessness" as narratives of racial progress because he sees through the gesture of moving while standing still, that is, the impression of progress while we remain entrapped in the old regime's concepts of Whiteness and Blackness.

George Sefa Dei is a natural king by heritage, Nana Adusei Sefa Tweneboah I, and an accomplished scholar by training and with the publication of *Reframing Blackness and Black Solidarities through Anti-colonial and Decolonial Prisms* he has demonstrated why he is accepted among his peers as one of the clearest thinking intellectuals of this generation.

Temple University   Molefi Kete Asante
Philadelphia, PA, USA

Acknowledgements

This book has been a product of my long years teaching, researching, and writing on Black and minority education and community politics. I decided to synthesize my ideas into a major collection on the challenges and possibilities of living, loving, and understanding Black and Blackness in contemporary times. I have never been someone to shy away from insistence on my Black identity and Blackness. I have often queried why a Black body would deem it necessary to emphasize that Black identity has little bearing and relevance to their social positionality and politics. For example, those colleagues who would insist that they be read as a generic "Scholar" period and not a "Black Scholar," or those who want to appease White worries by going to lengths to show their Black identity is not a profound identity for them in terms of guiding their frames of references and social reactions, etc. What are we running away from when we resist our Black identity? To make reference to essentialist Black identity as the source of discomfort does not cut it for me. There is no essential Black identity. There is, however, a Black identity that Black bodies can claim.

So many people have helped in the intellectual journey of speaking, writing, and politicking on my Black subjectivity and identity. The initial ideas on a piece on "Reframing Blackness through Anti-Colonial Prism" were presented in the UHURU Collective, a study group of graduate students working with me at the Ontario Institute for Studies in Education at the University of Toronto (OISE/UT). I thank the feedback received from the audience that helped generate further thoughts to a full-length manuscript. Along my academic journey I have been fortunate and privileged to work with a number of scholars, students, parents, and community workers who have helped shape my thoughts on Black scholarship and the imperatives of Black education. I want to thank Jacqui Jesso, Dr. Francisco Villegas, Fritz Pinto, Kate Patridge, Tracy Thomas, Aman Sium, Eric Ritskes, Chizoba Imoka, Dr. Isaac Darko, Suleyman Demi, Yumiko Kawano, Dr. Marlon Simmons, Dr. Mairi McDermott, Dionisio Nyaga, Anila Zainub, Shukri Hilowle, Jacqueline Scott, Andrea Vásquez Jiménez, Leroy King, Jacqui Spencer, Rogene Reid, Lwanga Musisi, Osholene Oshobugie, Elisha Lim, Charis Newton, Rick Sin, Pedro Moran Bonilla, Ximena Martinez, and Cristina Jaimungal of the University of Toronto and the Ontario Institute for Studies in Education [OISE] for providing additional feedback during various stages and sections of the manuscript. Such assistance consisted of reading, editing, and commenting on drafts of this paper. Jacqui Jesso and Dr. Francisco Villegas pushed me to turn what was intended to be a major paper for a refereed journal publication into a book and I am indeed thankful. But more significantly the research assistantship of Yousra Hassan Gendil and graduate assistantship of Brandy Jensen and Janelle Brady of the Department of Social Justice Education, OISE, University of Toronto, have been instrumental in bringing this book to fruition. These students went beyond the call of duty and worked tirelessly to strengthen the ideas and the literature to make this book the read as you enjoy it. I am also grateful for the participants in my OISE graduate courses: SJE 1925: "Indigenous Knowledges and Decolonization: Pedagogical Implications"; SJE 3914H; "Anti-Colonial Thought and Pedagogical Challenges," SJE: "Franz Fanon and Education: Pedagogical Possibilities"; and SJE1921Y: "Principles of Anti-Racism Education" for the learning and knowledge received in our class interactions.

Special thanks go to my close family members: our mother, Madam Agnes Koduah [Obaapanin Afia Donkor] of blessed memory, Nana Adwo Oku-Ampofo, Regina Ampadu Dei, Prince Yeboah Dei, Lashanda Durowaah Dei, Yashita Maame Agyarkoa Dei, Ernest Dei, Helena Dei, and Joyce Dei.

Finally, many scholars, researchers, students and communities have informed many of the ideas I speak about in this book. I remain grateful to them. While that is the case, I take full responsibility for the contents of this work, both for its strength and failings.

Contents

About the Author

George Jerry Sefa Dei Ghanaian-born George Jerry Sefa Dei is a renowned educator, researcher, and writer who is considered by many as one of Canada's foremost scholars on race and antiracism studies. He is a widely sought after academic, researcher, and community worker whose professional and academic work has led to many Canadian and international speaking engagements throughout the USA, Europe, and Africa. Currently, he is Professor of Social Justice Education and Director of the Centre for Integrative Anti-Racism Studies at the Ontario Institute for Studies in Education of the University of Toronto (OISE/UT). In both 2015 and 2016, Prof. Dei was awarded a Fellowship through the Carnegie African Diaspora Fellowship Program (CADFP), a prestigious top scholar program for educational projects at African higher education institutions. In the summer of each year of the award, Prof. Dei has been hosted by the Institute for Educational Research and Innovation Studies, University of Education, Winneba, Ghana. The Fellowship has allowed Prof. Dei to "give back" by assisting with graduate student mentorship, joint faculty research and publications, as well as the development of an African curriculum textbook. In addition to this Fellowship, Prof. Dei received the honorary title of "*Professor Extraordinaire*" from the School of Education, University of South Africa (UNISA) in August of 2012.

Professor Dei's teaching and research interests are in the areas of antiracism, minority schooling, international development, anticolonial thought, and indigenous knowledge systems. He has twenty-eight (28) books and over one hundred and sixty (160) refereed journal articles and book chapters to his credit. His recent books include *Teaching Africa: Towards Transgressive Pedagogy*, *Learning to Succeed: Improving Educational Achievement for All*, and an international reader titled *Indigenous Philosophies and Critical Education*. In 2012 he co-edited *Contemporary Issues in African Science Education* with Professor Asabere-Ameyaw, Vice Chancellor for the University of Education, Winneba, Ghana. In 2013, Professor Dei released *New Perspectives on Africentric Schooling in Canada*, Canadian Scholars Press, [co-authored with Arlo Kempf] and *Contemporary Issues in the Sociology of Race and Ethnicity* [New York, Peter Lang, co-edited with Meredith Lordan]. In 2014 he released three books (a) *Politics of Critical Anti-Racism*

Education: In Search of Strategies for Transformative Learning (co-edited with Mairi McDermott), New York, Springer Publishers; (b) *African Indigenous Knowledges and the Disciplines* (co-edited with Professor Glorai Emeagwali), New York, Springer Publishers; and (c) *Emerging Perspectives on African Development: Speaking Differently* (co-edited with Professor Paul Adjei), New York, Peter Lang.

Currently, Prof. Dei co-chairs the African Community Networking Committee in Toronto, an organization dedicated to the economic and social enhancement of African peoples in Canada. He was the first President of the Ghanaian-Canadian Union, an umbrella group of Ghanaian-Canadian cultural, ethnic, and religious associations in Ontario. He is on the Board of the AfroGlobal TV, and the National Scholarship Fund (formerly Harry Jerome Awards) of the Black Business and Professionals Association (BBPA). Prof. Dei was a member of the City of Toronto Mayor's Roundtable on Children, Youth and Education and also the Postsecondary Education Advisory Committee on First Generation Students. He is a Distinguished Fellow of the Molefi Kete Asante Institute, based in Philadelphia, USA, to advance the cause of Global African development. Prof. Dei has been a major proponent and a pioneering voice in the establishment of Black-focused/African-centered schools in Canada.

Prof. Dei is the recipient of many awards. He was a co-recipient of the 2016 Whitworth Award for Educational Research from the Canadian Education Association (CEA), awarded to the Canadian scholar whose research scholarship has helped shape Canadian national educational policy and practice. He received the 2014 Distinguished Teaching Award at OISE, University of Toronto, for excellence in teaching over the years. He is also the 2014 recipient of the Ludwik and Estelle Jus Memorial Human Rights Prize from the University of Toronto for his internationally recognized work on antiracism and social justice. His additional awards include the "Race, Gender, and Class Project Academic Award" in 2002 in New Orleans, the African-Canadian Outstanding Achievement in Education from *Pride Magazine* in Toronto in 2003, and the City of Toronto's William P. Hubbard Award for Race Relations 2003. He is also the 2006 recipient of the Planet Africa Renaissance Award for his professional achievements in the field of African education, antiracism, and youth and the 2007 Canadian Alliance of Black Educators Award for Excellence in Education and Community Development.

In June of 2007, Prof. Dei was installed as a traditional chief in Ghana, specifically, as the Gyaasehene of the town of Asokore, Koforidua, in the New Juaben Traditional Area of Ghana. His stool name is Nana Adusei Sefa Tweneboah.

Chapter 1
[Re]framing Blackness and Black Solidarities Through Anti-Colonial and Decolonial Prisms: An Introduction

Abstract I begin this chapter by positioning the self, personal, and political as intertwined. I write about Blackness from a complicated socio-political location as an African-born scholar, researcher, and community worker living on Indigenous people's Lands in North America. Indigenous people of this Land call this place Turtle Island. I come from a colonized African community struggling to reclaim our Indigeneity. I strategically evoke Blackness and Black subjectivity as part of an invention of an Africanness in Diasporic context to gesture to the particular intellectual politics I wish to pursue in this book. I share the overall learning objective to [re]conceptualize Blackness in a complicated and inclusive ways while acknowledging the many dimensions of Blackness. In my work, I attempt to offer a way of re-reading Blackness differently. I have decided to focus on a couple of interrelated issues to complement the extensive work of Blackness: (a) to include Africa[ness], as a strategic re-invention of Africanness in diasporic contexts; (b) to reclaim my African Indigeneity in global knowledge production as a way of knowing that speaks to history, culture, identity, African spiritual ontologies, and a politics of the African/Black body; (c) to undertake a conscious intellectual shift in reading Black/African diasporic presence on Indigenous peoples Lands from a discursive prism of "colonial settlerhood" and discourses of "complicities in our claims of citizenship" to one of "collective implications" and "differential responsibilities" so as to foster decolonization and, particularly, decolonial solidarities among colonized, oppressed, and Indigenous peoples; (d) to highlight questions of Black/African development and education and the responsibilities of the Black/African learner in the [Western] academy; and (e) to re-read Black[ness] in ways that speaks to the continental African subject who may decry the color descriptor of Black[ness]. Concretely, I see my work as part of decolonial and anti-colonial projects seeking to subvert imperial and colonial knowledges for action-oriented knowledging, grounded in African Indigenousness and the pursuit of politics, subject[ive] and resistance. Colonial and colonizing relations are ongoing [never-ended]. Rather than seeing

© Springer International Publishing AG 2017   1
G.J.S. Dei, *Reframing Blackness and Black Solidarities through Anti-colonial and Decolonial Prisms*, Critical Studies of Education 4,
DOI 10.1007/978-3-319-53079-6_1

them as "foreign or alien," they are continually "imposed and dominating" (see Dei 2000; Dei and Asgharzadeh 2001).

I begin this chapter by positioning the self, personal, and political as intertwined. I write about Blackness from a complicated socio-political location as an African-born scholar, researcher, and community worker living on Indigenous people's Lands in North America. Indigenous people of this Land call this place Turtle Island. I come from a colonized African community struggling to reclaim our Indigeneity. I strategically evoke Blackness and Black subjectivity as part of an invention of an Africanness in a Diasporic context to gesture to the particular intellectual politics I wish to pursue in this book. I share the overall learning objective to [re]conceptualize Blackness in complicated and inclusive ways while acknowledging the many dimensions of Blackness. In my work, I attempt to offer a way of re-reading Blackness differently. I have decided to focus on a couple of interrelated issues to complement the extensive work of Blackness: (a) to include Africa[ness], as a strategic re-invention of Africanness in diasporic contexts; (b) to reclaim my African Indigeneity in global knowledge production as a way of knowing that speaks to history, culture, identity, African spiritual ontologies, and a politics of the African/Black body; (c) to undertake a conscious intellectual shift in reading Black/African diasporic presence on Indigenous peoples Lands from a discursive prism of "colonial settlerhood" and discourses of "complicities in our claims of citizenship" to one of "collective implications" and "differential responsibilities" so as to foster decolonization and, particularly, decolonial solidarities among colonized, oppressed, and Indigenous peoples; (d) to highlight questions of Black/African development and education and the responsibilities of the Black/African learner in the [Western] academy; and (e) to re-read Black[ness] in ways that speaks to the continental African subject who may decry the color descriptor of Black[ness]. Concretely, I see my work as part of decolonial and anti-colonial projects seeking to subvert imperial and colonial knowledges for action-oriented knowledging, grounded in African Indigenousness and the pursuit of politics, subject[ive] and resistance. Colonial and colonizing relations are ongoing [never-ended]. Rather than seeing them as "foreign or alien," they are continually "imposed and dominating" (see Dei 2000; Dei and Asgharzadeh 2001).

I bring an intellectual politics to this work insisting on a non-hegemonic Blackness. It is a politics that takes into account nuances and complexities of the Black and African experience and the value of multiple knowings such that we do not present a singular way of seeing and defining Blackness. In complexifying what Blackness means in Canada, for example, I call for unpacking who and what is currently included/excluded in conversations on Blackness. I want us to reimagine "new geographies of knowledge" (see also Raghuram 2017), the varied and intersecting ontologies and epistemologies that inform Blackness and Africanness. We cannot uncritically substitute 'African' for 'Black' and vice versa without knowing what it entails. We need scholarship about Blackness equally grounded in diverse African peoples' learning experiences, research methodologies and ways of knowledge generation (see also Lebakeng 2010; p. 28, citing Teffo, 2002). We must search for new analytical systems for understanding the Black and African experience and our human condition in the global space of transnational mobility. I am emboldened to situate African Indigeneity in these discussions. Claiming African Indigeneity is resistance to "amputate" history, culture, and identity as the African body. African Indigeneity offers a way of knowing that speaks to history, culture, identity, spiritual ontologies, and politics of the African/Black body; and asserting Land, cultural, spiritual, and psychic memories as "living forces" we learn from. African ancestral cultural knowledges about Black[ness] symbolize beauty, purity, happiness, anger and resistance; a subversion of racist Euro-constructions of Blackness as deviancy, criminality, and dis-normal. Engaging African-centered thought becomes an intellectual subversion. I am reframing Blackness within African conceptions, epistemes and philosophies of an interdependent and interrelated universe (cosmology), social reality as "fundamentally spirit and spiritual with material manifestations" (ontology), and values systems that prioritize interpersonal relations, as well as collective, communal and community gain (axiology) [see Carroll 2014, p. 259]. I hope my readers will see this book as an intellectually rewarding and stimulating work from the position of an African scholar writing and speaking differently on Blackness, and also, offering an authentic, genuine response to Black and Indigenous peoples' solidarity. I want to be part of an audience or an epistemic community that can meaningfully engage in a kind of solidarity building and collective organizing that transforms not just ourselves but our varied communities.

The truth about Blackness is that it is consequential, complex, contested, and yet affirming. Blackness to me is not an objectified moment in time and space. There is a clear resurgence in Black/African identity in the ongoing colonial violence on our bodies. As a Black/African scholar, I bring a conception of "authentic" to my understanding of Blackness. This stems from an ontological lived experience grounded in decolonial and anti-colonial epistemologies. There is no measure of authenticity. But, there is a strategic deployment of the term to challenge the Western liberal prism steeped in the Euro-modernist processes of the production, interrogation, validation, and dissemination of "valid" knowledge. As Black learners, we must bring degrees of mindfulness to disrupt dominant academic spaces through our knowledge politics. Part of the task of transforming our academies is to take the conceptual understanding of Blackness to new and different levels as critical discursive encounters. Consequently, I see the claiming of Blackness and African [inter] subjectivity as an exercise of academic and political decolonization. Black and African bodies must refuse to think of ourselves as deficient or deficit under the gaze of modernity. We must critique "development" as benevolence rendered to people craving social improvement. When I say "we," I refer to all who read this book, and also, in particular to scholars and learners of Black and Africa Studies and scholarship. A critical scholarship on Blackness is, and must be, about anti-racist practice, and particularly resistance to anti-Black racism, as well as, the pursuit of decolonial and anti-colonial praxis. There are implications for the study of Blackness as "living knowledge" about ourselves, our histories, cultures, and identities. In a social context where Blackness is consumed daily [and yet many of these same consumers are unprepared to acknowledge the pain that comes with Blackness], academic theorizing about Blackness must also be made practical and meaningful for communities.

It is important for me to reiterate my vantage point as a Black/African scholar since Black subjectivity and Indigeneity in Diasporic contexts and spaces are political ventures. I expect and respect other scholars who may flesh out different and competing understandings from their own different stand points. My academic work and politics are heavily intertwined with my experience as a Black, African, and Indigenous scholar. Consequently, I see no need for such separation. This is a luxury that Black scholars in the Western academy cannot afford. I do not and will not claim to be speaking from a disinterested stance and position. As academics and researchers, our social locations affect the knowledge production process and our interactions and dialogues with those who co-produce knowledge with us. That production of knowledge is political. We all bring multiple and different understandings to the social world from our different subject positions and identities. We are never innocent nor neutral in producing knowledge—contrary to claims of objectivity. We bring our own vested interest when producing knowledge. Many times, the supposed objectivity of others, when closely scrutinized elucidates subjectivity. We are all informed by our histories, experiences, locations, and situatededness (Hall 1996, p. 447; see also 1991). In fact, our myriad and complex identities offer a complicated re-readings of power and privilege that is unattainable, contingent and temporal through arguments which claim objectivity and closed off difference. Knowledge and power are so intertwined. Questions of who has power to determine what is true, valid, rational, and scientific become a matter of urgency. To claim an identity is to know from that space of identification and social location. Through subjectivity, we are implicated in getting to know that we are never neutral in knowledge production and dissemination. While race, class, gender, sexuality, [dis]ability, and other markers of difference may demarcate us, the truth is that these identities (as relations of power) also imply asymmetrical power relations and dynamics. While we may find ourselves in shifting positionalities and realities, the power and privilege we hold does not necessarily decrease or vanish. Concomitantly, for some of us, privileges of class, gender, and sexuality may not always diminish the position of racial subordination that we occupy in the White Euro-colonial context. This does not mean that we are powerless or without agency. We resist continually and we become subjects and agents of our own history. But we must recognize the power of the colonial dominant.

The dominant group (while grudgingly acknowledging privileges) consistently speak of themselves as minorities in certain colonial contexts in relation to Indigenous populations (e.g., White Europeans in Africa). But it should be asked: "Are Whites in such colonial contexts 'colonial dominant', or can they aptly be referred to as 'Others' with access and privilege?" To be dominant is to be in a position of unearned power, authority, and influence. The position is supported by institutional structures to maintain and reproduce privilege and benefits of entitlements. Those structures are them [Whites] and they are the structure. The structures are also, a creation of the dominant. The structures are born out of dominance; and as such these structures cannot defy their own creator. The structure settled when their master enters but they become hysterical when the "Other" steps in them. It is not a question of numerical strength as any critical scholar with an understanding of power relations in White dominated societies will attest.

In global politics of race, power, and knowledge production, Whites everywhere, irrespective of demarcations of class, gender, sexuality, [dis]ability, etc., cannot be and are not "Othered" in ways that racialized minorities are. The process of "Othering" is a relation of power. For one to be Othered then the power to define space and bodies must be with somebody else. For our case the definer of spaces and bodies has historically been taken up by White people. It is not just about being different. It is about who has power to construct the "Other" as different and act accordingly to deny access to valued good and services of society (Dei 2008).

To clarify the power of "racial Othering," Goldberg (1993) discusses how the racial governance of modern states is informed by racialized knowledge production. Building on Edward Said's work *Orientalism* (1978), Goldberg indicates that naming the racial Other is essentially the Other (p. 150). No racial subject exists behind or beyond the invention of racialized knowledge—knowledge in the Other's name. It is production of the racial Other as stagnated for easy ordering and regulation. Practices of naming and knowledge production deny autonomy and naturalize the extension of power and authority over those who are named and invented. Mbembe (2001) also identifies this power dynamic as a central component of modernity. The principle of free will is embraced for the Western subject, which includes the right to levy critique and to validate only that which seems justified. The individual has the capacity to self-refer and to reject any absolutist claims.

Mbembe (2001) and Silva (2007) show that the racial subject, in contrast, cannot and do not speak for themselves. They are denied to represent themselves. It is a process of objectification meant to deny the racial Other the power to know themselves. For example, Jensen (2016) shows how Western-based institutions and governing bodies (such as the United Nations [UN], Western universities, the Canadian government, etc.) policies implicitly or explicitly target racialized or Indigenous groups where subjects are given voice only to validate statements and declaration, if they are given voice at all. Unlike the allegedly rational programs set out by Western-dominated institutions, human action by racialized bodies is regarded as stupid, irrational, or arbitrary, "always proceeding from anything but rational calculation" (Mbembe 2001, p. 8). Programs for racialized or Indigenous groups, or for Global South nations, are therefore deemed necessary and justified [or rationalized] to save them from their underdevelopment. A connection between rationalism, modernity, and the West is deemed as constitutive in this exercise of colonial power. In effect, then, racialization is much more than "Othering" human subjects. So, whether "Othered" or not in different contexts, White bodies maintain power and privilege which cannot be taken lightly. The insight of Silva (2007) applies, as she notes that the failure to conceive the racial as a productive signifier "limits the understanding of how [it governs] the contemporary global configuration, instituting modern privileged and subaltern subjects" (p. 7).

I have long maintained that groups can be racialized for different purposes (Dei 2008). Whites can be racialized when claiming power and privilege. As for Black, Indigenous bodies and racial minorities, our racialized subjectivities are meant for punishment. But it is also important to ask who has the power to racialize the "Other" as different and inferior? Clearly, racialization works differently on different bodies and not often with the same result, given that the "gaze" and contexts are continually shifting. Recent work on Whites in colonial and colonizing contexts show that rather than Whites being simply privileged through normativity and invisibility, they are equally privileged through non-normativity and hypervisibility (see Anonymous 2014). To be White [and to be such in the colonial context] is "an affirmative process of both an imagined (perceived/fantasized) and real identity and social position" (Anonymous 2014). However, the shifting nature of our identities implies bodies are always read differently and contextually, albeit with similar reactions and responses. For example, the experiences of dominant groups working in overseas/international contexts reveal the often ambivalent, contradictory, and shifting perspectives of international development from the viewpoint of development workers themselves. When doing "development" work, there is tension between the fantasy and reality of Whiteness and its association with wealth, mobility, and privilege (see Anonymous 2014). It is the hypervisibility of White[ness] that opens doors for Whites to do such work in overseas countries. A White body can easily move and command its acceptance in spaces. Spaces reorganize themselves to accept the entrance of the White body; historically and conceptually seen as the savior or liberator. Such work can be a privileged position, given all the benefits and the perception of altruism or "doing good." White bodies hang on to their identification with power and privilege, making them complicit even as they critique the "inferiority complex" demonstrated by some within the colonized population who would accord privilege and respect to Whites and allege the superior position of Whiteness. In the colonial encounter, the colonizer not only plays and preys on these perceptions, but cultivates it. Consequentially, it is important for us to see racialized dichotomies inherent in development work as a "colonial continuity"; as "Three World Theory" discursively constructed for developing states and populations and deem them underdeveloped, historically behind, and unable to fully self-govern—regardless of formal sovereignty (Escobar 1995; Goldberg 2006). It is also important to note that while the West seeks to "develop" its legally equal yet developmentally unequal racial Others, it also warehouses and excludes undesirable populations through racial definitions (Jensen 2016). Development becomes a civilizational moment of defining spaces and bodies as inherently incapable of entering progress. The practice of development reveals the way in which the "us" versus "them" divide sustains a false sense of Western/Northern superiority and the inferiority of the Global South. Such dichotomies of exaltation and privileging of Whiteness and the West while denigrating and attempting to control racialized Indigenous peoples in the Global South need to be disrupted.

I see myself as an anti-racist educator and community worker who has been involved in helping to develop Canada's anti-racist scholarship for many years. During these years, encouragement and deep connections were made and continue to be made between myself and many scholars and practitioners. These relationships reach across colonial moments with their unique cocktail of colonial logic(s) and geopolitical tensions. These years allowed us to offer each other the intimacies of our oppressions, our losses, our sufferings, our rage, and our healing. They also offered the intimacies of trust through sharing our experiences and our knowledges. Our alliances, our differences, and the honesty and risk of our conflicts exposed the ethics of our different works; clarified and shifted our gaze, despite resistance; and slowed us down when we moved in ways that overlooked or undermined each other's work along the way. This furthered our hope for one another and for all racialized communities in the work of surfacing and ending colonialism(s) in different ways. Indeed, at times our differences came as a surprise and were experienced as sudden and overwhelming blows. These blows created space between theorists, activists and communities and many silences came to follow and fill them. It is these spaces and these silences that we are invited to take a step into leveraging and advancing our antiracist and decolonizing work into new collaborative ways. In this work, I provide you with an account of one of these spaces; these blows. I return to Fanon's work as I recall his warning and his invitation regarding decolonizing efforts. In his classic text "*Wretched of the Earth*" he argues that, "Challenging the colonial world is not a rational confrontation of viewpoints. It is not a discourse on the universal, but the impassioned claim of the colonized that they are different" (Fanon 1963, p. 6). What I offer in this work is an impassioned claim that I am different, that antiracist scholarship is different, that Black/Africans living on Turtle Island (generally referred to as North America) are different. But this difference is not about our singularities, rather it is from a position of shared histories and experiences that are different, and contingent.

To the communities, activists and practitioners of antiracist and decolonizing scholarship, I deeply appreciate and respect the unique articulations and vantage points that I have been offered during times of collective struggles. Our different standpoints deepen our understandings of the profound reach of colonialism(s) and the malevolence of its scaffolding. Colonialism(s) impact us coincidentally and differently, although always violently, at varying degrees of direct intensity. This violence, so constant, can become difficult to name and to synthesize. This violence is wrapped and presented to one or a few racialized communities as gifts or special entry points. Simultaneously, or prior to, or soon after delivery, such "gifts" bring violent, often deadly, blows, to another racialized community or communities. Sometimes the measured, repeated, and too often, deadly blow is delivered to a community through a single body, repeatedly. For example: a hanging, a deadly police shooting, a rape, a failed interview, a sabotaged vote, or a missing and murdered woman. These blows are meant to remind us of our place and history. They are a way of creating us as different. Those blows narrate a story, a reminder of non-belongingness of the Other. Clearly, we rely on each other to amplify the tenor of our resistance to the violence(s) of colonialism(s), the denied psychopathology of colonial rage, and the conceit of its successes, achievements, entitlements, and its stolen endowments, Land and space. Should this work or our support for one another in this work be challenged or weakened? I ask that we stop and look closely at what is happening and invite the knowledge of our different colonial lenses. I ask this so that we can intelligently unpack, disarm, learn and then resist and overcome this weakness that opportunistically seeks out and thrives in moments of division. Our success depends on gathering up the strengths of our multiple analytic standpoints and practices as well as the strength and willingness for us to state and hear clearly what these different standpoints offer and what they reveal to us about our different works. This is essential to the ongoing development of knowledge and practice paths that galvanize us collectively and point us toward coordinates that help to surface and end colonialism(s) and be free of its rage.

This book attempts to offer an analytical standpoint and coordinates that can galvanize us collectively. I offer this in the shadow of an alarming critique. This critique weakens antiracist scholarship and practice, and also weakens Black/African peoples living on Turtle Island in a profound way. We must write to offer an antidote to the long established critique of how we as racialized, immigrant, African Indigenous bodies have been complicit in the domination of Indigenous peoples of the Land on which I call "home." The discussion continues to proceed as though we are here simply to partake in the sharing of colonial goods. The fact of our labor and contributions to this Land needs to be recognized. I am also forced to be here due to the colonial geo-politics of dispossession of our rights to Land, material existence, hopes, dreams, and aspirations of other Indigenous peoples; my own people. In the political economy of globalization, the clear majority of racialized migrants from Global South nations are involuntary migrants—forced to leave their own Land and home. Land appropriation is not living on someone's Land in perpetual strangeness. Of course, this development in no way absolves us of implications and responsibilities.

International development practice in Africa offers poignant lessons. Despite the purported efforts of the UN, World Bank, and International Monetary Fund (IMF) to alleviate poverty disparities in resources and living conditions between the Global North and Global South, poverty continue to widen and compel our migration to Canada and other northern locations. Recent data show that the number of billionaires is growing in both the Global North and South, along with inequality (Broad and Cavanaugh 2013; Danaher 2001). At its most extreme, poverty in the Global South is perpetuating what Mbembe (2003) terms death worlds, "new and unique forms of social existence in which vast populations are subjected to conditions of life conferring upon them the status of living dead" (p. 40). Concomitantly, in the 2008 documentary film *The End of Poverty?*, political scientist Susan George calculates that the Global South funds the Global North at a rate of $200 billion annually (Portello and Diaz 2008). So, while racial inequities are increasing within advanced liberal democracies of the Global North and impacting Black/African and Indigenous peoples in Canada, racially shaped inequities and colonial forms of rule continue to widen the gaps in resources and living conditions between Global North and Global South nations as well (Khan 2015). As will be explored in more detail later, these inequities are sustained and intensified despite, and perhaps through, formal race equality claims advanced through political and legal discourse within Canada and the UN. While Indigenous peoples in Canada and African/Black residents in Canada both suffer from racism and colonialism, it is also clear the migration from the Global South often takes place under coerced conditions.

More detailed background on the contemporary geo-politics of dispossession can be seen in how Global South debt, development, and poverty function within a self-sustaining logic of neo-liberal governance by the West (Jensen 2016). Neoliberal governance carried out by the UN, IMF, and World Bank exalts market relations in part by building upon and reinforcing imperial hierarchy of nation-states that can be traced to European colonialism and Western practices of empire (Stasiulus and Bakan 2005). The interconnected relationship of debt, development, and poverty in global governance becomes clear through policies like Structural Adjustment Programmes (SAPs). The UN Development Programme cites Global South debt as a barrier to development and consequently to poverty alleviation. Yet, Global South debt is constructed through the logics of capitalism and colonialism. For example, it is noted that the region of sub-Saharan Africa pays $25,000 per minute to the North, for debt incurred by these same collectors during colonial rule. Global South debt is used to justify SAPs. Despite claims that SAPs are necessary to address macroeconomic issues that impede Global South development, they are overwhelmingly shown to deepen poverty and reinforce the racial and colonial systems formally countered by the UN (Stasiulus and Bakan 2005).

The issue and magnitude of Global South debt, when considered in relation to poverty alleviation as the center of contemporary UN Development, may seem ironic. Requiring debt payments from states that are also the targets of UN Development Programmes seems counter-intuitive. Debt discourse posits an underlying rationale that developing nations are unable or less able to self-govern, and that indebted nations must be part of (or keep up with) the "modern" global economy. In the context of "raceless" UN policies, such as human rights and declarations to eliminate racism and colonialism is counterintuitive considering that SAPs function as an authoritative and paternalistic measure that defines states as governable. The constructed need for financial and governing assistance elides how neoliberal policies advanced through the UN, IMF, and World Bank create and reify vastly unequal conditions between the Global North and South. Global capitalism requires such disparities (Harvey 2003; Toussaint 2008) between the north and south for it to flourish. It erases how the very notion of "developing" nations and their need for governance is constructed largely by Western values carried out through global governance. While construed as necessary to address macroeconomic issues that impede Global South development, SAPs deepen poverty and reinforce the racial and colonial systems formally countered by the UN. SAPs replicate colonial and racial hierarchies even as the IMF and World Bank continue to sanitize the policy.

The IMF and World Bank are Western-dominated institutions indicted by some as neo-colonial structures. Since their inception, race remains external to the institutional discourses of the IMF and World Bank. The racelessness of UN discourse and policy further distances race as unrelated to the operations of these ostensibly objective and rational institutions (Jensen 2016). Goldberg (2009) notes how race has been explicitly removed from the register of institutions, shifting to micro-level relational aspects of everyday life on one hand, and to macro-level political strategizing of global interests on the other. Racism, when acknowledged, is individualized view of a socially dislocated person, rather than institutionalized inequality. This erasure of race in institutional policy and language occludes how Eurocentrism, as a paradigm, underwrites IMF and World Bank policies by creating institutional norms that structurally, and enduringly, position Global South populations and states in relations of inequality (Mongia 2007). SAPs are a prime example of how this relation of inequality impels many of us from the Global South to migrate to Canada and other Northern nations.

According to the IMF and World Bank, SAPs aim to create long-term or accelerated economic growth in loan-receiving countries by restructuring the economy and reducing government intervention. In a depoliticized discourse, SAPs simply operate according to a business-based model of governance. It is a kind of governmentality meant to rationalize state operations. The IMF and WB compel developing nations to agree to Structural Adjustment Programmes in a way that reflects and reinforces this nations' subordinate status within the imperialistic hierarchy of nation-states (Stasiulus and Bakan 2005). Developing nations that are subjected to structural adjustment typically have no financing options other than the IMF or World Bank. Structural adjustment is a condition of their loan, without which these nations are cut off from resources that can allow them to function internally and within the global economy. Less economic and political power means that developing nations must agree to loan terms set out by the IMF and World Bank despite their deleterious effects (Touissant 2008). Regardless of this coercion and egregious loan conditions, failure to pay back the loans renders such nations to financial deprivation from any other major financial institutions. Thus, when developing nations are subjected to Structural Adjustment Programmes, it means that they are under the regulation of the Breton Woods institutions. To obtain a loan, the IMF or World Bank largely determines and sets the parameters of their nation's inclusion in the global economy (Danaher 2001).

Despite the discursive construction of Structural Adjustment loans as consensual contracts; agreement to the terms of IMF and World Bank adjustment loans does not reflect consent. Although presented as neutral in liberal forms of governance, the term "consent" implies an unequal power relations (Brown 2003). Consent functions as an internal element of "debt" as a global governing technology by Northern nations. This is made possible by denying the power relations that both allow and are reinforced by SAPs. Likewise, the majority of Global South populations live under conditions that allow SAPs, and those experiencing their brutal effects, have little to no choice to migrate. Importantly, this situation of compelled migration is not limited to the outcomes of SAPs. Free trade agreements, the global currency system, Global South debt without the imposition of SAPs, and the Highly Indebted Poor Countries (HIPC) Initiative demonstrate how neo-colonial and neo-imperial forms of governance continue to dispossess and marginalize people in the Global South who are then forced to migrate in search of better living conditions or even for basic survival.

As a Black/African scholar, I am in constant search for intellectual peace. This is because my skin as a Black scholar is under the constant and continuous scrutiny from the Eurocentric gaze. My knowledge can easily be weighed, questioned, and rendered suspect. Based on my skin color, I am often seen simply as an "emotional" being. I am constantly being urged to be a 'rationale' thinker without questioning the basis of such Western logics of rationality. Nothing can shake me out of my intellectual confidence as a Black scholar in the Western academy. I may not be many things, but I am damn sure I have brains. Intellectual fool hardiness is not my cup of tea. But the academy is not a place for the Black scholar. Our presence is under a constant gaze, as subsequent discussions will show. Our experiences can be invalidated, our knowledge-base questioned; and when we are critical, our scholarship is not only suspect and labeled as "anti-intellectual," we are often seen as angry intellectuals without a cause. A Black scholar may make some inroads in the academy as a post-colonial rather than anti-colonial critic. But to achieve success it is hard work and often comes with an emotional, spiritual and physical lost of oneself. Many times, when I see Black and racialized bodies congregate in our academy, I often quip—"Wow, our universities are in decline these days, how did all these bodies get in? Surely they must be lowering standards"! You see I may joke or laugh about this, but I am dead serious. This is a dominant way of thinking that sees excellence as the prerogative of a group. The idea or prism of the "school to prison pipeline" follows from such thinking. In such cases Blackness can be subjected to and defined by an intellectual system of control. Black radical thinkers may be welcome with their anti-colonial politics but it sure scares the hell out of some people in the academy. Those who would insist they are the spokesperson for the Black race are not listened to, yet in the eyes of many we are that spokesperson. We are in the academy and our institutions need the few privileged among us to play this role.

Frankly, there has been so much time and energy devoted to developing ways to discipline and dismiss the Black body, we are clearly having a tough time instituting policies for Black educational, social, and political advancement. Of course, I do not expect White society to determine and dictate Black advancement. The sad reality is that the institutions, politics, and structural mechanisms currently in place continue to assert this colonial narrative. Any attempt for Black self-determination must consider colonial processes within and without the academic spaces. Therefore, the anti-colonial struggle is about body, mind, soul, and spirit (see Dei 2012). For the Black body that is continually, consistently, and constantly shamed; to reclaim Blackness and Black identity the challenge is equally about pride, self-determination, and self-preservation. The categorization of identity is deeply political. I am re-theorizing and reclaiming Blackness as a sense of ownership of my identity, the social place for the existence of such identity, as well as a recognition that such identity and the body matter always. Colonialism and colonial relations have an uncanny ability to self-preserve. Colonialism has continually reinvented itself to ensure dominance. This reinvention is not a postcolonial experience but an ongoing colonial experience—one that is a daily struggle for peoples at the receiving end of colonialism.

Critiques can serve to make our scholarship critical. But there are limits to being critical. As critical learners, we must continually ask ourselves how everyday practices connect to the materiality of privilege, power, and advantages. Anti-colonial engagements are always rife with questions of individual and collective responsibilities including owning up to one's complicities in colonizing relations. The anti-colonial scholar or community worker must never shy away from asking critical questions. In fact, for colonized, racialized, and Indigenous bodies we have no choice but to continually keep a critical gaze on society and thus, ourselves. The questions we ask must always be part of our existence and should speak to the everyday realities. It is imperative to understand that our everyday realities are deeply rooted in coloniality as Maldonado-Torres (2007, p. 243) posits, "we breath coloniality all the time and every day" and this is different than colonialism. Coloniality speaks to the everyday effects and realities stemming from colonization. Coloniality highlights the ordering of the conquerors and conquered based on the idea of race and this structuring resulting in the control of labor and resources (Quijano 2000). Through colonial and Eurocentric knowledge, Black bodies have been rendered homogenous. Coloniality highlights the lived realities of Black bodies being racialized based on assumptive inferiority and how this plays out into everyday interactions resulting in global power. We see this othering in Black bodies in all realms of life. From birth to death, the Black body is categorized, questioned, and disposed through time and across space. Our humanity has always been questioned. Papernick (2015a) notes there has been a "mythology of [racial] inferiority that is labeled as cultural difference" which in fact is "based on anti-Black racism" (p. 7). Black, colonized, and racialized bodies experience difference (e.g., social class, gender, disability, etc.) differently. When our difference is not denied, it is totalized or fetishized. We are the perpetual exotic "Other." The colonial encounter was an interaction of different bodies, differentially privileged on particular Lands. Therefore, the colonial question has always been a racial question *and* a Land question. We cannot separate the two. Any decolonization project that moves away from centering issues of race and Indigeneity as intertwined is bound to fail. *The interconnecting issues of political recognition, sovereignty, citizenship, identity, culture, history, belonging, and solidarity evoke questions of Indigeneity and race together.*

But, in centering race and Indigeneity in anti-colonial resistance, all sites of domination need to be simultaneously engaged if we are to transform our communities through decolonial struggles, especially in the context of the matrix of domination and oppression. The contemporary commodification of Blackness makes Black subjects unwelcomed in some spaces often deemed a desirable fetished object of possession as well, perceived as a valuable commodity yet also as a threat and repulsive all at once. This is a reality that ranges from popular culture to academic spaces to public policy. Making such conflicting realities clear in our discursive practices is not an attempt to speak from the victim stance. The hard truth is that there is an Eurocentric and White supremacist construction of Blackness and Black identity that has been mired in the subjugation of Black bodies and Black lives.

Of late I have been concerned about the ways discursive practices in the academy continue to reproduce and institutionalize White hegemony. Sara Ahmed's 2004 article *Declarations of Whiteness: The Non-Performativity of Anti-Racism* is useful here, as it critiques what she calls a "politics of declaration" within the academy and beyond. This politics re-centers Whiteness as institutions (as well as individuals) "admit" to bad forms of practice—in this case racism—and this "admission" itself becomes deemed as good practice. Lisa Lowe's (2015) analysis also applies to such declarations, which along with human rights and other legal and political acts of equality, operate as part of liberalism's economy of "affirmations and forgetting." This economy affirms various forms of equality while forgetting or eliding the historical and contemporary violences upon which the equality platform is built (Jensen 2016). It is not only that such admissions, declarations, or affirmations become "good practice" in and of themselves without redress or structural changes. These discourses are also productive; they have material effects. They work to authorize as much as they foreclose or occlude. To address this point, Ahmed rejects a definition of institutional racism that remains limited to what institutions fail to do, thus foreclosing an account of an ongoing series of practices that shape institutions—the norms that are established, reproduced, and reified. Ahmed (2004 n.p) states, "Racism would not be evident in what 'we' fail to do, but what 'we' have already done, whereby the 'we' is an effect of the doing," which helps clarify how institutional policies to eliminate racism fail to do so in their very articulation. The "we" in Ahmed's (2004) account reflects the dominant Western academy, as well as other institutions. The "we" is an effect of racism and colonialism; it operates through an unnamed Eurocentrism.

As learners, the spaces in the academy make us complicit in the power relations of our institutions. Therefore, we must ask, to what political projects are our discursive stances contributing to? How do our intellectual engagements help build community, especially among colonized, racialized, and oppressed populations? What does it mean to claim to share colonial experiences of oppression and domination? How do we broaden our existing epistemologies and discursive frameworks to include the possible range of different ways of knowing? How do we begin to name the un-nameable experiences we undergo daily as racialized, oppressed, and colonized bodies?

I do not ask these questions for the sake of asking. I believe deep intellectual reflections over these issues are critical to our collective survival. Our discursive practices themselves shape the direction, applications, and relevance of knowledge production. A radical scholar cannot occupy the liminal spaces of the academy without accentuating a distinctive voice, one that freely disturbs and subverts the silences and complacencies of the academy. But our discourses cannot be monologues. There are always competing and counter discourses. The problem, as we know, is that certain discourses—our counter-stories to dominant accounts—are never allowed at the table for contestations. We must understand the push back against certain voices if we want to transform our institutions. The Eurocentrism that epitomizes dominant narratives shows how counter-narratives are often measured within prisms, values, and standpoints. If counter-narratives are not articulated in ways that the dominant will legitimate, these narratives are discounted as unintelligible or anti-intellectual. This explains why certain racialized bodies are forced to speak within the tropes of acceptability and respectability. It also explains why the dominant validates and gives currency to scholarship that disguises or liberalizes power relations and power differentials when espoused by colonized, racialized, and Indigenous bodies. Despite pretense to the contrary, it is difficult to pursue a sustained critique of the economic and political structures as well as the culture of institutions to which we belong. In the academy, these constraints make the magnetism of Whiteness ever so powerful. We must hear multiple voices in the narration of counter stories to have a complete and full account of the "story." The call for "voice" is not a romantic representation, but instead, a re-politicization of voice in ways critical of the cooptation of subaltern and Othered experiences. For colonized bodies, we must reclaim our experiences, histories and the past in ethical and responsible ways. There is an ethical responsibility of the decolonial project. There must be a counter [if not a better] way to teach and promote decolonization in our schools, colleges, and universities. We need radical pedagogies that challenge and subvert dominant ways of thinking, and further promote education practices and relations among learners in a spirit of sharing, reciprocity, appreciation, and validation. Schooling as a racializing and colonizing project can be transformed through the affirmation of all identities, including racial, class, gender, sexual, [dis] ability, and spiritual identities of learners. Every learner embodies these identities. So, a decolonizing education must ask why some educators tend to dismiss, deny, or devalue certain identities and identifications as if these are irrelevant to schooling and education. Brown (2008), for instance, shares how as both a student and teacher, she has experienced and observed the destructive tension that arises when the hegemonic knowledge of the colonizer clashes with the repressed knowledge of the colonized. Through decolonizing education, learners can collectively disturb and subvert the colonial paradigm of validating knowledges, experiences, and histories through one prism, usually that of the dominant.

In addition, we must work against what Brown (2008) calls a "fashionable pedagogical" strategy, when teachers and instructors ask children and adult students of African descent to tell their own stories (p. 378). One can imagine that these students are often expected to be representatives of all Black matters. Brown (2008) poses a critical question: "…of what use is it to racialized students to bring forward their stories and experiences when there is no epistemic base upon which to validate and honor them within a critical and ethical framework?" (p. 378). Decolonizing education must therefore also engage this collective, not as an "imperial net" that forces alignment across differences, but rather as a political yearning for solidarity across differences. It must counter attempts to tokenize and/or homogenize stories of difference. Such education must seek to organically create a shared understanding of our collective identities. In decolonizing education, it is imperative to understand that the foundation of multiculturalism education is based on meritocratic ideals and has enabled the manifestation of White privilege, without the interrogation of its unearned privileges and its positionality in past and contemporary colonialization. Comeau takes essentialism further and suggests that multiculturalism does not only serve to essentialize marginal identities; it also "commodifies" culture and difference. Comeau (2005) problematizes multiculturalism as follows: "the consumption of commodified cultural differences remains central to the way Canadian national identity is imagined" (p. 11). The normalization of Whiteness in multicultural educational practices and lack of interrogation creates difficult realities for entry points into the interrogation of race and decolonizing education practices (Abawi 2017). The responsibility for Black bodies to historicize and narrate their own colonization becomes a tenant of liberal, multicultural education practices which purport that students have control of their own identities and histories, and is often only presented on the surface through food and dance.

A long time ago when speaking about colonialism and colonial oppression, anticolonial theorist Steve Biko asked colonized and oppressed bodies a simple question: "Why should we be concerned with a problem we did not create?" I do not think the answer is simply that as oppressed/colonized peoples, we are implicated or even complicit in colonial oppressions. There is something more we need to speak about: The importance of defining an agenda for political and social transformation, and setting goals on our own the terms of debate/engagement. The starting point in this task is reclaiming our subjectivities and identities.

It is in my professional, academic, and community role as an African-Canadian educator want to ground my re-theorization of Black identity and Blackness. Blackness is about knowledge production, representation, and politics centered on race, Indigeneity, culture, and history. Race and racial differences make difference meaningful because of the consequences of espousing difference for Black bodies and other oppressed or colonized groups. Unfortunately, critiques of race essentialism have only served to divert attention away from the shared, and yet diverse, experiences of colonization and oppression that racialized, Indigenous groups encounter. These experiences are neither similar nor singular. But they are relational and shared. I have long felt that when one is forced to deny their racial Blackness, it is part of an agenda that either stems from or tacitly supports anti-Blackness. Being asked to deny one's racial identity comes in many ways, including incessant contentions that any claims to a Black body ultimately totalizes a complex identity, as if we are only about race! We are constantly told to recognize that race is in a state of flux–fluid and constantly changing. Yet, I wonder how much of my Black identity keeps changing in a White supremacist context? How do we account for the porousness of Black identities in such contexts? The failure to distinguish the metaphor from the real permanence of skin color, racism, and racialization is intellectually nauseating. We can agree race is socially constructed. It is not a fixed or bounded category. But race is also real and has a permanence for some in the endurance of Black skin color and anti-Black racism.

When we resist an equally essentialist reading of race as always in state of constant flux, we are punished for it. From where I sit, the punishment [e.g., criminalization, denial of our humanity] of the Black body across various historical registers makes it difficult to swallow the contextual fluidity of race and skin color. The discomfort of speaking race meets its match in the popular conservative and the not so commonsensical refrain "we are all one race, the human race"! I would insist that there must be resistance even as we collectively and collaboratively exist, because not everyone—not every racial group, sits well in this space of uncontested "cohabitation." Racialized bodies in an oppressive context cannot simply join the celebratory mode of multiracial and multicultural formations and identifications. The sad bit is that for far too long many, including some Black, racialized, and Indigenous intellectuals, have uncritically welcomed calls for intellectual sophistication which merely espouse theoretical and political ambiguity in the name of hybridity and postcolonial engagement.

Many have mimicked Western intellectual traditions when theorizing about our identities and subjectivities in the vein of postcolonial theory. Homi Bhabha's ideas of hybridity, in-betweenness, and the liminal space are key aspects of the textuality theory (Bhabha 1994). The theory is relevant but only to a point when it comes to understanding Blackness in a White supremacist context. There are significant limits of Bhabha's post-colonial theorizing as it relates to the question of "elite culture and power" and particularly, the dynamics of Black social and political ecologies when read through time and history. We encounter huge drawbacks of an intellectual preoccupation with the "subjectivity of the interstitial space" devoid of broader questions of structure, materiality, and politics. Identity and subjectivity cannot be discursively engaged or seen simply as a "cultural discourse." There is a materiality to Blackness and Black identity in the White-dominated global society. In fact, as many have noted, the anti-essentialist character of Bhabha's theorizing ends up being equally essentialist as he is unable to escape from what he sets out to critique (see Moorhouse 2015). The "discourse of language" or "cultural identity," however powerful these may be, do not fully capture the relations between the Global South and North throughout history, nor the experiences of Black bodies in Euro-American, White supremacist contexts.

It is a false separation to claim an existential opposition between "theory speak" and "politics." We must understand that there is a conjunction of theory and practice that manifests itself in the everyday material lives of Black peoples globally. The mobility of labor and capital factor into the Black experience across transnational spaces. Uncritical claims of hybridity produce distance from the subjectivities it produces and the placement within a "third space" in the context of Blackness and the global political economy. Any intellectual placement in the so-called "third space" must allow for aligning practices of global capitalism with colonialism and anything which is "imposed and dominating", as opposed to "alien and foreign."

In bringing the materiality back to questions of the subject, I am arguing that we must acknowledge but not necessarily prioritize only the subjectivity of the interstitial space. I am also insisting that there is more to the claims of complexification, heterogeneity, contingency, flux, fluidity, shifting marginalities, cultural displacements, and the discursive spaces of "translation." The "third space" is not simply a space of cultural discourse. History is about human lives and recollections of history call for different responses. Black bodies resist with our identities, not because we are in situations constitutive of flux, fluidity, and displacement, but because we are conditioned in given historical moments through dominant-subordinate relations. It was colonialism and imperialism that created the core and peripheries, the centers, and marginal space.

Post-colonial discourses have under-theorized what Bhabha's hybridity means for Black bodies and the legal, political, and material consequences of identifying as "hybrid" in a racial context. Hybridity homogenizes the Black experience, further scripting our external location as a result of subjectifying our identities (see also Papernick 2015b in another context). Any discussion of the Black experience should be able to explicate how hybridity, as a concept, helps us understand the connections between imperial colonial culture, colonized cultural practices, and the experiences of Indigeneity. Hybridity, when evoked to account for the Black and African experience, fails to explain the differences in power and material inequalities between groups and peoples, a point Zeleza (1997) and Dirlik (1997) made a long time ago. Not all hybrid positions are equal in power and effect. Hybridity often obscures the fact that different spaces and bodies have their own internal and historical processes of knowledge creation which must be acknowledged in their own right. Therefore, we must be mindful of the potential for absorption and amnesia by modernist projects (see also Agyeyomah and Langdon 2009, in another context).

As I will argue later, Black and African bodies are influenced by the structural and capitalist bases of colonial imperialism such that an analysis of Black/African identities and subjectivities cannot be outside of a materialist paradigm. A key component of understanding Black/African identity and Blackness is Black agency and resistance to colonial subjugation. This knowledge must be foundational to a theorization of Blackness. The fluid identities of the Black subject do not in itself detract from a politics of the body for resistance to Euro-colonial domination. The postcolonial hybrid as a space/place of harmonious existence devoid of power is a misreading. Ideas of hybridity, in-betweenness, and the liminal space are significant. Yet, the postcolonial "hybridity and cosmopolitanism that serve to harmonize the universal" fail to acknowledge differences in power and material conditions of inequality between groups (see also Angod 2006; Dirlik 1997; Krishnaswamy 2007; Zeleza 1997).

In effect, any claims of the shiftiness of identity must embody power and resistance and allow for possibilities and transformations. Resistance and resurgence must be conceived broadly as encompassing different borders and spaces, and as residing in our voices, oral languages, cultural memories, histories, actions, and spirits to foster collective solidarities. There is a politics of diaspora and it is important to understand how Diaspora informs constructions of community, solidarity, and nationhood. It is also imperative to understand diaspora in relation to decolonization and the process of coming to know about Indigeneity, and that Indigeneity contains multiple histories and cultural memories. There are no straightforward, easy, and quick distinctions between Blackness, Africanness, and Indigeneity (see also Anderson 2007, 2009).

In re-theorizing Blackness I wish to anchor my ideas in the "necropolitics" (Mbembe 2003) of intellectual metaphorical and physical death when Black bodies are not allowed to affirm their full identities. This will include affirming our racial, gender, class, sexual, and [dis] abled identities as inclusive such that no identity is denied. It is a death politics when Black bodies are continually told to complicate our Blackness, which for the most part is a subtext, code word or a catch phrase to silence a discussion of the racialized identity of Blackness. How and why is it that those who affirm the power of racial identity are often accused of essentialism? Who (in terms of identity) is accused of this, and in what contexts? I do not dispute the many sidedness of Blackness. I have cautioned against a hegemonic understanding of Blackness. It is also important for us to temper our perpetual need to complexify and understand why Blackness is a strategic community's protective response to a "culture of Whiteness" (see also Hampton 2016). But what does it also mean for Black and African bodies to complicate their racial identity as more complex when in fact we continually experience this identity as "criminal," "violent," "disruptive," "angry," and "barbaric"? This must be part of the discussion. It is easy when we complicate a racial identity of Whiteness because it is power and privilege we want to deny. When called upon to acknowledge this identity, the dominant White body engages a politics of escaping the hard scrutiny of White power. The escape route is to trouble Whiteness as more complex than about power and privilege—that it is often demarcated by class, gender, sexuality, [dis]ability, etc. In effect, to deny White identity and Whiteness by assuming their complexities is not innocent. When an identity is being criminalized an essentialist politics is embarked upon, and we do not often hear concerns about complicating such an identity. It becomes hypocritical when calls for complexifying and complicating identities are not taken up in the context of the differential intellectual and political engagements of identity. Who is being asked to complexify and complicate identity—what is being asked, in what contexts, and why? Whiteness can claim multiplicity in identity as opposed to racialized bodies that are viewed in terms of an essentialized, singular identity. Whiteness, as the benefactor of racial privilege, can and does conveniently claim "racelessness" as well. Liberal discourses that proclaim we are all "one human race" with equal rights, and we live in a society that values multiculturalism, deny the fact that social inequalities and violences are structured through race itself.

The dominant often speaks of the dangerous proxy of race as if race is irrelevant. Yet race is real in everyday lives. Race is about Whiteness, White power, and entitlements. If identity is always discursively produced then why is it so easy to dismiss the lived experiences and accounting of marginalized bodies, particularly when we speak about what it means to live in a Black, African, or Indigenous skin in the settler colonial context of North America? For Black, African, racialized, and colonized bodies we know too well that when we are not at the table, though we can guarantee ourselves to be on the menu. We cannot dismiss the power of words. Words define us and can move us to act. Words also give meaning to our actions. But for words to have meaning we must insist on our own voices. We must cultivate the voice to challenge the hierarchies of significance that are continually accorded to different experiences, histories, and identities. We cannot sit quietly and allow race to become the disappearing act. We must connect our race and racialized identities to knowledge production.

Research, particularly among racialized and colonized communities and bodies, has always proceeded with an assumption to make the subject of study knowable. Everything exists to be known. The idea that a people may refuse to be "known" is not a point of conversation nor contention. What is not known is not knowledge. It is not valid experience. It is not something that we can talk of as shared knowledge. Spirituality, for example, is not valid knowledge. Spiritual identities do not exist and neither is the spiritual identity shared. It is through this process of making the "unknowable" knowable in particular ways that dominant bodies have assumed discursive authority over colonized groups and communities. Through a colonial Eurocentric rationality, differences structured along lines of race, class, gender, sexuality, and ability as sites of our myriad identities have been understood in terms acceptable to the dominant. To speak of identity and difference as shared and collective is always questioned in neo-liberal democracies that affirm us as merely individual subjects. There is no sense of shared history because this history also evokes acknowledging our complicities in colonialism and colonial relations as shared experiences and histories.

If dominant bodies researching the colonized also have the power to define them there is a big problem. It is problematic when dominant bodies research and define the colonized. Therefore, it is important to resist dominant constructions of Black identities, either as about differences or communities. If we believe identities are also discursive we can entertain room for sharing and negotiating our identities in ways that make room for counter voices and interpretations inclusive of other stances. For example, claiming a racial identity in a White-dominated context is also to claim shared histories and experiences of power, privilege, punishment, and resistance. It is not inconceivable or anti-intellectual to insist that racial identities are about both collectivities and individual experiences.

In re-articulating and re-theorizing Blackness, Africanness, and Black identity, I am searching for a perspective to affirm harsh realities or truths of the Black and African experiences in varying contexts. My intellectual objective is to begin to think of the Black/African existence as constructions and contestations on/over shared identities on our own terms, including the evocation of our own cultural knowledges, histories, and languages. Modernity has never been about "free and equal subjects" exercising a collective will to reconfigure human existence. Modernity is about colonial domination. As Mignolo (1995) long ago noted, both the "rhetoric of modernity" and "logic of coloniality" go hand in hand. The oppressive structures of modernity have their roots in colonialism and the colonial experience. Modernity is imposed through European colonial and colonizing encounters with the subaltern. Mbembe (2001) outlines how in social theory, modernity has been understood primarily in the perspective of Western rationalism (p. 10). The connection between modernity, rationalism, and Westernism has been posited as more than contingent—it is viewed as constitutive of all three. This alleged interconnection is used to distinguish the West from the rest of the world and to posit that its advancements have not happened anywhere else (Mbembe 2001, p. 10). The West makes a claim to modernity through universal ideas of progress and development that subaltern subjects lack. Such universal notions are quite contingent and they are very much based in colonial relations. To give one example, Western ideas of wealth are universal (not everyone believes that accumulation of objects or economic imperialism denote "wealth"). Also, attainment of this "wealth" is completely contingent—it has been built on slavery, colonialism, coerced labor, and empire. Barrett (2014), for example, explores the complexity of the transatlantic slave trade and the ways in which violence and racism were central to the Black body and the development of Western modernity. Furthermore, these processes of racial governance: slavery, coerced labor, and colonialism, persist in our contemporary moment through new discourses and practices (Lowe 2015).

Hence what is deemed to be modern[ity] is neither universal nor neutral. If modernity is a colonial project, then we need critical knowledge to decolonize our ideas about human history and identity formations. As many others, have noted within the intellectual space, modernity is normalized and universalized in multiple forms. Whiteness is "firmly upheld by conceptions of modernity" and the key question we should be asking is: "how do we move beyond modernity and conceptions that uphold colonial structures such as whiteness?" (Jaimungal 2015, p. 2).

Western cultural philosophy has been woefully inadequate in accounting for the Black/African experience and human condition. To this end, I see counter and alternative conceptions of Blackness steeped in Indigenous and decolonial prisms as a useful political tool for deployment. In other words, it is my contention that we can begin to challenge the dominance of Whiteness by affirming a positive force of Blackness which is about resistance from a social and epistemic location and identity. To be Black is to be an embodiment of struggle and resistance challenging White supremacy and dominance. For me calling oneself "Black" or "African" is claiming an identity that is synonymous with struggle, politics, oppression, and resistance. Evoking Black identity and Blackness for anything else is a betrayal. The logic of survival for Black bodies rests on a preparedness to define, fight, and insist on oneself and the collective, the existence of our collective humanity and destiny. In fact, Blackness finds its authenticity through the participation in anti-racist and anti-colonial struggles. When some of us reinvent our Africanness in a diasporic context, we do so in the spirit of healing, transformation, critique, and resistance.

Colonial formations are about the power of definitions. "Development" has been defined as a common good by the most powerful; yet many scholars and activists show how it perpetuates colonial and racial governance (see for example Escobar 1995; Toussaint 2008). The roots of development lie in the years immediately following World War II, when a key transformation occurred in the construction of poverty. Through an archaeology, Rahnema (1991) illuminates poverty's globalization after 1945 when two-thirds of the world was constructed as poor. This conversion took place through a mere statistical comparison of annual per capita incomes, and conceptions and treatment of poverty changed drastically through this transition. During colonialism, economic development of "the natives" was pointless. Even if colonial subjects could be enlightened in some capacity by their colonizers, a common belief circulated that they possessed no capability for technology and science (Escobar 1995, p. 22). In contrast, elimination of poverty became a vital component of Western governmentality after World War II that continues through UN Development today (Jensen 2016).

In *Encountering Development: The Making and Unmaking of the Third World*, Arturo Escobar (1995) discusses the vast implications of the Western "discovery" of mass poverty in Asia, Africa, and Latin America in the early post-World War II period. He reveals the construction of two-thirds of the world as poor as strategic in maintaining Western hegemony. The Third World was central to superpower rivalry in the Cold War, as continued access to raw materials and the formation of new markets were necessary for Western (US) capitalist expansion. Third World poverty thus became linked with anti-communism in the justification of development. It was argued that if not rescued from poverty, poor nations would succumb to communism out of desperation (Escobar 1995, p. 34). Therefore, the war on fascism that occupied the US and Europe during World War II was replaced by the "war on poverty" in the Third World, which came to play a key function in the rapid globalization of US domination as a world power (Escobar 1995, p. 21). As the West reluctantly accepted the untenability of sustaining formal colonial rule, the war on Third World poverty was indispensable in limiting communism, continued access to raw materials from the Global South, and setting up a US-dominated global capitalist system.

With a focus on relations of domination, Escobar shows how UN development was born from this Western project that "discovered poverty" and assigned it as an inherent feature of the Third World that needed to be changed. Mass poverty in the Global South was removed from any historical and relational context of colonialism and racism in this "discovery." In market societies, poor people were defined as lacking what other classes had in terms of wealth, and poor countries came to be defined in the same way in the post-war era. As poverty became known as the essential trait of the Third World, its elimination through economic growth and development became an unquestioned, necessary, and universal truth (Escobar 1995, p. 24). Poverty became a problem the answer to which was economic growth and development through Western-generated programs and policies implemented through the UN, World Bank, and IMF.

Yet without idealizing traditional societies or pre-colonial histories, massive poverty in the modern sense arose only when the spread of the free market severed community ties and deprived millions of people of access to water, Land, and other resources. Free market became the process of introducing rational and scientific practice as the only way to "development." This rationality meant the withdrawal of state welfare responsibility to citizens. The consolidation of capitalism made systemic impoverishment inevitable (Escobar 1995, p. 22). Rather than eliminating poverty, development has been a project of modernity that has created many failures for the Global South. In addition, free market rationality and a colonial mentality of rule continue to inform development (Jensen 2016). What we are witnessing today is mal-development, under the guides of "development." Neoliberal progress, a new form of colonialism, has emerged with the international financial community leading the war to plunder the wealth (material, physical, and human resources) of Black and African peoples and the Global South. We see this in the policies of institutions such as the World Bank and IMF which notwithstanding their expressed intentions on helping promote development in poor in underdeveloped communities, have succeeded in exploiting the Global South through debt repayments, tied aid, brain drain, free markets, and trade liberalization policies (Bond 2013; Crush 2002). There is a clear linkage of colonialism and neo-colonialism, Western civilization ideals, economic/material poverty, and Blackness. The racialization and feminization of poverty has its corresponding aspects in Black Diasporan communities, as well as in Africa itself.

While capitalism continues to be promoted as a beneficial and necessary means to end poverty within UN development, many also believe that it will benefit them through migration to the Global North. The Diasporic context has been presented as a place of desire and something for which we must all yearn. Global migration to the West has been a feature of the economic exploitation of Black, Asian, and Latin American populations. To say capitalism is foundational to the Black experience is neither a reductionist nor totalizing argument. It is an acknowledgement of how capitalism has brutally dictated the histories of the colonial experience for marginalized bodies, even as these bodies resist. Corporate capital has an assumed role as the final arbiters of life and death for many local communities. The material exploitative relations of global capitalism continue to script the lived experiences of Black, racialized, and Indigenous bodies and communities. But, as Dirlik (1997) noted, "the narrative of capitalism is no longer a narrative of the history of Europe [given that] non-European capitalist societies make their own claims on the history of capitalism" (p. 71). There are non-European versions of history to be told and economic inequities within many non-European communities have long histories that predate European capitalism. Indigenous economies existed and helped sustain communities prior to the advent of European colonial capitalism. The pre-colonial experiences of Black, African, racialized, and Indigenous communities also suggest varying colonial and post-colonial relations to European capitalism. Therefore, it is important for the so-called "global" to be understood in the context of current and historical differences.

The primacy of open markets and capitalism in the context of Western and Euro-colonial education, far from eliminating poverty, has intensified poverty, particularly, in Black/African and Diasporan communities, and by extension, the Global South. In Africa, there is a reason why the current focus on basic education (e.g., Education For All) as a strategy for poverty reduction has not borne its anticipated results. The failure of education to eradicate poverty in the imperatives of globalization has become a new form of Western imperialism. The encroachment of private and corporate capital in education has meant education for the highest bidder thereby leaving many people on the tracks. Globalization has been synonymous with poverty and social inequality. Nonetheless, poverty must be understood in terms of its multiple dimensions—economic, social, and spiritual. So, while I connect Blackness and poverty as induced by globalization to script the lives of certain bodies, I do not see such poverty as absolute. Poverty is relative because it is not just economic and material we are talking about, but also, social, psychological, and spiritual. The poverty for Black/African communities is largely an economic/material one. There is the "poverty of opportunity" as many local peoples in Black/African and Diasporic communities lack access to basic services, jobs, and education. Black/African peoples are having a difficult time achieving a reliable source of income to cover the economic and social costs for adequate health, education, housing, and transportation. Within many Black/African communities there is rising youth unemployment and underemployment as a major concern. I will return to these considerations in a later chapter.

The question is when we as Black/African bodies come into these spaces, how do we use the [new] location to articulate counter and oppositional stances? There are responsibilities for the Black learner as discussion in later chapters will show. Our location even in the margins of dominant spaces can be arenas to foster a clear sense of resistance for developing a clear sense of social purpose and meaning in life. Subaltern difference has always been acknowledged as a position and a location from where the marginalized can begin to re-theorize about their experiences. This space can, in fact, become a site of critical knowledge for shifting our discursive and political practices away from Euro-modernity. What we need are subaltern knowledges that are truly anchored in place-based epistemologies of the Indigenous and the marginalized world. We need such knowledges to offer a corrective and a counter re-visioning of our world and the human experience incorporating critical, non-hegemonic ideas about how we come to know, think, and act in a complex global world (see also Escobar 2004).

In *The Intimacies of Four Continents*, Lisa Lowe (2015) explores some of these historical differences that help explain contemporary experiences of African/Black and Indigenous peoples in Canada in the contemporary global context. Lowe shows how the "new world" of the late eighteenth and early nineteenth centuries, comprised of European settlers, Indigenous populations, and African and Asian peoples in the Americas, was inextricably linked to the rise of liberal modernity and global capitalism. Lowe clarifies, "...the modern distinction between definitions of the human and those to whom such definitions do not extend is the condition of possibility for Western liberalism, and not its particular exception" (p. 3). This well-formulated analysis of modern liberalism exposes it as commensurate with and integral to the *imbricated* processes of slavery, colonialism, capitalism, and empire.

Lowe (2015) reads across colonial state archives and liberal political, philosophical, and cultural texts to reveal how modern liberalism occludes its inherent violence through what she calls an "economy of affirmations and forgetting" (p. 3). Modern liberalism simultaneously makes universal promises of liberty, rights, wage labor, free trade, and emancipation while eclipsing or exceptionalizing the global asymmetries upon which those ideals are predicated. This illustrates how current differentiations based on race, nation, the Global north or south, or the discourse of modernization that creates different stages of development, are traces of liberal forgetting (Jensen 2016). Such racial "amnesia" shows the politics of Western "memory" itself, and reminds us that knowledge cannot be analyzed outside of the procedures of its own production.

Lowe's (2015) contribution helps to disrupt the settler/non-settler dichotomy in contemporary Canada by illuminating the intimate yet often buried connections between settler colonialism in the Americas, transatlantic slavery, and colonial trade of East Indies and Chinese indentured laborers and goods, and by assessing how racial and colonial governance have been *integral* to the rise of liberal governance globally (Jensen 2016). Despite separate historical scholarship on individual societies, regions and populations of these four continents, the sorting of knowledge by academic discipline has helped render the interlinked processes of empire distinct from one another. In addition, while other critical scholars have also demonstrated how liberal philosophy, culture, and governance have required and perpetuated colonialism, imperialism, slavery, and capitalism, Lowe's analysis is unique in its consideration of the *imbrications* of slavery, settler colonialism and imported indentured labor. Critical inquiries into each of these areas have not explored the interconnections of all three, often examining one or two of these phenomena in relative isolation from the other(s) (for example, Mawani 2009). Lowe shows how gaps and absences in these accounts say much about the politics of knowledge that help create the dominant history of our present day—an Anglo-historical narrative that contributes to development of an artificial opposition between racialized immigrants and Indigenous peoples in Canada. Lowe illustrates how intertwined histories of distinct yet connected racial logics helped form an Anglo-American settler imperial imaginary—an imaginary that continues to produce human difference in relation to liberal notions of "development" and civilization. Human difference, as Smith (2006) reminds us, is produced through distinct yet interconnected logics of White supremacy which are explored more below.

This separation helps fuel charges of settlerhood leveraged against racialized immigrants in the Canadian nation state today. Disrupting such a separation, Lowe (2015) reveals the colonial archive as intrinsic to the archives of liberalism, and illustrates how modern liberalism defined and delimited the "universal" human as one with European male attributes, while differentiating colonized populations as less than human. This distinction of "less than human" applied to all colonized populations, a point of historical and contemporary connection for African/Black and Indigenous populations in the Canadian nation state. Lowe demonstrates that, "*Liberal forms of political economy, culture, government, and history propose a narrative of freedom overcoming enslavement that at once denies colonial slavery, erases the seizure of Land from native peoples, displaces migrations and connections across continents, and internalizes these processes in a national struggle of history and consciousness*" (p. 3). Importantly, contemporary racial and colonial hierarchies are residual of these liberal forms of governance that simultaneously liberate certain subjects, while distancing or removing other subjects, regions, and ways of life from the "human" category.

These points show how we need to engage slavery, colonialism, indentured labor, and liberalism as a conjunction that continues in our contemporary moment. There are artificial separations created between racialized and colonial subjects through dominant narratives that supplement the forgetting of colonial and racial violence, with new affirmations that claim universal rights and multiculturalism (Jensen 2016). Transcendence of slavery, indenture, or colonialism has yet to happen, and claims to the contrary are the violent work of dominant discourses and historical narratives.

Importantly, Lowe (2015) demonstrates how racial hierarchies themselves emerged within (and reconciled) the contradiction between liberal claims of progress and universality, and the colonial and capitalist imperative to manage the labor, reproduction, and social organization of colonized subjects. Furthermore, she effectively traces subject categories and colonial and racial hierarchies throughout her study, revealing how they are not fixed or essential. She uses Foucault's (1978) genealogical method to investigate how such categories become established, what they help authorize, and what are the effects. Viewing categories as historically specific social constructions allows a tracing of their transformations and reinscriptions in particular places and times, the fictions they help to create and uphold, and the forms of governance organized around them. Lowe indicates that, "Liberal ideas of rights, emancipation, wage labor and free trade were articulated in and through the shifting classifications that emerged to manage social difference" (p. 9). The interconnectedness of different racialized and colonial subjectivities points to Smith's (2006) suggestion that we avoid oppression Olympics and instead look at how White supremacy racializes differently as we engage in anti-racist and anti-colonial solidarity work.

All the same, while such cultural and historical specificities and differences must be noted, they do not in themselves fully account for contemporary global forces defining human experiences (see also Papernick 2015a, b). We must pay attention to the ideological, institutional, and political structures that operate within the logics of capitalism to structure global social relations (see Dirlik 1997). A critical understanding of global economic relations through a race lens may help us uncover "the ideological and dominating practices of global capitalism that operate under the new forms of colonialism in the post [colonial] period" (Papernick 2015b, p. 3). Capitalism was very much linked to the historical forms of colonialism that asserted White global dominance.

Returning to Lowe (2015), she tracks global flows of people and the functioning of economies, illustrating how settler colonialism, indentured labor, and transatlantic slavery all became necessary for the construction of Anglo-American identities and the development of an Anglo-American led capitalist system. She rejects Western narratives of linear temporal progression from colonialism to liberal freedom, and uses a spatial analysis that exposes how the liberal subject at the center of imperialism is made possible only in relation to its racialized laborers in colonial spaces or spaces of exception. For example, Lowe shows how liberal promotions of abolition and freedom that secured Anglo-American identities as progressive and moral also helped reconcile the (partial) replacement of transatlantic slavery with indentured labor under global capitalism. Although slavery and the slave trade extended beyond formal abolition, narratives of abolition and freedom helped construct an intermediary category of Asian indentured labor that served both economic and identity purposes as the figure of the "coolie" could theoretically aspire to, yet never achieve, full freedom and personhood granted to White Europeans.

While indentured labor differs from slavery, Lowe's (2015) analysis makes clear how both are coerced forms of racial governance in the global capitalist economy which cannot be understood in isolation from one another. Understanding transatlantic slavery also requires an understanding of indentured labor, how both are commensurate with and authorized through liberal philosophies, and how different subjects are formed and organized through these distinct yet overlapping processes. The imbrication of slavery and indentured labor also clarifies that we must understand European liberalism in order to understand settler colonialism. Racial governance was underpinned by liberal philosophies which disavowed settler colonialism while narrating modern progress as the transition from slavery to freedom within the global capitalist economy. In addition, both slavery and indentured labor in the Americas relied on the continual colonization of Indigenous Lands. These modes of racial governance and their transformations are imbricated processes in an Anglo-led capitalist system, not sequential events (Jensen 2016). Slavery, colonialism, and coerced labor are ongoing in our contemporary moment of global capitalism and furthermore, Lowe (2015) posits that the contemporary biopolitics of neoliberal security regimes and states of exception are constituted in and through colonial differences.

This shows how White supremacy and capitalism, although working in different ways on different bodies, have always fostered colonial and imperial projects. When we ignore history we simply further the cause of global exploitation, social oppression, and marginality. Patriarchal and colonial structures and relationships of global capitalism have worked through time and again to impose social and economic inequalities on Black lives and subjectivities. Therefore, our intellectual and political practices, whether as Black, racialized or Indigenous scholars, students, or community workers, must continually account for the experiences of global capitalism. In understanding contemporary social and global relations, we cannot afford to lose site of the dominant force of capitalism and how it continues to impact human lives (see also Dirlik 1997). Capitalism and colonialism continue to work in tandem to confer unearned economic, social privileges and moral power on certain bodies. A recognition of the different forms of domination is important insofar as such analysis helps us to move politics forward and organize collectively and disruptively for change. If our conversations about the complexities of oppressions simply end up within the entanglement of oppressions, then it is "unfinished business." Beyond the complexities and imbrications of oppressions, we must fight to ensure the possibilities for collective social transformation. We can start by building anti-colonial solidarities on common ground—shared histories, experiences, and identities, while fully aware of differences of power, privilege, histories, and complicities.

The evocation of Blackness must name White supremacy and make it visible while dismantling it. Charles Mills' racial contract theory is relevant here, as it shows how White supremacy has crystallized over time with some people categorized as human and others sub-human. In his book *The Racial Contract*, Mills (1997) explains White supremacy as a global phenomenon characterizing modernity in which vulnerability to exploitation and access to beneficial opportunities rely most heavily on racial categorizations, as Whites are the only group granted full legal and social status. Mills posits, "Europeans set up a two-tiered moral code with one set of rules for whites and another for nonwhites. Although no single act literally corresponds to the drawing up and signing of a contract, there is a series of acts...which collectively can be seen...as its conceptual, juridical, and normative equivalent" (p. 20–21). While Mills notes that the racial contract theoretically could have been any "color," the racial hierarchies created through colonial modernity have placed Blacks at the bottom of the sub-human category assigned to all racialized people. White people continue to benefit from the racial contract and almost overwhelmingly accept racial privilege as a legitimate entitlement. Mills' global analysis helps us consider the implications of White supremacy on African/Black people on the continent and in diasporic contexts.

Elizabeth Martinez (2000) also conceptualizes White supremacy as a global phenomenon, defining it as, "A historically based, institutionally perpetuated system of exploitation and oppression of continents, nations, and peoples of color by white peoples and nations...for maintaining and defending a system of wealth... and power" (p. 1). Martinez makes clear that the White race was created historically and that erasure and denial of White supremacy's historical basis is indispensable in maintaining it. White supremacy plays out in intricate and often seemingly contradictory ways, for example by sometimes encouraging Global South migration to Canada only to exploit and socially exclude racialized immigrants upon arrival. Locating such practices within the logic of White supremacy reveals them as coherent, consistent, and ongoing (Jensen 2016). While race often goes unmentioned or the role of race is denied, White supremacy is naturalized and reproduced through interlocking laws, policies, social norms, institutional and spatial arrangements, and knowledge production. Martinez (2000) avoids labeling certain comments or actions as racist, and instead asks readers to contemplate how particular issues, laws, and situations relate to the system of White supremacy and to consider how their actions work to either oppose or uphold this system. Such a perspective is useful as we work in solidarity to decolonize. We must acknowledge how we are all implicated—yet in different ways, and find ways to work together to contest the pervasiveness of White supremacy.

Andrea Smith's (2006) work is useful as well, which outlines White supremacy as operating under three distinct, yet interrelated logics. The logic of slavery positions Black people as inherently slave-able and anchors capitalism, which ultimately commodifies all people while perpetually locating Blacks at the bottom of this hierarchy. Orientalism, another logic of White supremacy, was originally conceptualized by Edward Said (1978) as the West's construction of itself as superior to an exoticized, inferior East. Smith (2006) extends Said's definition beyond what may be called the Orient or East to include any racialized, foreign peoples or nations who may be designated threatening, inferior, or exotic. Orientalism serves as an anchor for wars and military occupations, as well as domestic and border security efforts allegedly designed to address all, and only, non-citizens. The third logic, genocide, holds that Indigenous people must constantly disappear so that White people can retain "rightful" claim over US Land, thus anchoring colonialism. Like Martinez (2000), Smith (2006) helps us understand how we are implicated in White supremacy in multiple, differing ways and how we can counter this system.

In contesting White supremacy, we must be clear that Whiteness and White supremacy will not name themselves. In fact, Whiteness does not look at itself. To this end, we cannot dismiss the potency of the Black-White paradigm in accounting for the experiences of racialized embodiments. Whiteness gets its meaning when it denies its own presence even as it affects the lives of racialized bodies. Black aesthetic representations are themselves about resistance. The early anti-colonial literary works of Aime Cesaire (1972) and Leopold Senghor (2001) bear this out. These literary representations not only exalted Black beauty and aesthetics, but also illustrate how we can carry forward our understandings of history, culture, language, and culture as Black radical politics.

As Fanon (1967) pointed out long ago, there are phenomenological, psycho-existential, macro-structural, and political implications of Black racialized embodiments. In the eyes of the dominant Blackness and Africanness have been signifiers of radicalism and uncivility. The criminalization of Blackness and the denial of African humanity cause anger, pain and resentment, and these emotions and experiences constitute legitimate bases of knowledge. To this end a re-theorization of Blackness must engage emotions as a good deal of race knowledge is produced along these lines (Latty 2015; Srivastava 2005, 2006). Blackness is emotionally laden and textured given the recurring denigration, silencing, and devaluation of the Black and African experience. For me not to express anger and deep emotion at such discursive practice is to be complicit at ongoing intellectual hypocrisy, particularly in the [Western] academy.

References

Abawi, Z. (2017). *Marginal voices: Indigenous and immigrant dialogue in education.* Kingston, Canada: Queen's University.

Agyeyomah, C., & Langdon, J. (2009). Building bridges from broken bones. In J. Langdon (Ed.), *Indigenous knowledges, development and education* (pp. 135–147). Rotterdam: Sense Publishers.

Ahmed, S. (2004). Declarations of whiteness: The non-performativity of anti-racism. Borderlands E-Journal. Retrieved from http://www.borderlands.net.au/vol3no2_2004/ahmed_declarations.htm.

Anderson, M. (2007). *When Afro becomes (like) Indigenous: Garifuna and Afro-Indigenous politics in Honduras.* Santa Cruz, CA: University of California Press.

Anderson, M. (2009). *Black and Indigenous: Garifuna activism and consumer culture in Honduras.* Minneapolis: University of Minnesota Press.

Angod, L. (2006). From post-colonial to anti-colonial politics: Difference, knowledge, and R. v. R.D.S. In G. J. S. Dei & A. Kempf (Eds.), *Anti-colonialism and education: The politics of resistance* (pp. 159–174). Rotterdam, NL: Sense.

Anonymous. (2014). (De)Constructing 'Others' with access: Hypervisible whiteness and transnational interracial intimacies in East Africa. Unpublished paper.

Barrett, L. (2014). *Racial blackness and the discontinuity of Western modernity.* Champaign, IL: University of Illinois Press.

Bhabha, H. (1994). *The location of culture.* London: Routledge.

Bond, P. (2013). *Looting Africa: The economics of exploitation (1).* London, GB: Zed.

Broad, R., and Cavanaugh, J. (2013). Number of billionaires is growing globally as inequality spreads. Occupy.com. Retrieved from http://www.occupy.com/article/number-billionaires-growing-globally-inequality-spreads.

Brown, W. (2003). Neoliberalism and the end of liberal democracy. *Theory and Event, 7*(11), 38–59.

Brown, Y. (2008). Ghosts in the Canadian multicultural machine: A tale of the absent presence of black people. *Journal of Black Studies, 38*(3), 374–387.

Carroll, K. K. (2014). An introduction to African-centered sociology: Worldview, epistemology, and social theory. *Critical Sociology, 40*(2), 257–270.

Cesaire, A. (1972). *Discourse on colonialism.* New York: Monthly Review Press.

Comeau, L. (2005). Contemporary productions of colonial identities through liberal discourses of educational reform. *Journal of the Canadian Association for Curriculum Studies, 3*(2), 9–25.

Crush, J. (2002). The global raiders: Nationalism, globalization and the South African brain drain. *Journal of International Affairs, 56*(1), 147–172.

Danaher, K. (2001). *Ten reasons to abolish the IMF and World Bank.* New York, NY: Seven Stories Press.

Dei, G. J. S. (1996). *Anti-racism education: Theory and practice.* Halifax: Fernwood.

Dei, G. J. S. (2000). Rethinking the role of indigenous knowledges in the academy. *International Journal of Inclusive Education, 4*(2), 111–132.

Dei, G. J. S. (2008). *Racists beware: Uncovering racial politics in contemporary society.* Rotterdam: Sense.

Dei, G. J. (2012). Subhuman: The trialectic space. *Journal of Black Studies, 43*(8), 823–846.

Dei, G. J. S., & Asgharzadeh, A. (2001). The power of social theory: Towards an anti-colonial discursive framework. *Journal of Educational Thought, 35*(3), 297–323.

Dirlik, A. (1997). *The post-colonial aura: Third World criticism in the age of global capitalism.* Oxford: Westview Press.

Escobar, A. (1995). *Encountering development: The making and unmaking of the third world.* Ewing, NJ: Princeton University Press.

Escobar, A. (2004). Beyond the third world: Imperial globality, global coloniality and anti-globalization social movements. *Third World Quarterly, 25*(1), 207–230.

Fanon, F. (1963). *The wretched of the earth.* New York: Grove Press.

Fanon, F. (1967). *Black skin, white masks.* (R. Wilcox, Trans.). New York: Grove Press. (Original Work published in 1952).

Foucault, M. (1978). *The history of sexuality (vol. 1): An introduction.* London: Allen Lane.

Goldberg, D. (1993). *Racist culture: Philosophy and the politics of meaning.* Malden, MA: Blackwell..

Goldberg, D. (2006). The global reach of raceless states. In D. Macedo & P. Gounari (Eds.), *The globalization of racism* (pp. 45–67). Boulder, CO: Paradigm.

Goldberg, D. (2009). *The threat of race: Reflections on racial neoliberalism.* Malden, MA: Blackwell..

Hall, S. (1991). Old and new identities: Old and new ethnicities. In A. King (Ed.), *Culture, globalization and world system* (pp. 41–68). New York: State University Press.

Hall, S. (1996). New ethnicities. In D. Morley & K.-H. Chen (Eds.), *Stuart Hall: Critical dialogues in cultural studies* (pp. 441–449). New York: Routledge Press.

Hampton, R. (2016). *Racialized social relations in higher education: Black Student and faculty experiences of a Canadian University.* Unpublished PhD dissertation, Faculty of Education, McGill University, Montreal, Canada.

Harvey, D. (2003). *The new imperialism.* Oxford: Oxford University Press.

Jaimungal, C. (2015). Notes on Foucault's concept of power. Department of Social Justice Education, Ontario Institute for Studies in Education of the University of Toronto [OISE/UT], Toronto.

Jensen, B. (2016). *UN Human Rights for Women: How race becomes an organizing principle.* Unpublished term paper. Department of Social Justice Education, Ontario Institute for Studies in Education of the University of Toronto, Toronto, Canada.

Khan, O. (2015). Ethnic inequality is widespread and a drag on the global economy. The Guardian. Retrieved from http://www.theguardian.com/public-leaders-network/2015/jan/20/ethnic-inequality-widespread-global-economy.

Krishnaswamy, R. (2007). Postcolonial and globalization studies: Connections, conflicts, complicities. In R. Krishnaswamy & C. Hawley (Eds.), *The postcolonial and the global* (pp. 2–21). Minneapolis, MN: University of Minnesota Press.

Latty, S. (2015). Cutting through the emotional tension: Towards a poetics of feeling in anti-racist research methodology. Unpublished Term paper. Department of Social Justice Education, Ontario Institute for Studies in Education of the University of Toronto [OISE/UT], Toronto.

Lebakeng, T. G. (2010). Discourse on indigenous knowledge systems, sustainable socio-economic development and the challenge of the academy in Africa. *CODESRIA Bulletin, 1 & 2*, 24–29.

Lowe, L. (2015). *The intimacies of four continents*. London: Duke University Press.

Maldanado-Torres, N. (2007). On the coloniality of being. *Cultural Studies, 21*(2), 240–270.

Martinez, E. (2000). What is white supremacy? *Catalyst Project*. www.collectiveliberation.org. Retrieved from http://collectiveliberation.org/wp-content/uploads/2013/01/What_Is_White_Supremacy_Martinez.pdf.

Mawani, R. (2009). *Colonial proximities: Crossracial encounters and juridical truths in British Columbia, 1871-1921*. Vancouver, BC: UBC Press.

Mbembe, A. (2001). *On the postcolony*. Berkeley: University of California Press.

Mbembe, A. (2003). Necropolitics. (L. Meintjes Trans.) *Public Culture, 15*(1), 11–40.

Mignolo, W. D. (1995). *The darker side of the Renaissance: Literacy, territoriality and colonization*. Ann Arbor: The University of Michigan Press.

Mills, C. (1997). *The racial contract*. Ithaca, NY: Cornell University Press.

Moorhouse, E. (2015). Who needs hybridity? Towards an anti-colonial, feminist theorization of "mixed race." Term paper, HSJ 3914H1 Anti-colonial though & pedagogical challenges. Toronto: Department of Social Justice Education, OISE, University of Toronto.

Mongia, R. (2007). Historicizing state sovereignty: Inequality and the form of equivalence. *Comparative Studies in Society and History 42* (02), 38–-411. doi: http://dx.doi.org/10.1017/S0010417507000539.

Papernick, S. (2015a, April). Colonial dominance in global capitalism. Unpublished Term paper. Department of Social Justice Education, Ontario Institute for Studies in Education of the University of Toronto (OISE/UT), Toronto.

Papernick, S. (2015b). Review of Arif Dirlik, 1997. The postcolonial aura: Third World criticism in the age of global capitalism. Oxford: Westview Press.

Portello, B. (Producer), & Diaz, P. (Director). (2008). The end of poverty? [DVD]. Retrieved from http://www.theendofpoverty.com/index.html.

Quijano, A. (2000). Coloniality of power, ethnocentrism, and Latin America. *NEPANTLA, 1*(3), 533–580.

Raghuram, P. (2017). Personal Communication. *Email invitation to 'Call for Papers'*. Open University, Milton Keynes.

Rahnema, M. (1991). *Global poverty: A pauperizing myth*. Montreal, Quebec: Intercultural Institute of Montreal.

Said, E. (1978). *Orientalism*. New York, NY: Vintage Books.

Senghor, L. (2001). Negritude and modernity or Negritude as a humanism for the twentieth century. In R. Bernasconi (Ed.), *Race* (pp. 143–166). Malden, MA: Blackwell.

Silva, D. F. (2007). *Toward a global idea of race*. Minneapolis, MN: University of Minnesota Press.

Smith, A. (2006). Heteropatriarchy and the three pillars of white supremacy. In *Color of violence: INCITE! Women of color against violence* (pp. 66–73). Cambridge, MA: South End Press.

Srivastava, S. (2005). You're Calling Me a 'Racist'? The moral and emotional regulation of antiracism and feminism. *Signs: Journal of Women and Culture in Society, 31*(1), 29–62.

Srivastava, S. (2006). Tears, fears and careers: Anti-racism and emotion in social movement organization. *Canadian Journal of Sociology, 13*(1), 55–90.

Stasiulus, D., & Bakan, A. (2005). *Negotiating citizenship: Migrant women in Canada and the global system*. Toronto: University of Toronto Press.

Teffo, L. J. (2002). Foreword. In L. A. Kassanga & T. J. Lebakeng (Eds.), *Paradigm shift in South African higher education* (pp. i–ii). Sevenga: University of the North Press.

Toussaint, E. (2008). *The World Bank: A critical primer*. London: Pluto Press.

Zeleza, T. (1997). Fictions of the postcolonial: A review article. *CODESRIA Bulletin, 2*, 15–19.

Chapter 2
Towards a [Re]Theorization of Blackness, Anti-Blackness, and Black Solidarities

Abstract This chapter uses a decolonizing framework and re-theorizes anti-Blackness and Blackness by highlighting previous existing literature and scholarship. I am interested in examining how other scholars have theorized Blackness; more importantly my work seeks to combine decolonial and anti-colonial theory. I am particularly interested in examining how scholars like bell hooks, Stuart Hall, Patricia Hill Collins, George Yancy, Jared Sexton, Cecil Foster, Rinaldo Walcott, and Saidiya Hartman, to name a few, have theorized Blackness. Some key areas I expand on include; the current Black Lives Matter movement; continual appropriation and consumption of Blackness, with a critical examination of post-Blackness as it relates to post-racial ideas about race-relations. Both Stuart Hall and bell hooks have written extensively on representation and how negative images of Blackness and Black people have been central to maintaining White hegemonic power. hooks calls for an alternative way to look at Blackness, in addition to a new way of looking at Whiteness. hooks argues, African American/African/Black people within the realm of the image. "Unless we transform images of [B]lackness, of Blackness people, our ways of looking and our ways of being seen, we cannot make radical interventions that will fundamentally alter our situation" (hooks 1992, p. 7). It is within this research that I seek to interrogate Blackness within the Canadian context to further examine the absence of representation within school curriculum, media, and Canadian cultural discourse.

Very long ago I recall a scholarly acquaintance asking me if it is possible to not speak of race at some point. My quick reply was why, and what is he afraid of? Upon later reflection, I enthused if he would ask the same question of gender, class, sexuality, [dis]ability, religion, language, and if not, why not? He got me going on a whole lot of things that I will not bore the reader with at this moment. Let me stay focused because race can be slippery and it can easily "vanish" around the table of public discourse. We foot dance around race. This is the ubiquity of race. It easily becomes the disappearing act where it rears its head. Needless to say my colleague lodged his query from a privileged racial position of White dominance. Unless racism ends, race will always be relevant. Anti-Black racism is one of the many pernicious aspects of racisms. Black and African peoples have continually endured this

© Springer International Publishing AG 2017   31
G.J.S. Dei, *Reframing Blackness and Black Solidarities through Anti-colonial and Decolonial Prisms*, Critical Studies of Education 4,
DOI 10.1007/978-3-319-53079-6_2

social cancer. If race is to become obsolete then racism must first be obliterated. Otherwise it will be foolhardy for anyone who is racially oppressed to not speak about race. Race is about everything outside of its impacts. It is convenient and indeed easy when advantaged by race to claim racial absence or neutrality.

To claim to re-theorize Blackness and anti-Blackness through a decolonizing framework is a tall order because of the tremendous amount of scholarship on Blackness. My overall learning objective is to complement the very extensive existing literature on Black racial identity, representation, and politics. This discussion is informed by some pertinent questions: What are the tools/frameworks Black and African diaspora can deploy to forge community and solidarity, and to resist anti-Blackness, anti-Black racism and other social oppressions? What critical analytical tools can be developed to account for Black and African lived experiences, agency and resistance? As well, what are the limits of the tools or frameworks for anti-racist, anti-colonial work (see also Sandhu 2014 in another context)? And, how do such critical tools or frameworks of Blackness and anti-Blackness assist in anti-racist and anti-colonial practice? In articulating Blackness and anti-Blackness as a framework for conceptualizing, analyzing and understanding the Black/African racialization and marginalization in Euro-Canadian/American contexts, this book helps strengthen anti-racist and anti-colonial pedagogies and politics. The focus on a Blackness and anti-Blackness framework helps to generate new insights of inquiry into African-centered perspectives, epistemologies, experiences, social relations and practices.

Let me put some questions on the table: How are Black and African scholars themselves theorizing Blackness? How are Black and African intellectuals vigorously resisting the misrepresentations of our Blackness, Africanness and our myriad identities? These are good questions to ask given that others have assumed discursive authority over Black lives, bodies and experiences. My project connects an anti-colonial/decolonial theorization of Blackness to an anti-Blackness thesis to demonstrate the worth of a social theory extends well beyond its philosophical grounding. As I have noted repeatedly, the social worth of an academic theory must equally rest on its ability to offer a social and political corrective i.e. to bring about social change for the better.

To begin the discussion in this chapter let me offer the intellectual rationale for a re-theorization of Blackness and anti-Blackness from where I sit. Clearly, this work builds on the existing excellent scholarship and knowledge on the Black experience in multiple contexts. One thing is for certain though: dominant bodies/scholars/groups do not get to define what Blackness and anti-Blackness is although they attempt to. Situated in North America, I also want to write a book about Blackness and anti-Blackness that extends the Diasporic milieu to speak to African peoples across a broad spectrum, including those on the continent itself as well. This is more than the fact that there are African-born learners in North American schools. Nor simply an argument although educators need to teach African Studies in Euro-American educational institutions from the position of a [re]conceptualized Black Studies as along with others I have long argued (see Dei 1995). For me this connection is important since there has been unfortunate intellectual musings around the term "Black" as a color descriptor with little relevance or application to the African conception of the human. However that may be, "the fact of Black[ness]" has become part of the lexicon of social and academic knowledge (Fanon 1967). We no longer have the luxury of simply dismissing these terms and substitute African for Black. It is just like the race concept—there is a political project as well. I hold on to this reading as it speaks to me: Black is African and African is Black! People are free to disagree. As Stewart (2016) enthuses, we need to see and understand the ways hegemonic "systems are put in place to perform anti-Black racism globally [and also how] these systems are used as 'divide and conquer' tactics to diminish any interest of Diasporic Africans and Black people to build and network a Pan-African movement [and] works to ideologically further disconnect Black people [everywhere] from their Indigenous roots and place of ultimate belonging" (p. 1).

In re-theorizing Blackness and anti-Blackness through anti-colonial and decolonial prisms, I engage my Black and African identity as a site of experiential knowing. I put forth a particular interest to reinvent an Africanness in Diasporic contexts where Black, Blackness and Africanness matter so profoundly. Hence, I offer a reading of Blackness and anti-Blackness that is relevant to African peoples everywhere, including those who may want to contest their Black [or African] identity. While we may insist on the existence of a Black or African community as contestable and heterogeneous, the community [like Black, Blackness, Africa] is not just a physical space, place and moment that can be defined by strict "temporal or physical limits" (Dilliard 2008, p. 279). For peoples of African ascent and descent we deny our Black identity and our own constructed Blackness at our own peril. When we fail to reinvent our Africanness in diasporic contexts we also continue the colonial tradition of severing/amputating peoples from their cultures, heritage and histories as sites of knowing, resistance and empowerment. No level or amount of academic complexification of our Black identities can take away our shared and contingent histories. At some point it simply becomes a conversation of academic elites needing to make themselves relevant to lost causes.

In this re-theorization of Blackness I infuse a reinvention of an "Africanness" with the discussion of "Diasporic Blackness" in very specific ways. Africanness takes my analysis back to pre-contact/colonial Africa when African peoples had discovered themselves and were not waiting on Europeans. Diasporic Blackness may center issues of historic specificity to the Black experience. But it does not mean there is no connection between the Black experience in the diaspora and African experiences on the continent and globally. All histories are about relations and connections. Part of the diasporic experience is still to deal with or to resist the sub-humanity of the African and the Black subject, our social and economic marginalization and the continuing legacies of enslavement and the question of Land displacement. These experiences shape the development of thought and action about what it means to be Black and to affirm our Blackness in particular contexts. Similarly, reinventing an Africanness in the Diaspora is to bring a deep awareness to what is still happening on the continent and, to connect that with the global African experience in terms of education, development, on-going colonialisms and the rapes of multinational corporations and the international finance capital of our human, cultural and material wealth and resources. Different bodies may come to an understanding of Blackness from specific locations and yet with shared concerns and politics. While Blackness is a negative for the dominant/oppressor, reclaiming Blackness may be subversive and liberating for the subordinated/oppressed especially when evoked for political and social transformation.

In both conceptualizations, "reinventing Africanness" and "Diasporic Blackness," it is important for us to acknowledge on-going global legacies of colonial genocides with particular impacts on Black, Indigenous and other intersectional communities and the displacement of African peoples and how this has deeply shaped the relations between Black, African and Indigenous peoples in North America, Africa and the global Diaspora. Identities [Black, African and Indigenous identities in particular] have been a site for colonial impositions. Today identity has been taken in the contexts of varied intellectual discursive spaces that sometimes normalizes dominant discourse and apolitical practices. There is some significance in asking: how are certain imposed Black identities being normalized within contemporary social formations of anti-Blackness and anti-Africanness? Also, how can we distinguish between current mobilizations of identity around cultural and ideological constructs of White nationalism and xenophobia (i.e., extreme Right discourses, neo-nazi) and the political and politicized mobilizations of identity for anti-colonial projects? As I write we are all witnesses to how in the United States, Donald Trump has mobilized around White popularism using a White nationalist identity construction of the Neo-Nazis to win votes for the US presidency. I would insist that we distinguish such practices from anti-colonial political mobilizations of identity to seek redress in legitimate historic injustices against Blacks, Indigenous populations and other oppressed groups. Such mobilizations are not in defense of power and privilege they are intended to resist oppression. It is significant to understand how identities (e.g., racial, class, gender, sexual, [dis]ability, and spiritual) are claimed as resistance to the politics of exclusion. We must understand that our social identities are not always defined in relation to others; but also, upon the recognition and affirmation of self and collective shared histories, and as an exercise of intellectual agency of the marginalized to know and define ourselves and our communities. This is the reason for an intellectual politics of subverting the construction of Africa, African diaspora and Black, which continues to exist within Euro-American ideologies.

2.1   How Have Black Scholars Themselves [and Others] Theorized Blackness?

A re-theorization of Blackness is not possible without first acknowledging the works of notable scholars who have written on Black identity and politics. Critical theorists contributing to the scholarship include bell hooks, Stuart Hall, Patricia Hill Collins, George Yancy, Jared Sexton, Rinaldo Walcott, Cecil Foster and Saidiya Hartman to name a few. In the following section I will discuss topics such as the Black Lives Matter movement; the appropriation, commodification and consumption of Blackness; the notion of "post-Blackness"; Black authenticity; Black citizenship and more alongside the theorizations of fellow scholars.

Representation and images of Blackness and Black people are important to critique because they define not only how we are seen but also how we see ourselves, since we can internalize negative images. bell hooks has written extensively on the power of representation, where she argues that "[t]here is a direct and abiding connection between the maintenance of white supremacist patriarchy in this society and the institutionalization via mass media of specific images, representations of race, of Blackness that support and maintain the oppression, exploitation, and overall domination of all Black people" (hooks 1992, p. 2). She calls for "radical intervention," for "fierce critical interrogation" of representation, and for "revolutionary attitudes about race and representation" (hooks 1992, p. 7). Like hooks (1992), I contend that since decolonization as a political process is always a struggle to define ourselves in and beyond the act of resistance to domination, we are always in the process of remembering the past even as we create new ways to imagine and make the future. hooks (1992) critically interrogates old narratives, suggesting alternative ways to look at Blackness, Black subjectivity, and, of necessity, Whiteness.

bell hooks reminds us that oppressive images of Blackness can also be constructed by people of color/Black people who may have internalized racism. As such, we must also be critical of what Black people are writing about. It is about *politics*. It is not an issue of "us" and "them." The issue is really one of *standpoint*. "From what political perspective do we dream, look, create, and take action?" (hooks 1992, p. 4). hooks believes that we experience our collective crisis as African American/African/Black people within the realm of the *image*. "Unless we transform images of [B]lackness, of [B]lack people, our ways of looking and our ways of being seen, we cannot make radical interventions that will fundamentally alter our situation" (hooks 1992, p. 7).

Stuart Hall's work has also been central to Black cultural politics, as he has written extensively on "the Black experience" and representation of Blacks in Britain (Hall 1997). The struggle to come into representation requires the critique of the fetishization, objectification and negative figuration of the Black subject (Hall 1997). The issue is not the absence or marginality of the Black experience, but with its simplification and its stereotypical character. Media images are powerful in that they can distort reality. That is why intellectual work has a role to play in helping to regain control of an image-dominated world by interrogating the image and asking hard questions rather than just accepting it at face value. Moreover, meanings do not occur in a vacuum. Humans are meaning-making beings. Hall discusses the production of meaning or "signifying practices." More critically, he notes *absence* means something and signifies as much as presence. This is relevant to my task of re-theorizing Blackness as we must interrogate the absence of Black persons as subjects within different terrains, such as the media, school curriculums, and Canadian cultural discourse. The task of re-theorizing Blackness lends on Hall's (1996) argument that identity should not be understood as singular, essential, ahistorical, given and fixed, but as something that is always *in process*.

Clearly representations, symbols, significations are as important as speaking to our lived/experiential realities as Black and African peoples. Black identity and subjectivity has never been about a "fetishization of culture and the past (see Keesing, 1989)." In fact, African-centered reading of culture is about process [something living and breathing], as well as folkloric productions, including material culture. We should utilize our local cultural knowledge and practices to explain/interpret our communities and our lives. Black/African identity and subjectivity is not just about process; it is also about non-material expressions folkloric productions, symbols, significations, as well as material/tangible artifacts, including sacred objects, motifs, "time honored images" and ancestral remains (see Howes 1996, p. 140) that speak about our past, culture, history and heritage. Acknowledging the tangible materiality and the non-material aspects of culture does not mean culture is a thing, an essence, or even a mere possession. Material objects and cultural artifacts can be a way of life/being as is the case when African peoples show a deep veneration of material remains—the dead body, bones, etc.

There is the power of a Black perspective. "Thinking Black" to borrow from Carter G Woodson's usage is about the necessity and urgency of Black intellectual thought in the Western academy that is steeped in our own cultural and historical perspectives. Recently, in a keynote address at my university, African American educational theorist, Joyce King (2016) alluded to the importance of a "search for Black intellectual independence" and what a declaration for such independence means Molefi Asante and others have been making such excellent points as well. There has been a consistent annihilation and nihilation of African and Black epistemologies. And yet there is excellence [defined in multiple ways] in our African-centered perspectives. Therefore, I take the re-theorization of Blackness as gesturing to the imperative and the ontological reality of counter-representations informed by Black and African epistemes. Black and African peoples [like other Indigenous peoples] have always recognized multiple readings of our world. We also recognize contestations, contradictions and complexities of culture, the past history. But we resist amputations of our past, histories and cultures not because we want these to imprison us. It is because they offer important lessons that can contribute to new imaginaries and new futurities for us. Our present is very much inclusive of the past and the future ahead of us.

Thus, I deeply concur with the call for Black, African, Indigenous, colonized and racial minority scholars to develop relevant "rich theoretical tool-boxes" for understanding our own experiences. In the current "geo-politics of knowledge" (Mignolo 2002), the contest over knowledge and power has serious ramifications for subjectivities and collective politics. The power to self-define and design our own futures readily comes to mind. The Black subject[ivity] is always in contention and is being contested. There is a pertinent question to be addressed: In what ways has the colonial and imperialist project perceived Blackness and the question of African Indigeneity as part of coming to know about ourselves? If one struggles to answer this question it is more because there has been the negations, devaluations and omissions in our politics of knowledging that I alluded to earlier.

2.2   Black Lives Matter Movement

#BlackLivesMatter is both a call to action and a response to the ways in which Black lives have been devalued. The Black Lives Matter movement is an intersectional feminist and queer proposition that began following the acquittal of George Zimmerman for the murder of Trayvon Martin in the summer of 2013 and was fuelled by the protests in Ferguson, Missouri after the death of Michael Brown. The movement is radically democratic in form and content, and is collaboratively organized. Some of the criticism of Black Lives Matter as "leaderless" comes from Black women often being rendered invisible. According to the organization's website, the Black Lives Matter Movement is not just concerned about police brutality, but also focuses on education, health, and social issues that affect Black lives. It goes beyond extrajudicial killings of Black people by police and vigilantes. Black Lives Matter affirms the lives of disabled Black people, Black-undocumented people, those with records, Black queer, cisgender and transgender people and all Black lives along the gender spectrum. It centers those that have been marginalized within Black liberation movements and they state that their aim is to (re)build the Black liberation movement ("Black Lives Matter: About Us," n.d.).

Interestingly, though Black queer women initiated the BLM movement, talks about violence towards cis, trans, heterosexual and queer women of color were largely absent from the dominant discourse in the beginning. Initially, the focus on state-sanctioned violence against Black men rendered Black cisgender and transgender victims invisible; however, many Black feminist activists subsequently came to speak against the silencing of the struggle of Black women. This shows that the movement has evolved as it is pushing for the recognition of Black humanity and now the challenge is to change the institutions responsible for its degradation. It is impossible to understand the intense policing of Black communities without putting it into the wider context of the decades-old War on Drugs and the effects of mass incarceration (Taylor 2016). The systematic over-imprisonment of Black people has conflated race, risk, and criminality to legitimize close scrutiny of Black communities as well as the consequences of the scrutiny. The entire criminal justice system operates at the expense of African American communities and society as a whole.

BLM has been criticized for being anti-White and racist—but let us be clear—declaring Black lives matter does not diminish any other life, rather, it is necessary to proclaim this as Black people are dehumanized, brutalized and killed every day. Moreover, statements such as "*all* lives matter" can be considered a form of anti-Black racism. Such a declaration is an example of the Euro-American tendency to centralize Whiteness as it fails to account for Black life and suffering. It is an attempt to erase an actual crisis under the guise of being fair. Moreover, "All Lives Matter" ignores context. The context of Black Lives Matter is that the value of Black lives remains under assault in the United States and around the world. #AllLivesMatter is often used as an attempt to question and dismiss the legitimacy and presumed "rationality" of #BlackLivesMatter (Carney 2016). Although #AllLivesMatter claims a certain universality that is inclusive of all groups, in practice it works to collapse the specificities of different groups' experiences in favor of a color-blind ideology that favors White supremacy. Moreover, the All Lives Matter phrase erases the long entrenched, specific histories of state repression that marginalized peoples have suffered under the guise of state protection (Gaber and Wright 2015). As BLM puts it, the movement stands for "the simple proposition that 'Black lives also matter.' " Other lives do not matter any less, but simply the movement is trying to reinforce the fact that ours always did, still does and will always matter. Moreover, the statement "Black lives matter" is not an anti-White proposition. Contained within the statement is an unspoken but implied "too," as in, "Black lives matter, too," which suggests that the statement is one of inclusion rather than exclusion. However, White people who continue to mischaracterize the affirmation of the value of Black life as being anti-White are suggesting that in order for White lives to matter, Black lives cannot. It is not until Black Lives Matter is true for All Lives Matter to be a reality, until then, it is *irrelevant* to the current experiences of Black people and it drowns out the real problems the BLM movement is trying to address.

The birth of this movement against racism and policing is shattering the illusion of a color-blind, post-racial United States (Taylor 2016). The BLM Movement works to address Black violability, defined as "a construct that attempts to encapsulate both the lived and historical experiences of Black people with state-initiated and state-sanctioned violence" (Lindsey 2015, p. 234). Specifically, anti-Black violence can be considered a performance of the modern American nation-state (Smith 2015). In other words, "state violence is a process of embodiment and subject making with plots, scripts, and spectacles that have tangible, material effects" (Smith 2015, p. 384). As Sexton (2015) argues, state violence gains and retains the aura of legitimacy at the direct expense of the legitimacy of one's very sense of self (p. 163). As we address multiple dimensions of state and state-sanctioned anti-Black violence, using an intersectional approach to contest Black violability is needed. Lindsey (2015) discusses how the Black Lives Matter movement speaks to the necessary acknowledgement of the tremendous work of Black women Black cisgender or transgender people, and queer people within contemporary racial justice movements. A long tradition of African American activism is the regular erasure of Black women Black cisgender or transgender people, and queer people from the historical record both as victims and activists. As such, the Black Lives Matter movement emerged out of an attempt to shift the masculine-centered narrative of contemporary anti-Black racial violence. As Lindsey (2015) shows, #BlackLivesMatter does not mean that only #BlackMenMatter. It is important to examine how gender and sexuality affect how we mobilize and organize for racial justice. The demands for recognition of the humanity of all Black people requires activists, allies and the broader US, Canadian and global publics to critically consider the impact of state violence on individual Black people, Black families, and Black communities worldwide.

One of the critiques of the BLM movement is that it has primarily been focused on the experiences of Black cis-gender men. However, Black queer people and Black transgender men and Black cis-gender and transgender women are often targeted as well in disproportionate numbers. They are targeted in different but also very similar ways as cis-gender men—shootings, police stops, racial profiling. They also experience police violence in distinctly gendered and sexualized ways, such as transphobia, homophobia, sexual harassment and sexual assault. Black feminist politics draws attention to the fact that Black cis- and transgender women and girls *also* suffer from state-sanctioned violence typically associated with Black cis-gender men and boys. The understanding is every time these same forces kill Black cis-gender men and boys, they are also victimizing, directly and indirectly, transgender men and boys and those Black cis- and transgender women and girls who raise and care for them. This violence encompasses the broad capacity of Black people to reproduce *as a people*, including "freedom from structural violence that might constitute conditions of livability" (Sexton 2015, p. 169). Sexton (2015) poses critical questions that are meaningful for the re-theorization of Blackness. He asks, "Black Lives Matter: how so and to whom, in what ways and by what means, when and under what conditions, precisely? Do Black lives matter only when taken together, or taken apart, or taken apart together?" (p. 159). This very precariousness of Black life brings into question Black citizenship, which will be discussed in the section to follow.

The BLM movement is not just limited to the United States, Twitter and other social media outlets have helped proliferate the movement across borders. Many young people are increasingly participating in the public sphere. Carney (2016) states that social media allows youth of color across the globe to engage in transnational discussions about oppressive systems and state-sanctioned violence. Yarimar Bonilla and Jonathan Rosa's (Bonilla and Rosa 2015) article discusses how social media or "hashtag activism" challenges dominant news organizations' representations of racialized bodies and usage of Twitter helps connect people over time and space much more quickly. In addition, today's pervasiveness of video-enabled smartphones, together with rapid mobilization of activist networks via social media, help boost the public salience of police brutality. The BLM movement is reminding us that while harm is always a possible outcome of the state's quest for urban health and safety, the probability of subjection to such harm is disproportionately distributed among populations along the lines of race, class, gender, sexuality, mental health and (dis) ability.

While Black Lives Matter participants called for police accountability and characterized the movement as anti-police-brutality but not as anti-police, conservative opponents depicted BLM as racially divisive, violent and "anti-White." The criticisms of BLM, especially accusations of the movement being anti-White, anti-police and "inherently racist" according to former New York City Mayor Rudolph W. Guiliani, are not new. Following peaceful BLM-organized protests against the police killings of Alton Sterling in Baton Rouge, Louisiana, and Philando Castille in Falcon Heights, Minnesota in July 2016, a heavily armed sniper gunned down police officers in Dallas, Texas leaving five of them dead. This shooting instantly moved such criticism from the background to the forefront—whereby the BLM movement was accused of being responsible for the deaths of the Dallas police officers. This goes to show just how racist the United States is when the horrid actions of one shooter is supposed to be reflective of an entire race, or in this case, a movement that aims to protect an entire race. The snipers' motivations were evidently fuelled by hate and their actions are certainly condemned by the movement.

One can argue that the backlash to BLM reflects a broad sense of unease among White people who worry about the cultural changes in the country and feel like they are being "marginalized"—the notion that Whites have replaced Blacks as the primary victims of discrimination. A recent study by Norton and Sommers (2011) Harvard Business School describes that Whites' belief about the prevalence of anti-White bias reflects a view of racism as a "zero-sum game," such that decreases in perceived bias against Blacks over the past six decades are associated with increases in perceived bias against Whites—a relationship not observed in Blacks' perceptions. Hence, the fact that White people tend to see race as a zero-sum game may actually impede progress.

Black Lives Matter and related protests have become part of a revitalized politics of intersectionality—whereby the recent waves of protests have focused on climate change, wages, immigration law, economic inequality, reproductive rights, access to healthcare, and voting rights. The movement highlights acute economic inequalities that affect a wide—but often not particularly visible—group of people in the United States and elsewhere. Moreover, this movement is shedding light on the necessity to re-theorize Blackness and how internalized stereotypes of the "angry Black woman" or "Black beast" feed into institutions that govern us and police us.

The discussion of Black Lives Matter is very relevant to the re-theorization of Blackness as it is also about the search for a new politics of educational futurity, and I insist on placing Black and African education on center stage. Picking up on Mbembe's (2003) "necropolitics," a framework to understand who matters and who does not, who is deemed worthy of loving and being killed, I ask: how do we define what and whose life is deemed worthy of education? How do we re-imagine the human that disturbs the creation of a universal learner that erases racial, class, gender, sexual, disability differences and the performativity of dominant identities in schooling? I grapple with another question: As Black/African scholar, what good is my academic scholarship and theorizing in the contexts of the struggles of "Black Lives Matter" organization when this work is not directed foremost to the continuing challenges of Black disposability, national/colonial settler state disregard of Black concerns, community anti-Blackness, the everyday capitalist commodification and consumption of Blackness and Black identity, and the persistent surveillance, policing and punishment of Black [and Indigenous and racialized] bodies as showing up in unwanted spaces, constitutive of Black transgressions? There is a particular responsibility of Black scholarship to be activist scholarship, unapologetic of Blackness and Black identity as political and politicized identities to challenge the normalization of every knowledge and social practice (see also Dei 2014) I will return to these questions.

2.3 Black Citizenship

The question of Black citizenship draws our attention to the unique relationship between Black/African peoples and the nation state and the negotiation processes in which Black people engage in order to navigate national belonging. For example, in his book *Black like who?*, Rinaldo Walcott (2003) is critical of how the fluidity of borders and America's influence on Canada can create a politics of exclusion and foster discourses of nationalism. He shows how this can hinder transnational political identifications that might be crucial for solidarity building (p. 33). The significance of media and technology for helping build coalitions and exchange information across borders, with Black Live Matters for example, is evident here. Walcott encourages questions of responsibility and ethics such as BLM that move beyond the nation. For example, he supports a "Diasporic sensibility" in making outernational identifications with other Black peoples.

As the persistent and escalating problem of anti-Black state violence in the Americas presents unique challenges to the discourse of race and national belonging, the need for transnational solidarities and Walcott's (2003) "Diasporic sensibility" becomes even more apparent. Many scholars contend that borders of Western nations themselves merely serve an ideological purpose, as the exploited labor of both legal and "illegal" immigrants is a structural necessity for capitalism's survival (Sharma 2009). A critical race analysis of immigration laws in Western nations illuminates the logic of race organizing society, rather than simply national origin. Sharma (2009) posits that within "national space," the racial or ethnic "Other" remains an object. In White settler societies, rights, privileges and social relations may be organized in such a way as to justify and legitimate discrimination against anyone defined as an outsider, including citizens. African/Black people are construed as outsiders in Western contexts, regardless of citizenship status. According to Canada's Constitution and those in other advanced liberal democracies, citizens of color ostensibly occupy the same rights and privileges enjoyed by White citizens. When race *is* explicitly addressed in law or policy, racial equality remains either the professed norm or goal. However, through implementation of law as well through the structure of law itself, the state employs race in classifying outsiders, eliminating and proscribing equal rights under the law. Far from a new phenomenon, state deployment of race in the legal and bureaucratic structuring of society has not changed; rather the techniques and racial subjectivities have been modified throughout time to uphold and mask the underlying structure of White supremacy. While nation-building is entrenched in the notion of the citizen, *racialized* citizens have never been fully embraced in White settler nations—politically or socially (Razack 2008).

As businesses and products cross borders freely under neoliberal policy, humans are allowed movement based on their capitalist utility. Neoliberalism has exponentiated what has been a historical commodification of immigrant laborers. When the economy has changed and certain occupations have fewer vacancies, Canada has returned to more restrictive immigration and temporary work permit policies. Refusing to grant citizenship to unauthorized immigrant workers guarantees the material benefits of cheap labor while avoiding many of the costs associated with recognition of worker rights (Sharma 2009). Despite Canada's Multicultural Policy, its immigration system reifies, alters, and creates racialized subjectivities through inconsistent inclusions and intrinsic exclusions. Abuse of non-citizens by government officials, employers, or citizens and the strengthening of a racist culture occur when racialized immigrants and refugees are "rightfully" denied the rights, entitlements and dignity expected of full "members of society." Basic needs such as health care, housing, and food may be denied based on a person's national origin (Sharma 2009). With the professed elimination of legal forms of racism, this racialization of space becomes an effective dividing practice, a mode of practicing racism that is enhanced through neo-liberalism. De Genova (2002) posits that "illegality" is an erasure of legal personhood designed not to physically exclude people, but to socially include them under imposed conditions of compulsory and protracted vulnerability.

Making this situation worse, racialized immigrants and citizens who access public benefits are often accused of abusing the system, as if basic necessities are reserved for (White) citizens. Cast as both criminal and undeserving sustains the inhumane treatment of Black/African citizens and non-citizens in Western contexts. Race thinking reconciles these contradictions and sanitizes the systemic violence that occurs through our exploitation and denial of fundamental human rights.

Race therefore continues to define not only *expressions* of citizenship and the kind of citizenship we practice but also the extent to which we are recognized as citizens—subjects at all, or even not worthy to live.

The nation-state's rules for engagement with Black bodies are not a cultural process of Black "citizenship" making—"producing consent through schemes of surveillance, discipline, and control" (Foucault 1977). Rather, they are a necropolitics of objectification—"contemporary forms of subjugation of life to the power of death" (Mbembé 2003, p. 39). Walcott (2003) shows that Black appeals for social justice in Canada remain unheard by those in authority, and he contends that this is because Black peoples continue to have an ambivalent place in the national imagination. Despite this ambivalence, Blacks and Blackness have always been central to the Canadian experience, even if most often they are not recognized as part of the Canadian good and ideal (Foster 2007). Black and Canadian become unstated opposite concepts in many national discourses that emerge on social issues. For example, the ubiquitous phrase "crackdown on crime" targets Black people without naming race while simultaneously reifying a White Canadian citizenry that is allegedly both law-abiding and non-racist (embracing multiculturalism). Another case occurs when the media frames Black murders by other Black People as "Jamaican crime" or "Somali crime," it projects a certain kind of ethnic blame that positions Blackness outside the nation (Walcott 2003, p. 12). This is strategic for creating divisions between Black communities. Walcott (2003) outlines Blackness as a sign that is always under contestation—"we are an absented presence always under erasure" (p. 27). He shows that we need to think within and against the nation, as Blackness can be a potential challenge to normative narratives of the nation (Whiteness), rather than something incorporated into these narratives. Furthermore, the recent Black migrant must not fall for the seductive discourse of multiculturalism that denies a longer Black presence in Canada.

2.4 Appropriation, Consumption and Commodification of Blackness

No human group has had their humanity denied or continually assaulted like African peoples. Africans continually have had to live with the sub-humanity of our existence. This racist thinking has always posed an existential threat to our collective survival everywhere. In fact, Dilliard (2008) makes an excellent observation that "no Black person has escaped the negation of our humanity, whether in the academy, the boardroom, on the farm, or in the streets" (p. 288). This must be a powerful justification for us to theorize Blackness in very inclusive ways. Such assertion is not intended to deny the historic and on-going atrocities against other oppressed groups, including the genocide of Indigenous peoples globally. It is also not to create a hierarchy of oppressions. It is fact of human history that the discomfort of race and Blackness makes the African experience an unpleasant history to be acknowledged let alone heard. We may tell it but it is also a question of who is listening to us. The African genocide was more than about our enslavement. And yet there is more to the state/official resistance and refusal to rendering apology for such human shame and even to pay reparations to African and Black peoples. I believe the resistance and refusal to act is not simply because of the question of how, for example, reparations can be justified. It has been done for others. There are African ascendants and descendants. My point is that we all know oppression and injustice when we see it and the least we can do is to apologize, atone for past and historic injustices and ask for forgiveness so that we can truly begin the healing process. To apologize makes it a bit easier to forgive, of course not to forget. Furthermore healing is important for on it rests the hope that we learn from the lessons of the past and history so as not to repeat them.

Colonization has standardly involved the denigration of native cultures and languages. When Blackness is appropriated to the exclusion of others, identity becomes political (Johnson 2003). A complicated dynamic occurs when Whites appropriate Blackness. Whites exoticize and fetishize Blackness, which bell hooks calls "Eating the Other." However, uncritical consumption of other cultures is a form of reductionism and dehumanization and *not* a form of anti-racism work. As Cornel West (1999) points out, "the irony in our present moment is that just as young Black men are murdered and imprisoned in record numbers, their styles have become disproportionately influential in shaping popular culture" (p. 518). "Black male bodies are increasingly admired and commodified in rap, hip hop, and certain sports, but at the same time they continue to be used to invoke fear. Black men are both held in contempt and valued as entertainment" (Collins 2004). This is nothing new. Black men *and* women have been viewed as a threat throughout American history while being accepted in roles that serve the benefit of White people (Ferber 2007).

In *Scenes of Subjection: Terror, Slavery, and Self-Making in Nineteenth Century America,* Saidiya V. Hartman argues that the complicated play between sufferance, sentience and spectacle that is at the root of the African American image in the United States has its foundations in the experience of slavery. Hartman contends, "the desire to don, occupy or possess Blackness or the Black body as a sentimental resource and/or locus of excess enjoyment is both founded upon and enabled by the material relations of chattel slavery" (Hartman 1997, p. 21). Hartman also recognizes the omission of the material reality of African American suffering from that spectacle (p. 33). The author elaborates by using an account of an abolitionist named John Rankin, which illustrates how when trying to make the slave's suffering his own, Rankin begins to feel for himself instead. As such, the captive body is exploited as a means to explore the dominant's humanity.

Furthermore, in "Can You Be Black and Look at This? Reading the Rodney King Video(s)," Elizabeth Alexander (1994) similarly maintains the primacy of the visual in creating the relation between Black and White subject formation, noting, "Black bodies in pain for public consumption have been an American spectacle for centuries. The deaths of Eric Garner, Terence Crutcher and Keith Lamont Scott were shown numerous times by several media outlets; the growth of social media has also increased the consumption of death of Blackness bodies. This history moves from public rapes, beatings, lynching to the gladiatorial arenas of basketball and boxing" (pp. 78–79). Alexander (1994) sees the experience of racialized terror as the unique property of African American identity formation because of its ability to visually codify a history of African American suffering in the United States into "a collective historical memory." Alexander provides examples of cases during the 1990s of prolific Black people such as Mike Tyson, Magic Johnson, Rodney King, Clarence Thomas that illustrate how African American bodies have been the site of which national trauma—sexual harassment, drug abuse, AIDS, racial and economic conflict—has been dramatized. Alexander (1994, p.79) adds that in each of these traumatic instances, Black bodies and their attendant dramas are publicly consumed by the larger populace. White men have been the primary stagers and consumer of the historical spectacles … mentioned, but in one way or another, Black people have been looking, too forging a traumatized collective historical memory which is reinvoked … at contemporary sites of conflict. The discussion of Black suffering being a spectacle is very relevant to the on-going videotaped police brutality which has sparked the Black Lives Matter movement in recent years. Black death, along with the brutalization of Indigenous people in North America, is a part of normal life here. The enslaved, chained or dead Black body to gaze upon or to hear about or to position a self against has become mundane.

Clearly, Whiteness has assumed its meaning in the context of a constructed negative meaning of Blackness through the project of Western modernity. The equation of Blackness with inferiority, criminality and deviance was intended to position White[ness] as superior, innocent, civilized, legal, rational, pure and pristine. By placing Black[ness] in the dark and primitive it served to offer a positive light to its opposite, Whiteness. Such was the basis of Euro-colonial theorizing about what was modern and the non-modern, primitive and traditional. Such splitting of traditional and the modern became false but appealing and seductive play of colonial difference (see also Lauer 2007) in another context. Part of our resistance as Black and African intellectuals theorizing Blackness should be about bringing counter interpretations to the term as discursive resistance. Our resistance has to be expressed in many forms to reinforce our multiple agencies and "agential knowing" (Daniel and Yearwood 2002).

Johnson (2003) is attentive to the Black-White paradigm as he discusses the essentializing effect of when White Americans construct Blackness, and the even more complicated dynamic that occurs when Whites *appropriate* Blackness. Appropriation often leads to commoditization. As Blackness is commoditized, literally and figuratively, it becomes a cultural product to be traded based upon its appeal to White majoritarian aesthetics. Black culture is commoditized and circulated through film, television, music, news and advertising. Moreover, Alston (2005) contends that anti-racism cannot afford to be simply responsive because commodification is real (p. 305). She argues, "valuing cannot sustain itself simply as a consequence of assertion (for example: Black is beautiful)" (p. 305). This is because in the industrialized West, hegemonic power structures such as White supremacy are adept at morphing deep expression of self-love and valuing into commodities in the marketplace (ex. appropriation of Hip Hop culture, dashikis and distorted nostalgia for the "Motherland").

As such, it is in reclaiming our marginalized identities as Black and African bodies that we decolonize ourselves. There is an understanding of African, Blackness and Black identity that has and continues to be produced and projected through the White and Euro-colonial imagination. An anti-colonial conceptualization of Blackness as Black subjectivity is more about process of coming to knowing, being and acting, a process of identity formation and an emerging political consciousness. A critical knowledge of Blackness would demand a re-theorization of Black and African beyond physical places, Land and space, and offer a response to on-going colonialisms, as well as Euro-colonial constructions of modernity. To reiterate, a re-theorizing Blackness speaks to the intellectual agency of Black and African peoples to articulate our own lived realities, conditions and experiences without being interpreted through Eurocentric conceptual frames of thought and Euro-colonial and racist conjectures of modernity. We urgently need to interrogate Blackness and modernity itself (see Foster 2007). It is in such interrogations that we are able to understand the "philosophical, anthropological, sociological and mythological" arguments developed in support and to sustain Whiteness as an Euro-colonial project of Western modernity (Foster 2007) and how counter discourses can and do resist dominant and colonial narratives and interpretations.

2.5 Post-Blackness

Post-Blackness is the idea that we live in a new racial age where people are not limited by their race. It is the belief that we have to transcend our Blackness and that "there are infinite ways of being Black and performing Blackness" (Touré 2011). However, there is much to critique about this stance. Firstly, lending on Stuart Hall, what is the *post* in post-Blackness? Post implies that there was once a stabilizing essence of Blackness, something that can be clearly defined, and thus we "have to move past it to progress"—we must trouble this! What are we moving past exactly? Moreover, how can you go past what you *are*—what you are currently experiencing? The way North America was founded all but guarantees that race will always be at the center of identity no matter how one defines it.

In fact, such notions of post-Blackness and post-racialism extend beyond North America in various global contexts. Although biological accounts of racism have been widely discredited, the idea that certain populations and nations are underdeveloped persists through what Goldberg (2006) refers to as "racial historicism." He posits that the major distinction between racial assumptions and the patterns of racial theorizing and governance they enable lies between racial naturalism and racial historicism. Naturalism pertains to the belief in the inherent inferiority of those who are of non-European descent, in some biological sense, to those who are European descendants. Historicism took hold as a counter-voice to naturalism from about the mid-1800s on, and it replaces the claim of biological inferiority with the idea that non-Europeans are historically immature or less developed. Racial historicism draws on historically based assumptions of the under-evolved nature of colonized populations in both colonial and settler colonial contexts. The move from racial naturalism to (primarily) historicism shifted notions of innate inferiority that justified slavery and apartheid, to claims of historical underdevelopment and unskilled ineptitude (even if admitted moral equality), that have fuelled much of the White abolitionist movement and patronizing anti-colonialisms (Goldberg 2006, p. 18).

The transition from naturalism to historicism demonstrates how modern states have presumed their own modernity in and through their elaborations on race (Goldberg 2006). Though historicism has not completely replaced naturalism (and at times the two converge), it is the dominant form that racial assumptions take in the current context. Racelessness, or alleged non-racialism and post-racialism on the part of states, is a logical outcome of racial historicism as it asserts formal racial equality under the law. Goldberg (2006) shows how color-blindness in the US, multicultural policies in Canada and Australia, non-racialism in South Africa, racial democracy in Brazil, and ethnic pluralism in Europe each reflect a claim to modernization through various versions of "racelessness."

Racelessness does not mean that views on race have become more enlightened, despite racial historicism's self-presentation through those terms. Historicism elides the significance of race, in part through positing the insignificance of race's historical effects—i.e. through claims of post-Blackness and post-racialism. Additionally, through the discourse of racelessness, the physically violent repression imposed under racial naturalist regimes (i.e. formal apartheid and colonialism) was supplanted by "the infuriating subtleties of a legally fashioned racial order" under racial historicism (Goldberg 2006, p. 46). As law became abstractly committed to formal equality, the color-blind constitutionalism of racelessness became a narrative of states' modernization and racial progress. Yet these commitments in words have not been reflected in deeds, or structures, of "raceless" states (see for example Gotanda (1995) and Harris (1996) for the US context). Racelessness was as much a refusal to address, let alone remedy, deeply embedded historically based racial inequities and inequalities as it was an expressed support of principles of race "blind" fairness and equal opportunity. Thus, we are far from a state of post-racialism or post-Blackness. Rather, the overt commitments to racelessness worked to re-shape these states in the face of civil rights, integrationist and demographic challenges to White privilege and power (Goldberg 2006).

Racelessness gained ground in the aftermath of World War II and came to dominate public commitment in a number of transnational contexts from the 1960s onward. Postwar reconstruction and economic growth in Western nations pulled postcolonial populations into North American and European metropoles, while the UN rejected racial naturalism as scientifically false and anti-Semitism became the dominant intellectual measure of racial prejudice (Goldberg 2006). As colonialism gave way to post-colonial forms of governance and globalized neoliberalism, racelessness became the mark of state rationality. That is, the formalized commitment to racelessness stems from states' self-promotion as rational and moral and the recognition of racially diverse states in the post-war context of increased migration of former colonial subjects and changing urban and employment demographics (Duffield 2006; Goldberg 2006).

If anything, we should be talking about post-Whiteness and what this truly could signify. White supremacy is built on the extermination of Indigenous peoples and the expropriation of their Lands, the enslavement, oppression and exploitation of Blacks, and the subordination and exclusion of brown-skinned peoples as citizens, all in an effort to create a White state. This cultural value is so pervasive throughout society that Whiteness is both the obvious and hidden norm against which most things are measured. To change this dynamic requires active intervention to disrupt the normal functioning of a society built on White supremacist foundations. Mutua (2006) argues that progressive Blackness *is* this intervention. It is the ethical and active participation in antiracist, anticolonial struggles from the standpoint of Black self-identity and Black communities' well-being. It aims to disrupt the normal economic, cultural, social and political workings of White supremacy and consciousness. Hence, the notion of post-Blackness is flawed as it keeps Whiteness untroubled, a system against which it demarcates itself. Post-Blackness is a limited tool for eradicating structural inequality.

Thinking through the nebulous concept of post-Blackness, I am reminded of post-racialisms. Similarly, post-racialism is a bankrupt concept because it ignores race and the underlying complexities of systemic racism. The post-racial underpinning to post-Blackness cannot be easily discarded—"post" means beyond race and Blackness. The success of a relative few African Americans is upheld as "proof" of the United States' color-blind ethos and as a testament to the transcendence of its racist past (Taylor 2016, p. 4). How far can we move away from race and Blackness?

Just as there is a limited way to be "authentically" Black, there are unlimited ways to perform post-Blackness. But this means that the performers must be able to embrace the fluidity of Black identity without being influenced or impacted by societal conventions. Post-Blackness is more concerned with individual expression as a path to liberation rather than a race-conscious group rights approach to the eradication of systemic inequalities. Moreover, the problem is that identifying oneself as "post-Black" does nothing to undermine White supremacy; in fact it does the opposite.

2.6 *Becoming* Black

The notion of *becoming* Black can be theorized in multiple ways. Firstly, we can think of it as a process of becoming *politically conscious*. Stemming from this notion is the argument that non-phenotypically Black people can *become* Black in their politics or at least as accomplices towards social justice. However, how do we balance the fluidity of Black identity with the permanence of racism? Because as Black identity expands, there are many Blacks who cannot claim the power of modern individualistic Blackness. Moreover, if we are to discuss "becoming Black," we should also address the notion of becoming White especially since the Black/White dichotomy foregrounds the theorization of Blackness and anti-Black racism. George Yancy (2005) for example, illustrates that race matters in how we philosophically conceptualize the world. He argues that despite their critical analyses of race, Black and Whiteness philosophers existentially live the sociopolitical dimensions of their Whiteness and Blackness. Although Blackness and Whiteness are systemically interlocked along axes of class, misogyny, heterosexism, political affiliation, etc., this does not negate the reality that America is structured in the form of a systemically racist Manichean (White-Black) divide. Yancy speaks to the Black-White divide from his own racialized positionality as a Black male, exposing the dynamics that continue to create and reinforce the color line between Whites and Blacks.

Yancy grounds Black identity within the semiotic and racist space of Whiteness. He argues that "our Blackness is structured through our historical agency, the narratives that we tell, and grounded within the existential crucible of Whiteness supremacy" (p. 255). Although such an analysis is structured along the Black-White Manichean divide, Blackness is never limited to or confined to the Whiteness gaze. According to Yancy, it is ever changing into historical reconfigurations. Yancy asks how Blackness and Whiteness are ways of *becoming* and not simply static descriptor terms. Similarly, Johnson (2003) also explores the meaning of "becoming" Black, whereby an individual becomes conscious of how racial categories uphold power dynamics in society and engages in some form of counter hegemonic activity as a result of this awareness. He proposes a distribution system that is non-racialized (p. 194) by stripping terms like *Black* and *White* of any social values.

Mills (1998) argues that the distortions about Africa's past—the "invention of Africa"—need to be contextualized not as contingently racist descriptions by individual bigots but as part of the grand project of denying African/Black personhood (p. 114). As such, one can theorize that *becoming* Black is a politicized process and identity that involves connecting with one's roots and history (see also Dei and James 1998; Ibrahim 1999). This means that we need to be critical of supporting simply Black people without interrogating their commitments and intentions, but their politics.

Asante's (2005) work is helpful here, as he explores the meaning of Blackness as an ethical trope. For Asante, Blackness is not reduced to skin color, rather, it signifies an ethic of resistance and human liberation. He cites Fanon's book *Black Skin, White Masks* (Fanon 1967) as a canonical text that revealed Blackness as an obstacle to "unfettered injustice and became, in the moment of psychological terrorizing, the ethic of resistance" (Asante, p. 203). "Blackness" for Asante acts as a descriptor that can also be applied to Whiteness that enact forms of resistance against justice and oppression. Blackness is not merely a phenotype phenomenon and there is not a form of confraternity among all people who are Black in complexion. "To be Black is to share the evolving political and social interests of oppressive people" (p. 204). This mirrors Clarence Johnson (2003), who also argues that non-Black groups can also *become* Black when they undertake transgressive forms of activity aimed at dismantling racial hierarchy (p. 178). Asante is against the notion that there are degrees of Blackness; it is either you stand with the oppressed and against oppression or you stand with the oppressor against liberation (p. 214). Moreover, he recognizes Blackness itself as a pursuit.

Importantly, my reframing of Black, Blackness and anti-Blackness anchors the question of African Indigeneity as an intellectual move to resist the erasure and denial of our African Indigenous presence. This negation is conscious practice steeped in the colonial and imperial projects. The erasure has been part of the ways colonial and imperial violence continue to be codified on Black and African bodies, places and spaces spanning across a broad spectrum (e.g., knowledges, cultural memories, histories, cultures and spiritualities). As noted earlier, one political resistance is to subvert the mythology of Indigenous as a theorization about a more physical location and to begin to understand the complexity of our relations to the Land wherever we find ourselves. In this context, the idea of Black and African can be made coterminous to culture, heritage, identity, politics and resistance, while not denying the power of the skin as epidermal schema.

In effect, this book seeks to recuperate Black identity and subjectivity to transform our consciousness through critical engagement of African and Black social thought. As a Black and African scholar my theorization and social engagements must embrace the "spirit" and "spiritual knowledge" of the African self and community. Spirituality is at the core of African Indigenous social thought and discourse, and undergirds African epistemologies. As Dilliard (2008) notes, this spirituality as African-centered thought is at the "very essence of African regardless of where we are in the world" (p. 278). The spiritual is a core axis of articulating a theory of re-inventing Africanness in Diasporic contexts. There is a realization that the spirit and spirit ontologies cannot be and were never colonized. We cannot de-spiritualize Black and African cultures in the Western-centric negation of the "spirit/spiritual" as legitimate site and source of knowing. So in re-theorizing Blackness and Black identity that reinvents an Africanness in a Diasporic context, I want to bring back the spiritual knowledge as consciousness and resistance. Those who have "problems' with the spiritual as a site of knowing do not have to agree with me; they can work through their discomfort in their own minds. But I surely do not want my knowledge to be dismissed as "anti-intellectual." It would be the height of intellectual arrogance for anyone to claim to know me and the epistemic community I share or identify with more than we know ourselves.

Shields (2005) long ago noted that spirituality functions as epistemology, that it offers a "system of explanation providing the framework for people to interpret their own life-world and formulate knowledge and truths from their experiences" (p. 8). Furthermore, spirituality as ontology allows us to appreciate the African way of being, seeing our realities and acting in our world to bring change. In other words, spirituality is expressions about how we live our lives in communities. In reclaiming spirituality as part of the re-theorization of Blackness and Africanness, African Indigenous languages are key to how we use our languages as tools for our mental, spiritual and intellectual decolonization as African peoples with implications for our shared and collective experiences in the Diasporic context. Language must, and do, shape our cultural and political standpoints. The interrelationships and dialectics of the spiritual and political as intellectualism also helps shape our understanding Black liberation through the affirmation of our Black and African identities and subjectivities.

Also, as already alluded to, while the focus on conceptual Blackness as Blackness built into language, culture, history and politics is important, I am not willing to let go or place under the intellectual carpet the idea of a continuing significance of skin color as a powerful racial marker with profound material and political consequences. When I say this I am simply gesturing to what already exists and not creating a "problem." Saying race is also skin is not fantasy but the reality. The skin [as epidermal body] is implicated if we speak of the embodiment of knowledge. It does not mean one knows better or worse by simply wearing the Black skin. It is merely an acknowledgment that the skin is relevant in knowledge production. Similarly, skin color is one of the [somatic] categories for Blackness and Whiteness even if less it is meaningful as Foster's (2004) work on modernity as a "failed quest for Whiteness" shows. We cannot simply dismiss some questions: what do we do with the knowledge that comes with wearing a Black skin in a White supremacist context? How is such body perceived and what are the entanglements of skin color as a politically and intellectually mobilizing force to resistance to Whiteness and modernity? How is it that throughout human history certain skin colors are met with punishment while others accrue privilege and power? If one is continually at the receiving end of punishment by their skin color it does not take a rocket scientist to figure out why they will repeatedly be asking these questions? We avoid talking about privilege and power because we know what it does for us.

2.7   Black Authenticity vs. Blackness as Cis-Gender, Heterosexual, Able-Bodied, Male, and Masculine

The notion of an "authentic" Blackness has always been contested. Neither masculinity nor femininity are authentically Black, neither are heterosexuality, homosexuality, poverty, wealth, or life in the inner city or suburbs. When speaking of authenticity, we have to be careful as to not foreclose any possibilities. The racialized lens through which we view the world and ourselves is enshrouded with other identity markers and contingencies (ex. gender, sexuality, class, etc.) that make a singular Black experience impossible (Johnson 2003).

Blackness has no essence; "Black authenticity" is contingent on the historical, social and political terms of its production. Foster (2007) also speaks of an authenticity that does not have to do with genuinity, but rather is open ended. Authenticity in this case is not based on a totalizing experience but rather, in the recognition that there can be no real authenticity—the same way there can be no essences. Instead, authenticity can be described as a spirit that suggests a feeling of acceptance even among those who are recognized as different and diverse (p. 301). Similar to Johnson (2003), Foster (2007) illustrates that there is no single definition of Blackness, rather contextual understandings of history, geography and politics are necessary.

This work by Johnson and Foster show how when trying to define a Black authenticity, the resonances depend on who is doing the evaluation. Johnson (2003) makes this point in his book *Appropriating Blackness: Performance and the politics of authenticity*, showing that Blackness does not belong to one individual or group. Rather, individuals or groups *appropriate* this complex racial signifier in order to set boundaries or exclude other individuals or groups. Authenticity can be problematic as it is another trope manipulated for cultural capital, according to Johnson. Nonetheless, there are ways in which authenticating discourse can enable marginalized people to counter oppressive representations of themselves.

In order to understand how Blackness is often viewed as being cis-gender, heterosexual, masculine, male and able-bodied we must take into account the system of White supremacy in which Blackness is defined and demarcated against. Since White supremacy is a system which shapes other forms oppression such as patriarchy, transphobia, homophobia, ableism and sexism, racism is also connected to these other systems of domination. Historically, Black nationalist discourses seemed to equate the Black male condition with conditions of *entire* Black communities (Mutua 2006, p. xiii). Thus, the argument followed that to remedy the Black communities' problem, the struggle against racism has to address the conditions of Black cis-gender men, to center on their predicament. In *Progressive Black Masculinities*, Mutua (2006) argues that the definition of progressive Black masculinities is grounded in the twin projects of *progressive Blackness* and *progressive masculinities*. She suggests that progressive Blackness is an anti-racist, and more generally and anti-domination project committed to the existential wholeness and well-being of Black people and communities, both materially and spiritually (p. xxii). Moreover, the project of progressive masculinities is similar but centers its efforts on reorienting men's concepts and practices away from ideal masculinity, which by definition, requires the domination of men over women, children and other subordinate, or "weaker" men.

In a re-theorization of Blackness, I offer an additional reading on authenticity. Claiming authenticity should not be read as pure, un-contaminated, nor as fossilized and bounded truth. Authenticity is about an epistemic saliency to the voice of the Black or African subject as having something relevant to say about their own histories, cultures and lived experiences. That voice is authentic in relation to the non-Black/African voice who has not lived that body and experience and yet claims to be an 'expert'. It is as simple as that. Our intellectual agencies are being repetitively assaulted to the point we cannot speak of our own experiences without having to respond to charges of romanticism, essentialism, or totalizing discourses. As Black and African peoples, our existence is always in question—and yet, not everything needs to be taken away from us. We may contest our communities and our ideas but a Black or African voice speaking about their own experience is authentic voice in relation to the dominant "expert" who claims to know us more than we know ourselves. We can and must be authoritative voices of our own individual, self, group and collective experiences recognizing the challenges, limitations, and yet possibilities in such stances.

2.8 Loving Blackness

bell hooks writes a lot about loving Blackness. She argues: "We cannot effectively resist domination if our efforts to create meaningful, lasting personal and social change are not grounded in a love ethic … . To give ourselves to love, to love Blackness, is to restore the true meaning of freedom, hope, and possibility in all our lives" (hooks 2001, p. xxiv). She addresses the meaning of love in Black experience today and calls for a return to an ethic of love as the platform on which to renew progressive anti-racist struggle and serve as blueprint for Black survival and self-determination. Loving Blackness is a real form of political resistance because it directly challenges the logic of White supremacist thought, which casts Blackness as something that *should not* and *cannot* be loved. Loving Blackness as an act of psychological and political decolonization, a process that challenges the dehumanization of Black and Brown subjects in their contact with White supremacy. Moreover, loving Blackness as a discourse of anti-racism moves beyond racial dehumanization of Blackness to *reclaim* Black life.

hooks (2001) argues, the most effective way of combating White supremacy, both external and internalized racism, is for individuals to love Blackness—not simply to love themselves in spite of their Blackness but *because* of their Blackness. She asserts that decolonization is the necessary groundwork for the development of self-love (p. 73). Our homes become sites of resistance, where we create the oppositional spaces where we can be self-loving. As such, how can we think of certain spaces as sources of oppositional power to White supremacy? In regards to the home, Collins' (2004) discussion of Black families as crucial foundations for resistance against anti-Black racism would be helpful for this conversation.

Re-theorizing Blackness must be a search for self and collective determination to give Black and African peoples' intellectual and political agency to fight anti-Blackness and anti-Africanness. We must have a locus of control over the story and how we tell these stories about ourselves, identities, histories, cultures and lived experiences. The telling of story must include a theory of Blackness empowering ourselves Black and African scholars/learners to define the problems and challenges afflicting our communities and to think through our own solutions. This will be a sort of "decolonial thinking and action" that emerges from and is developed on our own terms. It cannot be something forced upon us using normative and centrist systems of knowledge. It will primarily [but not exclusively] utilize our local cultural ways of knowing as Black African diaspora and continental African peoples and not simply deploying Western modernist thoughts or thinking processes. It will be based on a self, group and collective generated knowledge base. Theorizing Blackness and Africanness this way becomes an authentic measure interrogating and validating African-centered, Black epistemologies, and Black perspectives. It is an approach that takes culture and knowledge as intertwining political processes and projects riddled with power, ambiguities, contestations and contradictions. But it acknowledges the different cultural systems "that legitimately [allow us to] make sense of and interact meaningfully with the world" (Bishop 1998, p. 212).

Thus this project is also an urging to move beyond politically immobilizing postmodern critiques and the unending calls to complicate and trouble "Blackness" and begin to speak forcefully about the varied ways we can evoke Blackness in multiple spaces. As noted, this in itself is a requirement of thinking through new and creative imaginings and possibilities of the future. The "burden of Black representation" raises questions as to who, what, why and how of representation. Yet, in our academic interrogations what is often lost in dominant critiques is the idea of "affirming voice" as intellectual agency and resistance. We seek to define our own identities and to challenge racist interpretations and representations of our lives as Black and African peoples.

To speak of Blackness and Africanness as symbolic of positive difference is not, and must not simply be about a fixation of Otherness or a "fixity to Otherness" (see Keesing 1989, p. 37 in other contexts). Difference has been taken up in multiple ways. The colonial difference is about hierarchy, exoticization, inferiorization and over mythicization. We must be clear about the nature of our intellectual politics. We bring new and different meanings to challenge and subvert rigid orthodoxies. Claiming Blackness as political and politicized identity, difference and subjectivity is about agency and empowerment. In doing so we as Black/African bodies are resisting the persisting spurious claims to expertise and knowledge of the Black and African by the dominant. We are interrupting the discursive authority of the dominant to name us, our histories and identities, and to articulate our experiences.

2.9   Towards a Re-Theorization

My academic goal is not to impose any fixed, essentialized or totalizing readings or metanarratives of Blackness (see also Ladson-Billings 2000, p. 260). I acknowledge difference as significant and shun an approach that "reins in differences" (Daza 2008, p. 71). While I recognize the fluid, intersecting and contested nature of all social concepts, I am also fully aware of the prevailing fear of Blackness and the insidious attempts to delegitimize Black racial politics. I am also aware of the Euro-colonial racist hegemonic definitions and understandings of Blackness. But, I do not seek to present "authentic" knowledge about what Blackness is or is not. In fact, as already acknowledged my theorization of Blackness is always partial or incomplete, and also contested and very contestable. While I would not dispute such contestations as part of respectful scholarly debate, I would challenge and resist the intellectual arrogance of a scholar who purports to know Blackness when, in fact, they are working through a prism of the hierarchy of knowing. We all know differently, can and must speak differently as needed.

Our understandings of Blackness are situated in power relations. There are significant differences of race, ethnicity, class, gender, sexuality, [dis]ability, language and religion that complicate what we claim to know as Blackness. Patricia Hill Collins (2004) asserts that examining the intersectionality of race, class and gender is necessary in the analysis of Black sexual politics. An intersectional theoretical framework views race, class, gender, sexuality, ethnicity, and age as mutually constructing systems of power. Intersectionality permeates all social relations in society and has particular ramifications for Black people in Collins' work. She maintains that "developing an intersectional analysis of Black sexual politics has tangible political ramifications for anti-racist scholarships and activism" (Collins 2004, p. 11). However, our claims to Blackness when even our communities may be interrogated for our heterosexism, homophobia, classism, etc. does not dismiss the legitimacy of calls for the political affirmation of Blackness. While claims of Blackness may be imaginary I am still evoking it for intellectual and political work.

Returning to Collins, she discusses the Black/White paradigm of race in the United States, which is why she focuses on African American communities in her work. She recognizes how much African Americans share and at times intersect with many other groups in the U.S and globally, such as Indigenous peoples, Haitian immigrant populations, Latinxs (Dussel and Jaurengui, 2008) and others, and she makes the important point that the differences that exist among Black people should not detract from collective struggles for social justice. Similarly, I accentuate Blackness in a call for political mobilization and intellectual solidarity to resist Black racial oppressions for those who are part of an epistemic community with which I identify.

So, I complicate Blackness to a point. I distinguish between interrogating claims of authentic Blackness and mere dismissal or de-legitimization of Blackness. I resist the racist and colonial imaginary of Blackness. I raise this contention well aware of the very troubling incessant questioning of the existence of a [Black] community, as if communities were ever singular. I see the community in the existence of many communities, "communities of differences," and that the community is not neces-sarily for everyone to belong and/or identify with. As academic scholars, our intel-lectual pursuits are always guarded by politics. The politics of identity is not just about race. It can be identification with something else. No matter how hard we may try to deny this we all continually engage in a "politics of identity" that can be stra-tegic and selective. This point is of identity not just about race. It can be identified with something else. In the struggle for justice against oppressions, I equally worry as to what ends and purpose the unilateral fragmentation around difference can and/or does take us. I do not apologize for being part of an intellectual discursive praxis aimed at offering critical/alternative/counter/oppositional stances, understandings as well as compelling reasons, for our academy (schools, colleges, and universities) to address racism and particularly, anti-Black racism and anti-Indigeneity.

Like other Black, anti-racist educators, I have always had to respond to charges of hegemonic claims in racial constructs. For example, many critique traditional anti-racism as espousing a simplistic Black-White duality (Miles and Torres 1996). Clearly we need to be mindful of the complexities of identities. Black and White identities and constructions are neither homogenous nor bounded categories. They are not fixed opposites, but rather reflect continually shifting identifications. However, I maintain that scholars can still work with Black and White as significant concepts, constructs and signifiers in social formations. These are referent points in racialized societies and these identities can be claimed and mobilized in solidarity for anti-colonial projects and decolonization purposes. Regardless of the complexi-ties of Black, White, and other identities, a colonial dominance is expressed through a history that has inscribed and reinforced White bodies as significant power bro-kers. To deny this is intellectually dishonest. Not only are dominant conceptions of Blackness profoundly Eurocentric and imperialistic, but the denial of Black intel-lectual and political agency in articulating our own myriad understandings of Blackness and Black identity is part of the on-going colonizing practices of subjec-tifying the oppressed/colonized. The rethinking and re-evaluation of Blackness and Black identity has always been at the bedrock of Black anti-colonial struggles and resistance for self and collective empowerment, liberation and independence. Such rethinking and reframing of Blackness has also been a source of pride.

Race is salient in the constructions of Blackness, Whiteness, anti-Blackness, and particularly, in the maintenance of the logics and structures of White supremacy and global capitalism. There is no escaping the fact as to who is at the bottom of the global racial hierarchy. As Smith (2006) points out, Blackness has and continues to be equated with slaveability and the on-going criminalization of Blackness serves "as a logical extension of the Blackness as property thesis" (p. 67). A Black-White paradigm has served to structure and justify significant social relations, practices and histories in our communities (Smith 2006).

Therefore, an anti-colonial theorization of Blackness, while complicating the Black-White binary, must nonetheless affirm the potent force of the Black-White paradigm in recognition of the saliency of race, skin color and anti-Black racism in our societies. Skin color and anti-Blackness operate to fix African-descended peo-ple in a state of permanent visibility, and, paradoxically, selective invisibility

(Deliovsky and Kitossa 2013). Moreover, as noted in Dei et al. (2004, p. 92), the "economy of racial visibility," whereby skin color operates as a signifier of social value and moral worth, is a function of power. Deliovsky and Kitossa (2013) make an excellent point when they emphasize that the issue is not the phenotype of Blackness, as South Asians who can be darker than many African Americans and Africans would have different but shared experiences. Rather, the issue is the social construction of Blackness, along with the imagined ideal African phenotype, that is deeply grounded in Western culture and upholds the Black-White paradigm (Deliovsky and Kitossa 2013, p. 170).

The liberal pluralistic discourse such as multiculturalism and indeed some articulations of anti-oppression that ask us "to go beyond the simplistic Black-White divide" can be problematic. In their article *Beyond Black and White: When Going Beyond May Take Us Out of Bounds,* Deliovsky and Kitossa (2013) examine a selection of North American scholarly research that calls for "moving beyond" a Black/White binary paradigm and the implications for advancing this agenda for African descended peoples as well as other people of color. Some scholars suggest that this paradigm exclusively focuses on people socially defined as Black and White and excludes other racial groups such as Asian Americans. As such, these scholars argue that alternatives to Black/White paradigm are needed to capture the complexity of racism and process of racialization outside of this binary. Deliovsky and Kitossa ask what "moving beyond" means, and for whom? What are the implications and limitations of this call? How might we understand relations and dynamics of oppression and advantage or privilege from this viewpoint? Furthermore, if we are to move beyond, where are we moving to, and does this "place" have the analytical depth and clarity essential to the struggle for social transformation?

These articulations to "move beyond" can serve to deny the saliency of race and the Blackness in society and what can be termed the "severity of issues for Black bodies in White supremacist contexts" (Dei 1996). Deliovsky and Kitossa's (2013) work is relevant to discussions of multiracial coalition/alliance building. They support Sexton's (2010) views on the Black/White paradigm, whereby the call to move beyond is fundamentally flawed because it is built on an inadequate understanding of power relations that structure *what is, in fact,* a Black/White Manicheanism. Furthermore, the discourse sets up Blackness (interestingly enough, not Whiteness), and by extension people defined as Black, as an impediment to a multiracial coalition. Deliovsky and Kitossa note that uncritical acceptance of the "moving beyond" thesis creates an implicit allegation that African-descended peoples are complicit in the silencing and/or erasure of other voices in a multiracial alliance (p. 164).

History and social relations dictate that Africans are *not* granted the privilege of moving beyond a Manicheanism that situates them as the primary antagonist to the system of Whiteness. Thus, Deliovsky and Kitossa (2013) argue that to develop an epistemologically deep understanding of race, racialization, and racism in North America, the significance of anti-Blackness must be understood not as a superior form of oppression, but as a form that gives shape and context to the oppression of other racially marginalized groups (p. 173). The Black/White Manicheanism is a key factor in social differentiation of human beings in the West and is used to create racial hierarchies. However, it must be clear that this does not negate the absolute domination of Indigenous peoples and the theft of their Land through White settler colonialism, nor does it disregard colonialism and imperialism toward other people of color around the world. We must be critical of how and *by whom* the "move beyond" is narrated, especially since this would structure the relations between communities of color.

To clarify my position I would make the important distinction between the 'Black-White binary' which problematically assigns fixed notions of identity that create an oppositional division of two sides (Black and White) and a Black-White paradigm which is purely a prism, a lens of reading social relations and relations of power. It should be emphasized that the recourse to the 'Black-White prism' should not be read as a negation of the colonial impact on Indigenous/Native peoples since it is not gesturing to hierarchy of oppressions. The Black-White paradigm alludes to the fact of Whiteness as the norm to which everything else is referenced or measured (see Kincheloe and Steinberg 1998). It is a way of reading different identities with Whiteness and White identity as the anchor or base to which other demarcations are read. The re-theorization of Blackness must make this important conceptual distinction while simultaneously questioning the call to go beyond this binary by asking: what are we afraid of? Whiteness has powerful global currency and reach.

Whiteness is neither diminished nor rendered any less powerful by class, gender, sexuality, [dis]ability, and ethnicity. The Black-White paradigm alludes to the constitutive significance of race and racial identity. The paradigm engages intersections of race, class, gender, sexuality and [dis]ability while underscoring that although Whiteness is demarcated by sites of difference, there is a racial polity and sanctity of White (Johal 2007) that is not diminished by these intersections. Engagements of intersections and interstices must be distinguished from the dominant's quick and easy embrace of intersectional discourses as a saving grace and escape from critiques of White dominance. This race to intersections smacks of the joy and desire to spread oppressions around so we can all be held accountable for some form of oppression around race, gender, class, sexuality, and disability. While I do not dispute our relative complicities in oppressions, I have argued repeatedly that we cannot minimize the power of the White colonial dominant. We may all be oppressed and become oppressors simultaneously. Yet, the power of the colonial White dominant to oppress on the basis of skin privilege is notwithstanding intersections of class, gender, sexuality, [dis]ability and ethnicity. White identity and claims of White can mitigate against experiences of oppressions while at the same time serving to intensify oppressive relations. What I am arguing then is that dominance is inscribed within social institutions such that White privilege is perpetuated irrespective of Whiteness' intersections with other social markers in White bodies. Elsewhere (Dei 2013) I have cautioned against the possibility of intersectionality being co-opted to refute the saliency of race and Blackness as a primary entry point for domination studies. When people do not want to hear about racial injustice and therefore argue that others are equally oppressed, this is the deliberate and conscious refusal to examine racism to which I am gesturing. Just as the failure to connect oppressions and identities can be dangerous, so is the unilateral fluidity around difference that suggests identities are unstable, unending, relational and continually intersecting. I have already argued that, "the most seductive, fashionable, and perhaps, uncritical postcolonial and postmodernist readings [of intersectionality] have tended to flatten out identities with [unending] claims of fluidity, flux, contingencies, and contestations … " (Dei 2013, p. 4).

But admittedly, we can no longer afford to simply understand Whiteness [like Blackness] in a romanticized and/or idealized way. There is a clear visibility and hypervisibility of Whiteness, White-passing and White presenting in the global context, often understood within popularized narratives and the ways in which such well-rehearsed narratives continue to operate in contemporary society. It is no longer enough to simply argue that Whiteness maintains its power and privilege through claims to a mythic and oppositional Blackness. The Black-White relation and imaginary calls for a far more complex interrogation and understanding. The anti-Blackness thesis allows us to challenge popular narratives and myths of the Canadian nation-state as raceless and racist free, as welcoming of immigrants and promoting of diversity and inclusion. Such interrogation helps illuminate Blacks'/Africans' experiences in Canadian settler colonial contexts. The discussion also calls on us to be attentive to not only how Indigenous scholars are theorizing settler colonialism, but also how Black scholars are theorizing anti-Blackness. The Black/African bodily presence on Indigenous soil makes us [as Black/African bodies] implicated in White colonial settlerhood practices. But as is shown in later subsequent chapters rather than intellectually dilute the pervasive force, power and influence of the colonial dominant in settlerhood practices, it is maintained that Blacks/Africans have shared responsibilities to the Indigenous struggle for self-determination and Indigenous sovereignty on Turtle Island. Similarly, Indigenous peoples have shared responsibilities in pursuing political solidarity work in the on-going colonization of African Lands.

A critical reading of the Black/African experiences in Canada reveals the nature, extent and purpose of race and racial identity, and the efficacy of political strategies and struggles using racial representations to challenge systemic racism (see Benjamin 2003). The saliency of Black/African identity and the potential for Blackness to be deployed as a decolonizing framework, through a discursive analysis of Black resistance and activism, point to significant lessons for anti-racist, anti-colonial theorizing and political activism. As already mentioned, the Blackness/anti-Blackness framework for decolonization acknowledges differences among Black/African diaspora populations, as well as other colonialized and Indigenous peoples. But it is a framework that engages a collective struggle and vision notwithstanding the complexities of such histories and experiences (see Sandhu 2014 in another context). No population is homogenous and the claim to a collective Black identity is not necessarily informed by an essentialized reading of Black[ness] and Black racial identity. It is informed by shared histories and identifications which are not necessarily uniform. It is intended as a political reclamation of Blackness in the White colonial context. But such political reclamation also calls on us not to essentialize difference, but to embrace intersecting identities and oppressions. The identity of Blackness is constructed through shared histories of oppression and marginalization in the nation state based on collective experiences, heritage, ances-try, geography, and places of origin. It is this shared human condition that fore-grounds solidarity across Black, African diaspora and African communities to ensure a commitment to decolonization, collective resistance, reciprocal relations, action, renewal, and sovereignty.

Long ago, I insisted that for racialized peoples, our identity is all we have and we must be careful when asked to amputate or dislodge a part of our identities (racial, gender, class, spiritual, etc.) (see Dei 1996). Particularly, African bodies must con-front and resist the temptation of erasing our racial experience through intellectual rhetoric that the race concept is not a useful analytical tool. This stems more from the discomfort of speaking race rather than a realization that race is meaningless. Meaningless to whom we may ask? Race is neither meaningless nor inconsequen-tial to the oppressor who wants to subjugate and deny others of their dignity, bene-fits and access to social goods and services. An awareness of one's Black racial identity is a personal, political, and ideological project. Such awareness, when col-lectivized for change, becomes a decolonization framework for anti-racist anti-Black racist and anti-colonial resistance. The material and political implications of race as a socio-historical construct calls for an understanding of race as a complex relational identity. Race is a socio-historical condition that must be affirmed as part of our being (Omi and Winant 1993; Lopez 1995). Du Bois (1903) long ago affirmed Black racial identity as an important step in challenging White supremacy. The continuing significance of Whiteness means post-racial perspectives that dismiss the political and intellectual meaning of race through denials and erasures only act to sustain the dominance of Whiteness and White power. This is why Omi and Winant's (1993) call for scholars to acknowledge the on-going material, social, and political consequences of race and racial identity is so important to political activ-ism around racism and social oppression. Race continues to have social, economic, and political relevance, whether as a site or source of privilege, or punishment for others.

Poststructuralist critiques of essences and essentialism are always amusing to me. That the subject and subjectivities are always in flux is enticing, if not seduc-tive. But this stance is also dangerous. While I reckon with a call for inter-subjective knowing, I am also left with the question as to whether there is indeed an essence to, about or of capitalism, or to aspects of our identities other than race. Who and what are we? Are we simply floating signifiers without any core sense of being? I am using my Black subjectivity and identity in these discussions while being fully aware of their limitations when claimed as sites of identifications. I am just not holding my breath waiting for the postmodern stance of troubling, complicating, and my existence to come to a halt. The fact that no one has ever been only one thing or one-dimensional is a fundamental way of knowing and understanding human lives. But I would rather spend time naming the ethical grounds on which to do our work as scholars. So, for example, how do we address the critical anti-colonial and decolonial work that grounds itself in the importance of naming our existence, in terms of the realness, reality, concreteness and materiality of life? There has been much written on intersectional and interlocking forms of analysis, sometimes used interchangeably. What is still needed is a fuller explication of the intricacies and complexities of engaging each of these frameworks in critiques of oppression that foreground particular sites of difference as a point of departure.

Our social categories themselves are not the problem, but rather the interpretations we imbue onto these categories as analytical tools categories need to fully operationalized. Who says what, how, and why has always been consequential. Weheliye (2014), in particular, notes how those who took up the questioning of the Western universal "[hu]man" from a situated position, be that from an anti-racism or Black feminist framework, were often marginalized in the academy as speaking to localized, specific situations and therefore not adequately "theoretical" or transposable. The saliency of race as a concept addresses the ways in which race comes to inform how bodies can be read within the constellation of identitarian hierarchies as instigated and perpetuated through discourses of colonialism and modernity. The troubling of Western humanist thought and subjectivity, therefore, ought to be located in each of these conversations, as well as marked as a key thread bringing these positions into conversation with each other.

For example, working with student voice can be a possible site of educational critique and transformation that troubles Western humanist thought and subjectivity. In this work I ask, "How does coming to voice become a project of decolonization?" (hooks 1994; Weheliye 2002). hooks (1994) and Freire (1970) amplify the way in which voice can at once be resistance through speaking oneself into being and recognition (moving the individual from an object position to a subject position), and simultaneously a self-empowering practice. Additionally, in previous work (Dei 1999, 2005) I note the epistemic saliency of marginalized voices in anti-racism work. Voice, then, can become a counter-narrative, bringing in experiences that de-center the Euro-Enlightenment epistemological hegemony in conventional schooling and education. Anti-racist and anti-colonial theorists work with voice as an articulation of agency, experience, and cultural memory (Dei 2005; Mohanty et al. 1991; Wahab 2005; hooks 1994).

This underscores how teaching and learning must be relational and dialogical. It is about coming to know and using the knowledge responsibly. Academic responsibility requires that we disrupt racial and colonial discourses and narratives, but in the spirit of humility of knowing. Intellectual arrogance emerges when we dismiss ideas without a proper acknowledgement of the limits of our own knowing.

References

Alexander, E. (1994). "Can you be Black and look at this?": Reading the Rodney King video(s). *Public Culture, 7*(1), 77–94.

Alston, K. (2005). Knowing Blackness, becoming Blackness, valuing Blackness. In G. Yancy (Ed.), *White on White/Black on Black* (pp. 297–308). Oxford: Rowman and Littlefield.

Asante, M. K. (2005). Blackness as an ethical trope: Toward a post-Western assertion. In G. Yancy (Ed.), *White on White/Black on Black* (pp. 203–216). Oxford: Rowman and Littlefield.

Benjamin, A. (2003). *The Black/Jamaican criminal: The making of ideology* (Ph.D. Thesis, University of Toronto).

Bishop, R. (1998). Freeing ourselves from neo-colonial domination in research: A Maori approach to creating knowledge. *Qualitative Studies in Education, 11*(2), 199–219.

Black Lives Matter. (n.d.). *About us.* Retrieved from http://Blacklivesmatter.com/about/.

Bonilla, Y., & Rosa, J. (2015). #Ferguson: Digital protest, Hashtag ethnography, and the racial politics of social media in the United States. *American Ethnologist, 42*(1), 4–17.

Carney, N. (2016). All lives matter, but so does race: Black lives matter and the evolving role of social media. *Humanity & Society, 40*(2), 180–199.

Collins, P. H. (2004). *Black sexual politics: African Americans, gender, and the new racism.* New York: Routledge.

Daniel, B., & Yearwood, M. (2002). African-Canadian women's bodies as sites of knowing and no-ing. In S. Abbey (Ed.), *Ways of knowing in and through the body: Diverse perspectives on embodiment* (pp. 253–258). Welland: Soleil.

Daza, S. (2008). Decolonizing researcher authenticity. *Race Ethnicity and Education, 11*(1), 71–85.

DeGenova, N. (2002). Migrant "illegality" and deportability in everyday life. *Annual Review of Anthropology, 31*, 419–447.

Dei, G. J. S. (1995). (Re)Conceptualizing Black studies in Canada. *Canadian and International Education, 24*(1), 1–19.

Dei, G. J. S. (1996). *Anti-racism education: Theory and practice.* Halifax: Fernwood.

Dei, G. J., & James, I. M. (1998). 'Becoming Black': African-Canadian youth and the politics of negotiating racial and racialized identities. *Race, Ethnicity and Education, 1*(1), 91–108.

Dei, G. J. S. (1999). Knowledge and politics of social change: The implication of anti-racism. *British Journal of Sociology of Education, 20*(3), 395–409.

Dei, G. J. S. (2005). Social difference and the politics of schooling in Africa: A Ghanaian case study. *Compare: A Journal of Comparative and International Education, 35*(3), 227–245.

Dei, G. J. S. (2013). Reframing critical anti-racist theory (CART) for contemporary times. In G. J. S. Dei & M. Lordan (Eds.), *Contemporary issues in the sociology of race and ethnicity: A critical reader* (pp. 1–14). New York: Peter Lang.

Dei, G. J. S. (2014). The African scholar in the Western academy. *Journal of Black Studies, 45*(3), 167–179.

Dei, G. J. S., Karumanchery, L. L., & Karumanchery-Luik, N. (2004). *Playing the race card: Exposing white power and privilege.* New York, NY: Peter Lang.

Deliovsky, K., & Kitossa, T. (2013). Beyond Black and White: When going beyond may take us out of bounds. *Journal of Black Studies, 44*(2), 158–181.

Dilliard, C. (2008). When the ground is Black, the ground is fertile: Exploring endarkened feminist epistemology and healing methodologies of the spirit. In N. K. Denzin, Y. S. Lincoln, & L. T. Smith (Eds.), *Handbook of critical and indigenous methodologies* (pp. 277–292). Los Angeles: Sage.

Du Bois, W. E. B. (1903). *The souls of Black folk.* Oxford: Oxford University Press.

Duffield, M. (2006). Racism, migration and development: The foundations of planetary order. *Progress in Development Studies, 6*(1), 68–79.

Dussel, E., & Jaurengui, C. (2008). *Coloniality at large: Latin America and the postcolonial debate* (pp. 225–258). Durham, NC: Duke University.

Fanon, F. (1967). *Black skin, White masks.* New York: Grove Press.

Ferber, A. (2007). The construction of Black masculinity. *Journal of Sport & Social Issues, 31*(1), 11–24.

Foster, C. (2007). *Blackness & modernity: The colour of humanity and the quest for freedom.* Montreal: McGill University Press.

Foucault, M. (1977). *Discipline and punish: The birth of the prison.* New York: Pantheon.

Freire, P. (1970). *Pedagogy of the oppressed.* New York: Herder and Herder.

Gaber, N., & Wright, A. (2015). Protecting urban health and safety: Balancing care and harm in the era of mass incarceration. *Journal of Urban Health, 93*(1), 68–77.

Goldberg, D. (2006). The global reach of raceless states. In D. Macedo & P. Gounari (Eds.), *The globalization of racism* (pp. 45–67). Boulder, CO: Paradigm.

Gotanda, N. (1995). A critique of "Our constitution is colorblind". In K. Crenshaw, N. Gotanda, G. Peller, & K. Thomas (Eds.), *Critical race theory: The key writings that formed the movement* (pp. 257–275). New York: The New Press.

Hall, S. (1996). Cultural identity and diaspora. In P. Mondia (Ed.), *Contemporary postcolonial theory: A reader* (pp. 110–121). London: Arnold.

Hall, S. (1997). *Representation: Cultural representations and signifying practices.* London: Sage.

Harris, C. (1996). Whiteness as property. In K. Crenshaw, N. Gotanda, G. Peller, & K. Thomas (Eds.), *Critical race theory: The key writings that formed the movement* (pp. 276–291). New York: The New Press.

Hartman, S. V. (1997). *Scenes of subjection: Terror, slavery, and self-making in nineteenth-century America.* New York: Oxford University Press.

hooks, b. (1992). *Black looks: Race and representation.* Boston, MA: South End Press.

hooks, b. (1994). *Teaching to transgress: Education as the practice of freedom.* New York: Routledge.

hooks, b. (2001). *Salvation: Black people and love.* New York: William Morrow.

Howes, D. (1996). Cultural appropriation and resistance in the American Southwest: Decommodifying Indianness. In D. Howes (Ed.), *Cross-cultural consumption: Global markets local realities* (pp. 138–160). Routledge: London.

Ibrahim, A. (1999). Becoming Black: Rap and hip-hop, race, gender, identity, and the politics of ESL learning. *TESOL Quarterly, 33*(3), 349–369. doi:10.2307/3587669.

Johal, G. (2007). The racialization of Space: Producing Surrey. In G. Johnson & R. Enomoto (Eds.), *Race, racialization and antiracism in Canada and beyond* (pp. 179–205). Toronto: University of Toronto Press.

Johnson, E. P. (2003). *Appropriating Blackness: performance and the politics of authenticity.* Durham, NC: Duke University Press.

Keesing, R. M. (1989). Creating the past: Custom and identity in the contemporary pacific. *Contemporary Pacific, 1*(2), 19–42.

Kincheloe, J., & Steinberg, S. R. (1998). Addressing the crisis of Whiteness: Reconfiguring White identity in a pedagogy of Whiteness. In J. L. Kincheloe, S. R. Steinberg, N. M. Rodriguez, & R. E. Chennault (Eds.), *White reign: Deploying Whiteness in America* (pp. 1–29). New York: St. Martin's Press.

King, J. (2016, November 3). Blackness in the academy and in activism. Keynote address, 'Decolonizing Conference' marking the 20th Anniversary of the Centre for Integrative Anti-Racism Studies (CIARS). Ontario Institute for Studies in Education, University of Toronto, Toronto, Canada.

Ladson-Billings, G. (2000). Racialized discourses and ethnic epistemologies. In N. K. Denzin & Y. S. Lincoln (Eds.), *Handbook of qualitative research* (2nd ed., pp. 257–277). Thousand Oaks, CA: Sage.

Lauer, H. (2007). Depreciating African political culture. *Journal of Black Studies, 38*(2), 288–307.

Lindsey, T. B. (2015). Post-Ferguson: A "herstorical" approach to Black violability. *Feminist Studies, 41*, 232–237.

Lopez, L. J. (1995). The social construction of race. In R. Delgado & J. Stefancic (Eds.), *Critical race theory: The cutting edge* (pp. 163–175). Philadelphia: Temple University Press.

Mbembé, J.-A. (2003). Necropolitics (L. Meintjes, Trans.) *Public Culture, 15*(1), 11–40.

Mignolo, W. (2002). The geopolitics of knowledge and the colonial difference. *South Atlantic Quarterly, 101*(1), 57–96.

Miles, R., & Torres, R. (1996). Does race matter? Transatlantic perspectives on racism after 'race' relations. In V. Amit-Talai & C. Knowles (Eds.), *Re-situating identities: The politics of race, ethnicity, and culture* (pp. 24–46). Peterborough, ON: Broadview Press.

Mills, C. W. (1998). *Blackness visible: Essays on philosophy and race.* Ithaca, NY: Cornell University Press.

Mohanty, C. T., Russo, A., & Torres, L. (1991). *Third world women and the politics of feminism.* Bloomington: Indiana University Press.

Mutua, A. D. (2006). *Progressive Black masculinities.* New York: Routledge.

Norton, M., & Sommers, S. (2011). Whites see racism as Zero-Sum game that they are now losing. *Perspectives on Psychological Science, 6*(30), 215–218.

Omi, W., & Winant, H. (1993). On the theoretical concept of race. In C. McCarthy & H. Crichlow (Eds.), *Race, identity and representation in education* (pp. 3–10). New York: Routledge.

Razack, S. (2008). *Casting out: The eviction of Muslims from western law and politics.* Toronto: University of Toronto Press.

Sandhu, D. (2014). *Theorizing brown identity.* Unpublished MA thesis, Ontario: Department of Social Justice Education, Ontario Institute for Studies in Education of the University of Toronto (OISE/UT).

Sexton, J. (2010). Proprieties of coalition: Blacks, Asians, and the politics of policing. *Critical Sociology, 36*(1), 87–108.

Sexton, J. (2015). Unbearable blackness. *Cultural Critique, 90*(1), 159–178.

Sharma, N. (2009). The racialization of space and the spatialization of belonging. In A. Itwaru (Ed.), *The white supremacist state: Ethnocentrism, imperialism, colonialism, racism* (pp. 221–242). Toronto: Other Eye.

Shields, C. M. (2005). Liberating discourses: Spirituality and educational leadership. *Journal of School Leadership, 15*, 608–623.

Smith, A. (2006). Heteropatriarchy and the three pillars of White supremacy. In *Color of violence: INCITE! Women of color against violence* (pp. 66–73). Cambridge, MA: South End Press.

Smith, C. A. (2015). Blackness, citizenship, and the transnational vertigo of violence in the Americas. *American Anthropologist, 117*(2), 384–387.

Stewart, C. (2016, November 3). Personal Communication on 'Academic Statement of Interest'. University of Toronto.

Taylor, K.-Y. (2016). *From #BlackLivesMatter to Black Liberation.* Chicago: Haymarket Books.

Touré. (2011). *Who's afraid of post-Blackness? What it means to be Black now.* New York: Free Press.

Wahab, A. (2005). Consuming narratives: Questioning authority and the politics of representation in social science research. In G. J. S. Dei & G. Johal (Eds.), *Critical issues in anti-racist research methodology* (pp. 29–52). New York: Peter Lang.

Walcott, R. (2003). *Black like who? Writing Black Canada* (2nd ed.). Toronto: Insomniac Press.

Weheliye, A. G. (2002). "Feenin": Posthuman voices in contemporary Black popular music. *Social Text, 20*(2), 21–47.

Weheliye, A. G. (2014). *Habeas viscus: Racializing assemblages, biopolitics, and Black feminist theories of the human.* Chapel Hill, NC: Duke University Press.

West, C. (1999). *The Cornel West reader.* New York, NY: Basic Civitas Books.

Yancy, G. (2005). Whiteness and the return of the Black body. *The Journal of Speculative Philosophy, 19*((4)), 215–241.

Chapter 3
Reframing Blackness, Anti-Blackness, and Decoloniality

Abstract This chapter employs the "anti-colonial" to refer to a theorization of colonial and re-colonial relations and the implications of imperial structures on: (a) processes of knowledge production, interrogation, validation and dissemination; (b) the understanding of Indigeneity as both a process and identity; and (c) the pursuit of agency, resistance and subjective politics (Dei 2000; Dei and Asgharzadeh 2001). We must define Black/African identities in order to subvert racist imaginaries. Rooted in European colonization is the hatred of the Black subject; the denial of humanity along with the hatred of Black culture, aesthetics, language, politics and civilization. It is why I argue that there must be a call for Black racial and cultural pride, especially to resist the denigration of Blackness. This research aims to reframe how Blackness is defined and what it means to Black in a White-dominated society. I argue that Black racial and political awareness is important for Black resistance and survival. The White identity has access to privilege and power; race denial only seeks to mask the ways in which race is used as a tool to dominate and oppress. Those who denounce and deny race are unaware of their own privilege. Thus it is crucial for Black subjects to be aware of racial identity and it is important for Black subjects to subvert this notion of "post-Blackness." Race awareness is key in mobilizing and advocating for equity.

It is significant to distinguish dominant articulations of Blackness from those asserted by critical Black theorists and community workers. In critical Black scholarship, Blackness is evoked as an identity and experience with shared, contested and contingent histories. Much more than racial identification, Blackness is about knowledge of culture, politics and history of the Black experience. It is an identification that comes with a political consciousness, Black agency and resistance. Blackness claimed in this way works with a decolonizing perspective. Such a critical understanding of Blackness counters anti-Blackness—which usually manifests through dominant articulations that equate Black people with inferiority, criminality, violence and barbarism. Anything against the positive affirmation of Blackness constitutes anti-Blackness.

© Springer International Publishing AG 2017
G.J.S. Dei, *Reframing Blackness and Black Solidarities through Anti-colonial and Decolonial Prisms*, Critical Studies of Education 4,
DOI 10.1007/978-3-319-53079-6_3

The coloniality of Western discourses, including theories, is also challenged through Indigenous/Black/racialized self-perspectives on how we understand our human condition and how far we are willing to assert our intellectual agencies in defining our experiences and lived histories. Arguably, dominant [Western] perspectives, while perhaps indispensable, are incomplete and inadequate in helping us to understand the complexities of human histories and everyday social experiences. There is a need, therefore, to decolonize dominant epistemologies by grounding Black and Indigenous scholarship in subaltern perspectives that uphold epistemic traditions of knowledge of oppressed peoples globally. In order to be successful we need to continually remind ourselves to bring differentiated approaches to theorizing the anti-colonial moment.

In bringing conceptual innovations to discursive analyses of Blackness, I employ the "anti-colonial" to refer to a theorization of colonial and re-colonial relations and the implications of imperial structures on: (a) processes of knowledge production, interrogation, validation and dissemination; (b) the understanding of Indigeneity as both a process and identity; and (c) the pursuit of agency, resistance and subjective politics (Dei 2000). Discursively, I approach the "anti-colonial" as a theorization of the scattered colonial hegemonies that continue to affect the lives of Black and other Indigenous, colonized and oppressed bodies in global spaces and settings. The anti-colonial asserts experiential knowledge of the colonized for a transformative agenda. The anti-colonial argues that any theorizing must start from practice, specifically, that the intellectual questions we pursue must always start from the ground. Our best intellectual pursuits start from where we are rooted, and we foreground our everyday lived experiences in our discursive analyses.

The processes and histories of [Euro] coloniality raise some important questions for anti-colonial practice/work. Emerging understandings and theorizing must reconfigure coloniality in complex ways (see Grosfoguel 2007; Mignolo 2007, 2011; Quijano 2000, 2007) so as to bring international perspectives and dimensions to decolonial politics. The complexity and myriad aspects of colonialisms also mean that our understandings of coloniality must be revealed in the particular ways we come to define Black/African identities to challenge and resist the racist imaginaries. The logic of coloniality works when racialized, Indigenous and colonized bodies are denied their subjectivities. The politics of subjectification of Black lives and experiences demand a redefinition of Black identities to upend racist and hegemonic definitions of what Blackness is. Consequently, part of the project of liberatory and emancipatory discourses is to examine and promote alternative and counter assertions of Indigenous/racialized/colonized identities and identifications. For example, liberatory discourses expose how racist immigrant imaginaries are constructed through culturalizing state discourses, which are not innocent. Therefore, to resist is to work with Black/Indigenous/racialized articulations of identity and culture rather than dominant [culturalist] readings of Black/Indigenous/racialized identities within Euro-American hegemonies. Blackness is or can be oppositional to Whiteness given the ways Whiteness assumes representational authority as not Black.

Anti-Blackness and anti-Black racism are intertwined. Anti-Black racism is a particular negative reading, reaction and concrete response/action to Blackness. This racist reading and practice is framed by a racist thought. Specifically, anti-Black racism is a particular practice of social racism directed at Black/African peoples for our alleged sub-humanity and our supposed roots in a "dark continent" (see Benjamin 2003). In following other pioneering works (Sexton 2010, 2015; Hartman 1997; Smith 2015; Benjamin 2013), I conceptualize anti-Blackness as ideological practices of denigration and inferiorization of the Black/African subject in order to seek advantage and justify unequal treatment. Such inferiorization and denigration can be about the Black racial identity, but it extends to Black culture, aesthetics, language, politics and civilization. Anti-Blackness is more than a repulsion of the Black subject. It is also about racial and cultural hatred that has roots in European colonization of Black African diaspora and African peoples and our alleged sub-humanity. The ideology was built on a manufactured notion of White superiority to the Black subject. It was designed to subjugate the Black/African identity in order to maintain material, political and symbolic advantage of Whites over the Black race. The ideological practice was both an imperial project and colonizing mission. The understanding of anti-Blackness recognizes that while we accede to the myriad forms of racisms, the saliency and pervasiveness of anti-Black racism in a White supremacist society cannot be downplayed (Benjamin 2003). The different racisms and oppressions operate in asymmetrical power relations among groups, with the Black race always at the bottom of the racial hierarchy. It is for this reason that the politics of anti-racism require that race be kept in the foreground in the axis of oppression and the permanence of skin color as a powerful marker of human differentiation be noted. Racism directed towards Black people purely (but not exclusively) on the basis of skin color differences has always existed even as language, ethnicity, culture, gender, etc. have become equally powerful markers of human difference in contemporary times.

In theorizing Blackness and anti-Blackness, the call for Black racial and cultural pride is significant given the historic denigration of Blackness and the association with criminality and violence. Black identity is affirmed both as a racial consciousness and political awareness of what it means to be Black in a White-dominated society and the resistances that are required for Black survival. To be Black is to understand one's racial existence as a socio-political and historical condition. For example, if race has been used as a tool to dominate and oppress, it must also be an avenue to seek redress, to resist, and to seek liberation. If White identity has been a source of unearned privilege and power, then to resist such advantage gained at the expense of other bodies is to accord agency to the Black subject. To deny race is a luxury for those privileged by their race. For those punished for their race, an awareness of racial identity is an important tool for survival. It is precisely for this reason that we cannot ask Black bodies seeking representation in our schools, workplaces, media and other institutional spaces to simply think of themselves as raceless. Race can be a mobilizing or rallying point for Black action, such as the call for Black teachers in our schools and for Black people to hold positions of power and authority within our institutions. The tropes for speaking about merit, excellence, objectivity and intelligence have been White and White-centric. To counter such readings we cannot simply argue for the abolition and erasure of Whiteness, contrary to claims by Ignatiev (1997) and others. Rather we need alternative and oppositional viewpoints that stress White as just one of many identities.

There are some relevant issues of note in theorizing Blackness to counter anti-Blackness. As I have noted in previous work, a particular modeling of Blackness appeals the most to Whites/dominant groups—one that is known and accepted to entertain and acquiesce to Whiteness (Dei 2008). As alluded to earlier, claims to Blackness and in particular, claims of essentialized Black identity, are about political consciousness. However, such claims of resistant politics which challenge Black peoples' subordination and inferiorization are detested and always called into question by the dominant. This questioning is at the root of anti-Blackness, which espouses the notion of Black genetic inferiority in the White imagination. There is a severe and visceral nature of racism directed towards African peoples. This is compounded by a racist attempt to elevate the White body while denigrating the Black body. The Black body has always been inferiorized, and the significance of color in the mind of the racist cannot be dismissed. George Yancy (2005), an African American philosopher who writes out of his "personal existential context," makes this clear in his article *Whiteness and the Return of the Black Body* (p.215). Yancy's entry point to the discussion of Blackness is the *Black* body. He argues that to theorize the Black body, we must turn to it as the site of racial experience, and how this is fundamentally linked to the oppressive modalities of the "raced" White body. Yancy theorizes situations where the Black body's subjectivity, its *lived* reality, is linked to the White imaginary, resulting in what he refers to as "the phenomenological return of the Black body." These instantiations are embedded within and evolved out of the complex social and historical interstices of Whites' efforts at self-construction through complex acts of erasure vis-a-vis Black people.

So while we may insist on identities being fluid and transient, it is equally important to recognize the permanence of skin color as a salient marker of identity throughout human history. The mythologization of Whiteness as good[ness], pure and innocent and Black[ness] as devilish, evil and criminal must be problematized and countered and not merely dismissed. Yancy (2005) also makes this claim, asserting that it is not only the "Black body" that has to be interrogated, but the White body must also be demystified from its status as norm, beautiful, innocent, pure and noble (p. 217).

It is a powerful reading that has material and political effects and consequences in society. We trouble this reading by showing human complexities, but also through acknowledging the coloniality of Whiteness and White power. Many times the acknowledgement of human complexities works to negate and deny the powerful effects of the coloniality of Whiteness.

In contemporary social formations we must watch for anti-Blackness in new forms and to note these as perhaps "Black expressions." The Black body has always been held hostage to White compassion and White work. Pictorial depictions of naked Black bodies were always intended to show our animality or sub-humanity. When juxtaposed with Whiteness, these depictions restore the innocence that only Whites can administer to Black bodies in the context of hypocritical love and compassion. This, in itself, constitutes a new form of anti-Blackness. The irrespon-sible birthing of so many children by undisciplined Black mothers, and the lambast-ing of delinquent and missing Black fathers are all part of the White ideological message of the imperial savior and the over-burdened White man. The image pres-ents Whiteness as the capacity to heal and restore the true essence of everything through compassion and love. Today, we are witnessing a new slavery/enslavement, one that presents the child who must save themselves their family, community, and country, and the economic crisis that propels globalization and transnationalism (Koffman and Gill 2013). There is the White rush to security under the guise of sav-ing children, saving innocent undifferentiated clusters of Black bodies with compassion.

We must also think about hybridity, but not in the conventional post-colonial way in which it is thought or spoken of. We can think of hybridity in the sense of the White body, the White deep psyche that desires the Black body next to it, perhaps to envelope and devour it so that the Black body—inside the White—will eliminate the on-goings of White work that has to occur outside the body. The White body wants in some ways to absorb the Black body, to have it, to contain it where it can-not resist or engage in solidarity work or defend against Whiteness. This ensures that the White body is sustainable, no longer with external threats of possible dis-obedience and resistance. In fact, Whiteness and White work cannot exist without the Black body, separation, and arrangement. The Black body must always be pres-ent outside. Perhaps it would be more efficient to incorporate the Black body into the very body of the White. That is, to love the Black body to death so it is emptied yet still present. This also helps alleviate some of the tensions of White work. This work requires no struggle against the Black body, no resistance—but co-optation and consumption.

3.1 Blackness, Anti-Blackness, and the Theoretical Principles

In this section, I summarize foregoing ideas borrowing from my earlier writing (see Dei 1996) to advance ten theoretical principles that foreground the understanding of Blackness. The focus on these principles is an arbitrary decision that is more about the limits of my own knowing. The theorization of Blackness to counter anti-Black-ness is situated in debates about the nature of race and racial identity and the par-ticular strategies needed to challenge systemic racism using critical, essentialist, anti-essentialist and socially constructed notions of race. In this context, engaging race is a requisite entry point to anti-racist and anti-colonial practice for the explicit purposes of addressing racisms and social oppressions. Similarly, a redefinition of Blackness is a critical theoretical prism for the subversion of dominant discourses and representations of Black and African peoples in Euro-American contexts, and the challenge of White supremacy. In countering the anti-Blackness discourse and practice, the advancement of a shared Black identity, notwithstanding any heterogeneity and complexity, is a commitment to a collective resistance against racism and colonialism.

The first principle in theorizing Blackness to counter anti-Blackness acknowledges the coloniality of White power and Whiteness in advancing knowledge about the existence of different races. The idea and concept of different races was produced in service of White colonialism, and later capitalism. It was Whites, specifically White European explorers, who granted to themselves the power to define others as "different." This definitional power is about the "coloniality" of Whiteness. Colonial power fostered ideas about the existence of "races"—specifically that physically constituted self-evident "races" distinguished between human groupings. With European colonization, the idea of race became an essential feature of early societal formations as White explorers searched for social explanations and answers about the nature and consequences of human differences in everyday social relations—particularly in the allocation of social goods and services. Thus, race and racism were historically encoded in White European power and belief systems. Elsewhere (Dei 1996) I have noted that Reynolds and Lieberman (1993) long ago argued that "the origins of the race concept must be appropriately tied to Western European philosophical and belief systems, and particularly, to the colonial and imperial expansion activities" of the Western powers and economic capital in the seventeenth century (see Dei 1996, p. 40–41). Race, at the time, was a powerful and useful concept for sorting out human variation observed by European explorers, conquerors and colonizers. It was this practice of sorting groups on the basis of perceived physical differences that paved the way for racism as a social practice. In other words, the presumed existence of different races made racism real and consequential. In fact, Dei (1996, p. 41) further reiterate that as Reynolds and Lieberman (1993) enthused, a self-righteous racial ideology was developed to legitimize the ruthless exploitation and subjugation of non-Europeans. Particularly for Black bodies, this relevant history must be engaged with the concept of race critically evoked in its different and complex ways to challenge anti-Black racism and anti-Blackness. Consequently, the evocation of Blackness must openly name Whiteness and White supremacy, neither of which are named or acknowledged in dominant discourses. Hence, the importance of not letting go of the "Black-White" paradigm becomes clear. Similarly, an understanding of Blackness must affirm the power of colonial dominance and what it means to complicate "identity" depends on who is speaking and why (e.g., White bodies denying power and privilege & Black, racialized and/ or Indigenous bodies pursuing resistant politics).

The second principle of Blackness as counter to anti-Blackness is located in part within the problematic discourses of biology. In the biological sense, the race concept was used to categorize people on the basis of perceived differences of intelligence and physical prowess. An important justification for the enslavement of African peoples was that we were considered to be a "sub-human" species, like cattle. We supposedly did not have the "same" capacities for language, communication and culture as our European oppressors. Most of this discourse occurred within what was perceived and promoted to be the neutral, rational Eurocentric science of biology. This racist knowledge survived the test of time and became a dominant ideology over the years. Biddiss

(1979) has pointed out that "the development of racial theories was central to the dominant ideas of European bourgeois civilization and aesthetics (e.g., ideas of intelligence, character, physical prowess and beauty). Thus eighteenth and nineteenth century ideas reified the concept of race within this theoretical lens of biological determinism." Connections were made between supposedly scientific and mystical approaches to race. Racial ideas were presented as pseudo-religious thought, later adapted to a more secularized society (see Biddiss 1979). Throughout human history this intellectually unsophisticated discourse of biology has been fused with an equally problematic understanding of culture to explain human differences and to provide justifications for unequal treatment of individuals and groups. Theorizing Blackness as a challenge to anti-Blackness must engage this discourse of biology, even as we discount it. The metaphor of the social construction of race is powerful but it has not eliminated the discourse of biology. For the Black/African body, our perceived inherent inferiority is still a cornerstone of anti-Blackness and anti-Black racism.

The third principle calls for a critical reading of embodiment. There is a process of coming to know through one's racialized embodiment. Therefore, to assert one's Black identity is to reflect upon and embrace one's embodiment, and the epistemic significance of such racial embodiment (Dei 2007). Embodiment then is about how the Black body is read and perceived and the visceral reactions it evokes. To be Black is to be aware of such embodiment and what it means to embody the practice of Black identity/Blackness in positive (solution-oriented) ways as opposed to oppressive and dominating trends. Affirming a strong Black identity to challenge anti-Blackness is about a personal racialized embodiment. The Black body is a signifier of difference, but also of practice. The embodiment of race and racial identity is salient and consequential given the material, social, emotional, psychological and intrinsic implications of racial identity, and the "spirit injury" that results from the social and emotional effects of racism. A theory of Black identity consequently alludes to the experiences of being Black, the consequences of embodying this identity in a racist culture, and the particular resistant politics for which it calls. There are meanings encoded on Black bodies. This embodiment is not a biological reading of the Black body as much as a socially constructed dominant understanding of Blackness as violent, criminal, deviant and evil. Anti-Blackness is a repulsion of a Black identity that is not subservient, but challenges the dominant [and usually negative] interpretations of Black identity. However, affirmation of a positive Black identity cannot be seen simply as a reaction to this negativity. It must be read as the intellectual agency of Black peoples to define ourselves in ways that subvert dominant claims to know us more than we know ourselves. Affirming Blackness is a celebration of who we are. It is a definition in our own terms and not through Euro-colonial and racist lens. Such affirmation by extension is a response to anti-Blackness. It also points to the fact that in mounting a critique of anti-Blackness, we are simultaneously celebrating Blackness (see also Sexton 2011). Embodiment of Blackness is about the process of coming to know through one's racialized embodiment in a White supremacist context. Such racialized embodiment is emotionally filled, emotionally textured and consuming. Hence Black spirituality and emotions constitute a foundational knowledge base of Black racialized identity. Any re-theorization of Blackness must engage these sites as anti-racist knowledge, demanding spiritual and emotional accountability of the [Black] body (see also Latty 2015; Srivasta 2005, 2006).

An important question is the body as a site of knowing and socio-political space. This intellectual stance is an appreciation of the embodiment of knowing and the fact that we have "somatic" or "bodily knowings" (Heshusius 1994). This includes conscious and dysconscious knowings, as well as feelings, intuitions, emotions, and our psychic, sacred ancestral and cultural memories. I have often asked: what does it mean to inhabit a body and what are the implications for our knowing for those of us wearing a Black or African skin in a White supremacist context? The embodiment of self and knowledge is a political claim not a biological knowing. But it alludes to the social, material, historical, intellectual, spiritual and cultural legitimacy of Black and African peoples in matrix of knowing.

The fourth principle opines that advancing a theory of Blackness as intellectual and political counterpoints to anti-Blackness must work with both the idea of race as identity as the beginning [not the end] of politics, as well as the urgency to consciously challenge and subvert the construction of Black/African identity within Euro-American hegemony. Rather than deny the idea of race or argue for its dismissal because of a lack of scientific basis, we must recognize its political, material and symbolic effects as a strategy to confront racisms in its myriad forms. We must speak race. We cannot deal with anti-Blackness simply by denying race as a useful concept. Race has powerful effects notwithstanding its lack of a scientific basis. Racism is consequent to the reality of race. In fact, the silence around race is far from neutral and will not make racism go away. In effect, a theory of Blackness and Black identity that works against racism merely responds to that which "already exists," i.e. the idea of different races ranked within a hierarchy, with differential abilities to acquire, exhibit and express culture (Dei 2007, p. 53). Hence, a theory of Blackness challenging anti-Blackness explicitly and unapologetically names race as consequential and essential to identity and identity formations, community politics and resistance. Thus, engaging race is a requisite entry point to anti-racist/anti-colonial projects aimed at addressing systemic racism. To remain silent on race perpetuates racism. Race does not beget racism; rather it is racism that makes race real.

The fifth principle frames an intellectual and political project for affirming Blackness in the context of complexities of identities. The principle acknowledges that anti-Blackness is a strategic practice/political evocation intended to elevate Whites as the dominant group. It is a relational identity practice that defines the other as the opposite of the dominant. In other words, anti-Blackness maintains its full effects by insisting on White superiority over Black inferiority. By perceiving Blacks as not Whites, Blackness is "justifiably" equated with darkness, laziness, dirt, and criminality while Whiteness is about light, purity, innocence, and cleanliness. Blackness becomes repulsive, unwelcoming and hostile, while Whiteness is attractive, welcoming and friendly. Such binary notions are not innocent practices. It allows for a discursive space and positioning of Black[ness] as terror in the White imagination. This principle also theorizes a continuity between physical types or entities known as races and human culture and character, suggesting that these physical differences among human groupings invariably determine cultural differences. Such reasoning serves to explain the pathologization of Black/African cultures as disease and poverty stricken and the root causes of social decay. A culture of poverty thesis of Black/African culture contrasts sharply with the progress and enlightenment thesis of the White family and White culture whose values need emulating to ensure social success. In global development practice we have the whole discourse about the White "imperial savior," and Black Africa as a "basket case." Through this discourse Africa/Black is rendered impure through the White gaze. We are told that the problem with Africa is that it needs to modernize! Africa needs a "culture adjustment program," where our social values and cultural norms are in tune with a global capitalist competitive market. In such discourse, as I have also noted elsewhere (Dei 2014, p. 27) there is also the conflation of modernity and the modernist project. This Black/White or Africa/Europe split is an "attractive allegory" that offers up a "ridiculous" and "misleading imagery" (Lauer 2007, p. 292–4). In fact, there is an over-simplification of African culture and sadly, the colonial context and "the colonized mind is still a factor in African development" (Lauer 2007, p. 289). No one can counter hegemonic racist readings of Blackness and Black identity more so than Black/African bodies living these experiences. We must not allow the colonial dominant make the insulting claim that they know us more than we know ourselves (Prah 1997).

The sixth principle speaks to how ideas of "hybridity" and "in-betweenness" as liminal spaces are constructed as significant within particular historical and colonial contexts. Postcolonial "hybridity and cosmopolitanism serve to harmonize the universal," failing to acknowledge differences in power and material conditions of inequality between groups (see also Dirlik 1997; Krishnaswamy 2007, p. 3; Zeleza 1997). A theorization of Blackness cannot over-prioritize the subjectivity of the interstitial space. Any analysis of Black identity and subjectivity must equally be situated within a materialist paradigm. For instance, a key dimension of Black identity is the materiality of the body in the White-dominated global capitalist society (see Smith 2010). The mere acknowledgment of the shiftiness of identity is empty if it fails to embody resistance and the possibilities of (re)imagining and (re)organizing collectively, differently and disruptively for social change.

The seventh principle of Blackness as counterpoint to anti-Blackness asserts that speaking about Blackness and anti-Blackness addresses how social existence is essentially about asymmetrical power relations among groups. The binary of the oppressor and oppressed is a co-relational existence. While this binary must be understood in terms of its intended political consequences, it still needs to be complicated and rendered ineffectual. However, we must not fall into the postmodern trap of essentializing difference and flattening all differences in the plural discourse of "we are all oppressors and simultaneously oppressed." The fact of the colonial dominant or oppressor must not be downplayed. While we are all oppressed and become oppressors at some point in our lives, we are oppressed and become oppressors differently and in complex ways. Oppression is about power and we all are within asymmetrical power relations, even as we all have claims to power in different ways and forms. For example, as already alluded to, throughout human history White populations have claimed the power to define other social groups as different. This has had profound consequences for those who are or have been Othered. The

Othering process is about power, and while demarcations of class, gender, sexuality, and disability are worthy of note, these social divisions have not obfuscated the power of the colonial dominant (see Johal 2007). This is an anti-colonial reading of power that acknowledges its relational status and yet its differential effects for different groups. Clearly, anti-Blackness is one of the many faces of social oppression. The challenge to anti-Blackness [like other forms of racism] is a struggle against all other forms of oppression (e.g., racial, gender, class, sexual and disability oppressions). It is a collective struggle. Just as anti-Black racism has different manifestations of gender, class, sexuality and disability, so too do oppressions have myriad faces. Anti-Blackness achieves its full effects through intersections of race with gender, class, sexuality, disability, etc. Similarly racism, sexism, classism and ableism are all different forms of social oppression. Therefore, addressing anti-Blackness like other racisms and oppressions calls for collective efforts among oppressed peoples.

The eighth principle of Blackness as counterpoint to anti-Blackness asserts that speaking about Blackness and anti-Blackness on settled/stolen Lands is also about colonial-settler-oppression politics. Black experience is integral to colonialism[s] and White colonial settlerhood but as I will expand upon in subsequent chapters. Discussions about Black and Indigenous solidarities should be about "responsibilities," "implications" and "internal colonialisms," rather than "complicities" (colonial membership) and "settlers" (violence/genocide/dispossessions). Linking Black people to settlerhood is not only a dissonant construct, but also intellectually dishonest, especially when history is considered. There is a coterminous status of race and Indigeneity. There are no easy, neat or quick distinctions between Blackness and Indigeneity (Anderson 2007). This principle works with the knowledge that all co-shared spaces have the tendency to pit oppressions against each other and as such, engaging such spaces demands a critical scholarly gaze. The fact that Black bodies are situated within colonial and neo-colonial [settler] contexts has implications for decolonization and social justice struggles. Anti-Blackness, while constituting a different form of social oppression, has powerful connections with the oppression of Indigenous peoples. Yet the colonial project of the nation-state can utilize an oppressed group to oppress others. This is how the power of the colonial dominant works. A clear manifestation is when oppressed groups begin to compete and make distinctions among themselves in "oppression Olympics" (Smith 2006). Black/African peoples, Indigenous, non-Indigenous peoples, including Whites, must work in solidarities to challenge White colonial relations and White supremacy. This struggle requires the acknowledgement of implications and responsibilities and an understanding of how solidarities are themselves riddled with asymmetrical power relations. Unfortunately, such discussions of racialized groups and Indigenous communities within colonial settler relations usually pit oppressed groups against each other through hierarchies, despite intersecting marginalities. The engagement of Black and racialized bodies in White colonial settler relations often degenerates into a form of anti-Black racism, thereby contributing to let White-colonial settler subjects off the hook. An anti-colonial framework can help bring Indigenous communities and Black and other racialized peoples, including so-called immigrant bodies, all together to oppose the colonial dominant.

This solidarity work to contest both settler colonialism and anti-Black racism views Land as a place of coming to know and a place of experiencing relationality and connections with others in our worlds. Claiming Land is about an assertion of self-hood and collective identity. Land also constitutes a basis of onto-epistemological existence and pursuing strategies of anti-colonial resistance. Since colonialism did its dirty job over/on Indigenous peoples, Lands, and our identities, it is from such levels that we can legitimately lodge critiques and resistance (Alfred 2005, 2009; Corntassel 2003, 2012). The claims we make over Land must allow for alternative readings that are not hegemonic. While Land is a significant unifier of the colonial encounter and experience among Indigenous and colonized peoples, it is always important in doing political struggles everywhere to recognize the Lands on which we stand in solidarities with Indigenous Peoples (Amadahy and Lawrence 2010). All this notwithstanding, claims to Land must not operate with hegemonic orthodoxies or from a hegemonic knowledge base. We must bring multiple readings of our relations to Land so as to trouble/complicate how we come to define our respective entry or starting points for all decolonial/anti-colonial engagements. For example, while Land is sacred, revered and has a sanctity that is shared by Indigenous peoples, it is also important to understand Land as a site of violence, pain and suffering for Indigenous as well as other colonized, disenfranchised racialized groups. Land and racial dispossessions are co-relational and intertwined. Land and place-based politics in the context of violence onto colonized bodies and racial dispossessions make this co-determinant status apparent. The dispossession of Indigenous Lands everywhere is intertwined with racial, gender, class and sexual biopolitics. Race need not be pitted against Land or Indigeneity and vice versa. In his conception of the "coloniality of power," Quijano (2000, 2007) notes race as a fundamental organizing principle structuring the multiple and varied hierarchies of the global system (Grosfoguel 2007, p. 217). That is, we see in the coloniality of power the way race (White supremacy) organizes our worlds. So it is an important question to pause and ask: Why do many Black bodies react differently to their designation as "settlers" on stolen Indigenous Lands? Is it a question of denial of complicity, a "race to innocence" (Fellows and Razack 1998), or something broader? The fact of the matter is that questions of colonial/racial displacements, Euro-colonial and imperial pre-occupation of African soils, and the impoverishment of Black neighborhoods cannot be dismissed lightly. Any attempts to negate, dismiss or make light of such concerns is tantamount to anti-Blackness. If "Black lives matter" in settler colonial contexts, then any critical discussion of settler-colonial relations must touch on how anti-Blackness is entwined in historical and contemporary social structures.

Decolonization must be broader than simply about relations to Land because of how questions of materiality and ontology go hand in hand. The subjectification of Indigenous, Black and colonized bodies constitutes a significant problem within schooling and educational practices. The importance of reclaiming Indigenous positive (solution-oriented) traditions and histories as a continuity of past, present and future practices and resistance of the colonized presence are also about decolonial and anti-colonial struggles for spiritual rebirth, regeneration, health and emotional well-being.

The intellectual agency and power of claiming an African Indigeneity that is anchored on the reverence to Land and its teachings, as well as the interface of culture, society and Nature is also important to note. Such theorizing of Black/African identities as sites of knowing seeks to validate African peoples' own understandings of our worlds. Embedded in the African Indigeneity is the spiritual as ontology and epistemology. In other words, our spiritual ontologies and epistemologies as Black and African peoples espouse particular understandings of culture, and the principles of connections, relationships, interdependence, co-operation, sharing, reciprocity, generosity, mutuality and the idea of "connected knowings" as critical to knowledge about self, others, group and community (see also Bishop 1998 in another contexts). Equally important is the ontological reality of the "unity of being" of the African self/personhood and the existence of a metaphysical realm as a component of the human and the social world, all as part of the world of living (see also Mazama 2002). As humans we are neither separate nor distinct from the cosmos but are part of the one world (physical and metaphysical, human, animate and inanimate objects). Such worldview poses a strong challenge to Western science and scientific knowledge.

The ninth principle of theorizing Black identity and Blackness must emphasize global dimensions in resisting anti-Blackness in contemporary social formations. It is thus important for us to bring a global/transnational understanding to Blackness (e.g., globalization of anti-Black racism; being "Black" in Diaspora; the urgency of reinventing an Africanness in Diasporic contexts; and ways in which the politics of diaspora inform community building and solidarities). Black/African bodies in Diasporic contexts share struggles. Globalization and decolonization are major challenges. There is a globalization of racisms in which the use of color as a basis of racializing Black bodies as inferior to Whites has global dimensions. While Whiteness has global currency, Blackness on the other hand has global deficits. We face mounting challenges in the education of our children and resisting the devaluations of our cultures and knowledge systems. One of the biggest challenges in theorizing the African/Black existence is defining what it means to be African today and in the global context. Our humanity and subjectivity are always under threat and in question. We need anti-colonial education that empowers our young learners to be proud of their identities and identifications. We especially need all our people to understand what it means to be Black/African in the global context. It is more than a question of a search for a collective Black/African identity. Black/African peoples and our heritages have a lot to offer for the future human world; we are an integral part of global future. We are Africans and also global citizens. Our collective success closely hinges on global development. We have had to contend with centuries-long extreme oppression and exploitation. Our resilience and resistance demand that we reclaim the leadership role of human civilization and help shape the future of the world. Notwithstanding differences, we can move forward with a collective vision, a future that we not only dare to dream together, but more importantly, that we create together and of which we share the outcomes together. A theorization of

Blackness and anti-Blackness must therefore be broad enough to empower ourselves not only mentally, economically, politically and socially, but also spiritually—to use all aspects of our "humanness." The redefinition of Blackness must move away from materialistic/Eurocentric ideology to a more communal paradigm, to understand and respond to the cultural, political and socio-economic changes that impede our identities. This is one powerful way to counter anti-Black racism and negative portrayals of Blackness.

The tenth principle is Blackness must be read and understood in the prism of collective anti-colonial resistance. Fanon (1963) long ago noted the phenomenological, psycho-existential, macro-structural, political, and material implications of Black racialized embodiment, and the continuing "subjectification" of our bodies—i.e. "the dialectical process of sense making and being made" (Coloma 2008, p. 11). There is thus a need for a politics of de-subjectification, authentication, territoriality and detoxification [see Fanon]. Claiming Blackness is an affirmation of the continuing struggles to purge ourselves of the "psycho-existential complexes" and "psycho-affective features" battered and imprinted on us over the course of the colonial experience and through colonizing and imperial knowledges (see also Coulthard 2007, p. 450; see also Dei 2017). Blackness must be reclaimed for political purposes. We must also rethink Black resistance broadly as encompassing and residing in different spaces, voices, oral narratives and cultural memories, actions, and spirits, in order to foster meaningful, collective anti-colonial solidarities.

Collective solidarities for resistance must evoke an interlocking analysis of Blackness as race, gender, class, sexuality and [dis]ability as essential to a politics of social movement. There is a constitutive symbiotic relation of Black identities pointing to the complexities of political work as viewed within the "matrix of oppression" and the "simultaneity of oppression" (Collins 1991). How do Black bodies navigate the multiple forms of oppression that intersect to create different impacts on their lived experiences? We must pay attention to the relationship between their lived experience with gender, class, [dis]ability, sexuality and ethnicity in order to highlight the impact of intersectionality on Black bodies. We must ask certain questions such as: what is an integrative analysis and the relevance for studies of oppression and subjectification? What does such integrative analysis bring to the Black experience? And, in what ways can we be attentive to social differences and the co-determining status, while foregrounding key issues of race, gender, class, sexuality or language depending on the situational and contextual variations in intensities of oppressions?

Scholarship about Blackness must also respond to Black and African peoples' concerns, hopes and aspirations, and particularly what our intellectual projects as learners mean to our people and communities. Black and African scholars must be answerable to our communities however contested, diverse or heterogeneous these communities are. Our scholarship cannot study our communities "from a distance." Our scholarship cannot be about scholar detachment, separation or abstract claims of objectivity and science. Our scholarship about Blackness must subvert Western hegemonic systems of knowing that historically have articulated majority interests over our communities. There has been and continues to be a reproduction of coloniality (values, knowledge and practice) in everyday schooling and education that has served to undervalue, marginalize and negate the Black experience. This has been pursued while simultaneously affording power, privilege, discursive and authorial control over our lived experiences both to "experts" using largely a Westocentric narration of us framed in the lens of postmodernism.

A traditional critique of anti-colonial Black struggles has been that they have evoked the "nation," "community," and to some extent "family" in ways that can be exclusive by denying differences and heterogeneity and reinforcing hetero-patriarchal norms, which thus opened up these struggles to [mis]appropriations by more conservative elements from the Right (see also Smith 2006). Therefore in re-theorizing Blackness from a decolonial perspective, we must also be attentive to questions of community and communal relations, difference, inclusivity and power relations within these struggles. A decolonial approach to Blackness must work with a model of heterogeneous communities, and focus on forging community rela-tionships. But above all else, Black, Indigenous, and otherwise colonized and oppressed peoples must nurture our hopes and dreams and embrace new imagina-tions as we contest and design futures. How we mobilize ourselves is key to our success. We can run or shy away from our identities or we can reframe and embrace all of our identifications. We can also begin to explore radical possibilities to find hope in the midst of global despair. We must examine the political economic impli-cations of colonial and anti-colonial discourses and begin to historicize the place of theory in our lives as oppressed, colonized, Black and Indigenous bodies. We may not want to talk about Blackness because of its political edge. We may not want to engage it, because to some it is an essentializing and totalizing concept. But Blackness is a political evocation. We cannot be restricted by the double standard of Euro-modernity and we need to transcend the boundaries of so-called modernity.

We know how the criminality of Black bodies works with essentialist notions of Blackness; yet when Blackness is mobilized for political action and response, cries of a totalizing narrative ensue. Modernity is a colonial project, specifically a Euro-colonial totalizing project which universalizes the particular. What makes this Euro-colonial modernist project frightening is that it is an unfinished business, yet we can help sow the seeds of its demise. Modernity is unsettling. Hence, we must see it as a site of contestation, political struggles and resistance. While there are many entry points to the struggle, I contend that claiming Blackness as a site of empowerment, resistance and agency can be useful. There are colonial and imperial differences worthy of note for an anti-colonial reclamation of Blackness, such as differences in histories, processes and resistances to colonization, and subaltern politics of resis-tance. Yet the political and intellectual evocation of Blackness in all its complexity, tensions and complications can speak to some of us very well.

References

Alfred, T. (2005). Sovereignty. In J. Barker (Ed.), *Sovereignty matters: Locations of contestation and possibility in Indigenous struggles for self-determination* (pp. 33–50). Lincoln: University of Nebraska Press.

Alfred, T. (2009). Colonialism and state dependency. *Journal of Aboriginal Health, 5,* 42–60.

Amadahy, Z., & Lawrence, B. (2010). Indigenous peoples and Black people in Canada: Settlers or allies? In A. Kempf (Ed.), *Breaching the colonial contract: Anti-colonialism in the US and Canada* (pp. 105–136). New York: Springer Publishing.

Anderson, M. (2007). *When Afro becomes [like] Indigenous: Garifuna and Afro Indigenous politics in Honduras.* Santa Cruz, CA: University of California Press.

Benjamin, A. (2003). *The Black/Jamaican criminal: The making of ideology.* Unpublished.

Biddiss, M. D. (1979). *Images of race.* Leicester: Leicester University Press.

Bishop, R. (1998). Freeing ourselves from neo-colonial domination in research: A Maori approach to creating knowledge. *Qualitative Studies in Education, 11*(2), 199–219.

Collins, P. H. (1991). *Black feminist thought: Knowledge, consciousness, and the politics of empowerment.* New York: Routledge.

Coloma, R. S. (2008). Border crossing subjectivities and research: Through the prism of feminists of color. *Race Ethnicity and Education, 11*(1), 11–27.

Corntassel, J. (2003). Who is Indigenous? 'Peoplehood' and ethnonationalist approaches to rearticulating Indigenous identity. *Nationalism and Ethnic Politics, 9*(1), 75–100.

Corntassel, J. (2012). Re-envisioning resurgence: Indigenous pathways to decolonization and sustainable self-determination. *Decolonization: Indigeneity, Education & Society, 1*(1), 86–101.

Coulthard, G. (2007). Subjects of empire: Indigenous peoples and the 'politics of recognition' in Canada. *Contemporary Political Theory, 6,* 437–460.

Dei, G. J. S. (1996). *Anti-racism education: Theory and practice.* Halifax: Fernwood Publishing.

Dei, G. J. S. (2000). Rethinking the role of Indigenous knowledges in the academy. *International Journal of Inclusive Education, 4*(2), 111–132.

Dei, G. J. S. (2007). Speaking race: Silence, salience and the politics of anti-racist scholarship. In S. Hier & S. Bolaria (Eds.), *Race and Racism* (pp. 53–66). Orchard Park, New York: Broadview Press.

Dei, G. J. S. (2008). *Racists beware: Uncovering racial politics in contemporary society.* Rotterdam: Sense Publishers.

Dei, G. J. S. (2014). Reflections on "African development": Situating Indigeneity and Indigenous Knowledges. In A. Abdi & E. Shizha (Eds.), *Indigenous discourses on knowledge and development in Africa* (pp. 15–30). New York: Routledge.

Dei, G. J. S. (2017). Reframing education through indigenous, anti-colonial and decolonial prisms. In P. McLaren & S. Soohoo (Eds.), *The radical imagine-nation* (Vol. 2). New York: Peter Lang.

Dei, G. J. S., & Asgharzadeh, A. (2001). The power of social theory: Towards an anti-colonial discursive framework. *The Journal of Educational Thought, 35*(3), 297–323. New York: Peter Lang.

Dirlik, A. (1997). *The post-colonial aura: Third World criticism in the age of global capitalism.* Oxford: Westview Press.

Fanon, F. (1963). *The wretched of the earth.* New York: Grove Press.

Fellows, M., & Razack, S. (1998). The race to innocence: Confronting hierarchical relations among women. *The Journal of Gender, Race & Justice, 1,* 335–352.

Grosfoguel, R. (2007). The epistemic colonial turn. *Cultural Studies, 21*(2–3), 211–223.

Hartman, S. (1997). *Scenes of subjection: Terror, slavery, and self-making in nineteenth century America.* New York: Oxford University Press.

Heshusius, L. (1994). Freeing ourselves from objectivity: Managing subjectivity or turning toward a participatory mode of consciousness? *Educational Researcher, 23*(3), 15–22.

Ignatiev, N. (1997). The point is not to interpret whiteness but to abolish it, Talk given at the Making and Unmaking of Whiteness Conference, University of California, Berkeley. Retrieved 11–13, from April http://racetraitor.org/abolishthepoint.pdf.

Johal, G. (2007). The racialization of space: Producing surrey. In G. Johnson & R. Enomoto (Eds.), *Race, racialization and antiracism in Canada and beyond* (pp. 179–205). Toronto: University of Toronto Press.

Koffman, O., & Gill, R. (2013). "The revolution will be led by a 12-year-old girl": Girl power and global biopolitics. *Feminist Review, 105*, 83–102.

Krishnaswamy, R. (2007). Post-colonial and globalization studies: Connections, conflicts, complicities. In R. Krishnaswamy & C. Hawley (Eds.), *Postcolonial and the global* (pp. 2–21). Minneapolis, MN: University of Minnesota Press.

Latty, S. (2015). Cutting through the emotional tension: Towards a poetics of feeling in anti-racist research methodology. Unpublished Term paper, Department of Social Justice Education, Ontario Institute for Studies in Education of the University of Toronto.

Lauer, H. (2007). Depreciating African political culture. *Journal of Black Studies, 38*(2), 288–307.

Mazama, M. A. (2002). Afrocentricity and African spirituality. *Journal of Black Studies, 33*(2), 218–234.

Mignolo, W. D. (2007). Delinking: The rhetoric of modernity, the logic of coloniality and the grammar of de-coloniality. *Cultural Studies, 21*(2–3), 449–514.

Mignolo, W. D. (2011). Geopolitics of sensing and knowing: on (de)coloniality, border thinking and epistemic disobedience. *Postcolonial Studies, 14*(3), 273–283.

Prah, K. (1997). "Accusing the Victims—In my Father's House." A Review of Kwame Anthony Appiah's, *In My Father's House'. CODESRIA Bulletin, 1*, 14–22.

Quijano, A. (2000). Coloniality of power, ethnocentrism, and Latin America. *NEPANTLA, 1*(3), 533–580.

Quijano, A. (2007). Coloniality and modernity/rationality. *Cultural Studies, 21*(2/3), 168–178.

Reynolds, L., & Lieberman, L. (1993). The rise and fall of "race". *Race, Sex & Class, 1*(1), 109–127.

Sexton, J. (2010). Proprieties of coalition: Blacks, Asians, and the politics of policing. *Critical Sociology, 36*(1), 87–108.

Sexton, J. (2011). The social life of social death: On Afro-pessimism and Black optimism. *Tensions Journal, 5*, 1–47.

Sexton, J. (2015). Unbearable blackness. *Cultural Critique, 90*(1), 159–178.

Smith, A. (2006). Heteropatriarchy and the three pillars of White supremacy. In *Color of violence: INCITE! women of color against violence* (pp. 66–73). Cambridge, MA: South End Press.

Smith, A. (2010). Indigeneity, settler colonialism, white supremacy. *Global Dialogue (Online), 12*(2), 1–13.

Smith, C. A. (2015). Blackness, citizenship, and the transnational vertigo of violence in the. *The Americas, 117*(2), 384–387.

Srivastava, S. (2005). You're calling me a 'racist'? The moral and emotional regulation of antiracism and feminism. *Signs: Journal of Women and Culture in Society, 31*(1), 29–62.

Srivastava, S. (2006). Tears, fears and careers: Anti-racism and emotion in social movement organization. *Canadian Journal of Sociology, 13*(1), 55–90.

Yancy, G. (2005). Whiteness and the return of the Black body. *The Journal of Speculative Philosophy, 19*(4), 215–241.

Zeleza, T. (1997). Fictions of the postcolonial: A review article. *CODESRIA Bulletin, 2*, 15–19.

Chapter 4
Blackness and Colonial Settlerhood: A Purposeful Provocation

Abstract This chapter seeks to clarify and simultaneously trouble several key concepts that inform or have been assumed through the popular call to "decolonize
anti-racism." For example, Lawrence and Dua's (2005) thought-provoking article
Decolonizing Antiracism. These concepts include Euro-colonialism and settler
colonialism; settlerhood and settler White colonial discourse and settler colonialism; complicity and implication; and responsibility. My argument is that neither I,
nor any other Black/African residing on Turtle Island, can be referred as a settler,
and charged with complicity as Lawrence and Dua (2005) long ago claimed. Instead,
the chapter provides new coordinates for collective and global mobilization by troubling the politics of "decolonizing solidarity" as the intellectual flavor of the
moment. This is done by offering Indigeneity as an international category and as a
coordinate for decolonizing (and) antiracist work. Ideas put forward in the chapter
are aided by many who add complexity and nuance to decolonizing (and) anti-racist
scholarship and praxis. It is opined that theorizing the Indigenous as an international
category allows us to mobilize as an international category and as an international
collective of multiple anti-racist communities that can build solidarities with
Indigenous Peoples and their decolonizing work. Indigeneity provides a category,
and a collective, that can mobilize support for decolonizing work that reaches
Indigenous Peoples across the world.

We must steadfastly desist from doing what the colonizer wants. I do not write this
chapter to claim innocence nor to apportion blame. I feel it is important for me to
place on the table how my political and intellectual unease with a number of historical and ongoing divides spurred on by the colonial tactic of "divide and conquer."
So I ask: What does it mean to be on the Land of the Huron-Wendat and Petun First
Nations, the Seneca, and the Mississaugas of the Credit River, especially, if I insist
on claiming my African Indigeneity? How does our work as Indigenous and Black
scholars and community activists strengthen and support each other's aspirations
and collective existence? How can we stop feeding on the colonial antagonisms and
colonial divides that separate us from each other as colonized peoples? How do we
come to grips with our different entanglements with settler colonialism, anti-Blackness and anti-Africanness? In questioning the "ideas that hold us apart" how do we

© Springer International Publishing AG 2017
G.J.S. Dei, *Reframing Blackness and Black Solidarities through Anti-colonial
and Decolonial Prisms*, Critical Studies of Education 4,
DOI 10.1007/978-3-319-53079-6_4

also begin to question those "ideas that hold us together"? As an African Indigenous body questions about settler colonialism, Land and Indigeneity register differently and complexly for me. I fully grant the fact that there can be no decolonization for me unless I confront the Land I occupy from multiple understandings as a starting point in claiming my African Indigeneity. My Blackness is African and is also Indigenous. While my communities confront shared issues clearly it does not mean the issues are singular nor the same.

There is a yearning to define my belonging to a place, space and Land. But everywhere the search for belongingness is only critical to decolonial praxis if one is allowed to stake a claim of their Indigeneity. While I would agree that decolonization must be "culture specific" and located in particular histories of place, space and Land, our decolonial politics must also be astute enough to engage with the multiple and variegated forms of colonialisms and colonization happening across space, time and places. For those of us whose identity is continually in question and/or being constructed and challenged having something, some place and Land to hang on to or to claim our own cannot be trivialized. The question is what politics we choose to pursue when we come into certain spaces/places? Like many who are reading this book my journey in the academy has included a resistance to the "insistence" of measuring up to Euro-colonial constructions of "knowledge," "standards," "merits," "excellence" and what is deemed to be "intellectual." Many of us as colonized bodies are continually forced to respond to the dominant's tendency to view counter and oppositional discourses as "anti-intellectual." We have been seduced to search for validation, legitimation and acceptance in dominant [White] colonial spaces. We have been seduced into mimicking theories that hardly speak to our lived experiences as Black, African and Indigenous subject. What is disturbing is that alongside this "mimicry," there has been a consistent assault on the African heritage and our cultural ways of knowledge.

The resulting effect is the way many of us have become "intellectual imposters" (Nyamnjoh 2012) in the Western academy, we operate with a spiritual damage as "wounded souls" and "dis-membered bodies" (Anzaldúa 1987; Anzaldúa and Moraga 1981) and we are not our true authentic selves. We must and have to disrupt the "politics of knowledging." Erasing the Indigenous presence has always been a colonial project everywhere. This in itself cannot be allowed to float around unchallenged. We must be interrupters in the "Journey of Compliance" where there is a particular politics of knowledging that has only succeeded in reproducing and enforcing the "coloniality of power." In becoming a subversive and an interrupter, I make no apologies speaking differently. This is because speaking differently has been a form of resistance for many of us. Many of us are struggling to shed the roots of Western academic scholarship in terms of the exploration, disruption and renaming the world of the "Other." If we are serious about *drastically changing* the colonial and re-colonial foundations of some of our disciplines and discussions in the academy then we should re-imagine the academy and knowledge production differently.

I stake six discursive positions/stances in reclaiming my own politics of knowledging and the understanding of settlerhood implications. First, *there is an African*

Indigenous and Indigeneity. This is a refusal to erase, deny and amputate African subjects claim to their Indigeneity and the epistemological and ontological claims of the African Indigenous. I stake a claim to an African Indigeneity as a form of intellectual interrogation and discursive curiosity of why some people would deny the African Indigeneity in the first place? What are we afraid of? After all, if we are to define "Indigenous" as the first/original occupants of the Land, how can we dislodge and even deny claims of colonized peoples who still occupy their Lands as non-Indigenous? African peoples are Indigenous to a place of their origin. In fact this denial runs counter to a political and intellectual project to develop relevant "rich theoretical tool-boxes" and to "pioneer new analytical systems for understanding our communities steeped in our home-grown cultural perspectives" (Yankah 2004, p. 25). I articulate my African Indigeneity using Indigenous cultural framings that also learn from Indigenous peoples on Turtle Island, in the context of the Canadian settler state as well as the global Diaspora, grounded in the teachings of the Land, as well as working to create decolonial and anti-colonial solidarity for authentic Indigenous futures.

Second, *there is an urgency for thinking through the possibilities of new authentic Indigenous futurities.* The thinking through process must transcend borders to work with multiple counter epistemic stances in order to reimagine our communities. In order for the search for Indigenous futures to be collectively shared, it must also rest on struggles of Indigeneity across different Lands, spirits, waters, spaces, places, times and moment. This collective project can only help in articulating new ways of imagining new global futures. The use of authentic is not to gesture to romanticism, purity nor a non-contamination. It is about something being genuine, real and grounded. This authenticity rest on the epistemic saliency of the colonized, oppressed and Indigenous to be able to posit their own futures in ways that make sense to them and not be subjected to the insulting reading and practice that futures can be designed for others. There is an "authentic Indigenous" if we to disrupt the assumed discursive authority of the dominant to speak of Indigenous realities. We may also speak of "Indigenous cultures" and "Indigenous peoples" as linked and coterminous these can also be separated for an analytical discussion, especially in the Diasporic contexts. There is the materiality of Indigenousness which insists that we make bold claims to Indigenous/Indigeneity as international perspective to retain our sanity in the madness of the political economy of the [Western] academy. This is what I have called the search for a "trialectic space" (Dei 2012) for some of us.

Third, is the *dialectic of Indigeneity and decolonization.* The search for Indigenous futures is about decolonization. And, just as much as decolonization cannot happen when there is a settler/occupier [she/he must seize to exist], decolonization cannot happen solely through Western science knowledge [scholarship] (see also Kerr 2013, 2014). Why? There is and has been the coloniality of Western science, i.e., science has been a tool of colonization. For example, the omissions, negations and devaluation of African Indigenous intellectual traditions in school curriculum are a case in point. Decolonization is not simply for the non-authentic Indigenous body (see Dei 2015). Indigenous bodies need to decolonize just as much as the colonizer and oppressors.

Fourth, is the fact that there is the power *of Indigenous theorizing.* There is an understanding of Indigeneity that has and continues to be produced and projected through the White imagination and the Euro-colonial construct of modernity and overmythicization. Europe does not define the Indigenous for me; and neither is Europe is not the advent of human history. The world did not begin with Europe. Theorizing Indigenous and Indigeneity as more than about a more physical location to understanding the complexity of our relations to the Land, waters, sky, seas, and how colonial violence continues to be codified on bodies, places and spaces that span across a broad spectrum (e.g., knowledges, cultural memories and bodies). In effect, as well be expanded upon later, an anti-colonial conceptualization of Indigeneity is about process, identity, political consciousness and resistance. It must mean something for us to insist that the "Indigenous" resides in bodies, cultural, spiritual and psychic memories, histories and cultural knowledges.

Fifth is the significance of *affirming Black and Indigenous resurgence through decolonial and anti-colonial solidarities in Diasporic contexts.* In the Euro-American contexts, these two groups have been under perpetual colonial assault. We are living through our different entanglements with the historical processes of enslavement, genocide, and Land dispossession. There have been countless enunciations of the clear evidence of the physical exterminations of Indigenous populations in the Americas, this atrocities of residential schools in North America. While some may ask us to go beyond the inhumanity of human enslavement we know that today anti-Black racism and anti-Blackness impact us all. They implicate each and every one of us. Anti-Black racism operates in every facet of our society. We see it in the way Black bodies become disengaged in schools, we see it in the way Black bodies are underrepresented in institutions, and we see it in the way the media attempts to sensationalize the tropes about Black people (the violent Black man, the angry Black woman). These tropes are imbued with anti-Black racism; they are not just about stereotypes about Black people. Anti-Black racism is entrenched in the way our society and its institutions are set up to operate. Anti-Blackness and anti-Black racism is part of a colonial system. We need to recognize that colonialism is not simply an event that happened in the past. It is a system; it is an ongoing project in very global space. Research has proven that anti-Black racism works through colonial systems in society. It is easy to ignore anti-Blackness because we (as a society) have become so used to it. When one becomes so used to seeing something, it becomes normalized (kind of like the air). If we are all to remain deeply committed to equity, social justice, we all need to recognize that anti-Blackness exists in our communities, homes, and minds. Naming anti-Black racism, anti-Blackness and colonialism is one step that can help bring visibility to these important issues.

It is important then for us to talk about anti-Blackness and anti-Black racism where they happen and it is how they can be addressed and stopped. We need to talk about how colonial systems privilege and marginalize certain bodies differently. However, if the goal is to decolonize, we must guard against colonial logics that overly rely on articulations and accentuations of tensions and divisions and refocus our attention on strengthening our solidarity. Going beyond the colonial logic of creating and accentuating tensions, divides and divisions. We are currently witnessing resurgence of Black and Indigenous critical solidarity, friendship and alliances. We must continuously search for healthy alliances that build on both historical and contemporary Black, African and Indigenous solidarities (i.e., while we recognize that our histories are not similar nor single they are connected and attempts at building anti-colonial solidarities through "decolonial thinking" (Mignolo 2000, 2008). We must not succumb to the racist logic of feeding on colonial divides). The idea of "shared" colonialisms and oppressions should create opportunities for solidarity among Indigenous peoples worldwide with an interest in challenging and subverting colonial, racist logics. A subject location on Indigenous peoples Land, space, territory in a Diasporic contexts becomes a moment to revitalize and reclaim our own local cultural knowledges informed by/steeped in local culture, history, identity and politics, instead of the exclusion of these as valid sites of knowing.

Lastly, is the *"burden of representation"* of Blackness in a politics of knowledging. I allude to the politics of claiming Blackness. In working with what has been termed "conceptual Blackness," I would not want us to get rid of Blackness as seriously about skin color racism. It is one of the ways we can come to fully grasp the complexity of anti-Blackness. Representing Blackness is a burden of the oppressed/colonized/racialized just as for the oppressor/colonizer/dominant for the question Blackness raises: Who, what, why and how of representation? There is always politics of reclaiming and the resistance to unlearning and un-naming that is usually complicated by the interpretations and meanings we bring to authenticity. The politics of who is representing whom needs to be complicated. Representing Blackness beyond skin color through theory illustrates a particular kind of intellectual agency that is important to understanding Blackness. However, such kind of intellectual agency does not affirm that the voice of the bodies which are doing theorizing beyond skin color is cognizant of their social location. It is also a burden of representing given the difficulties of finding resolution to the challenges of cultural appropriation of what Black means. For example, as noted by Howes (1996) in another context, there are many misrepresentations through cultural appropriations that can cause much harm and damage to a "people's sense of cultural integrity" of who they are (p. 144). We must always resolve then to bring responsibility to the knowledge we are allowed to have and come to know.

In this book, I have purposely reserved an important statement of personal location for this chapter. The delay is strategic and intentional. I write about Blackness as a resident in Toronto, a settler city of Turtle Island. For me this residence is about responsibility and collective politics given that I am coming from a place where Euro-colonizers also have settled on our Lands and the processes of Euro-colonization are still ongoing. But more specifically, in this chapter my goal is to "manage the density" of scholarly critiques about the need to "decolonize anti-racism" and "decolonize solidarity" and what I see as a troubling reading that unfortunately continues to shape ongoing discussions of Black and White colonial-settler relations. Anti-racism emerged as a community practice practically (but not exclusively) within Black local communities. It is Black scholars who pioneered the field of anti-racism studies just as we did with Transnational Feminism. Given the politics that spurred anti-racism studies, I am concerned by calls to "decolonize anti-racism". However, I do see the potential for solidarity in offering a direct response. Therefore, in an attempt to build solidarity and reshape the conversation, I offer a direct response to those who have thoughtfully called for an action to "decolonize anti-racism". Most importantly, I want to be heard as much as I should. I also want others to be heard when they speak and write. I want to be heard in a constructive and instrumental value, both theoretically and materially, to Black and Indigenous futurities. In the discussion that follows, I will first engage some of the key concepts and ask why we do this dance of making Black peoples complicit in colonial settler practices. It is my hope to lay bare a justification for a new dance, one that will take Indigeneity as an international category, show the links of race and Indigeneity as strictly interwoven, and implicate all—including Indigenes on their own Lands.

I will clarify and simultaneously trouble several key concepts that inform or have been assumed through the popular call to "decolonize anti-racism," for example in Lawrence and Dua's (2005) thought-provoking article *Decolonizing Antiracism*. These concepts include Euro-colonialism and settler colonialism; settlerhood and settler White colonial discourse and settler colonialism; complicity and implication; and responsibility. My argument is that neither Black/African nor people of color who reside on Turtle Island can be charged with complicity in the appropriation of Indigenous people's Lands in the way Lawrence and Dua (2005) affirm. My argument is based on a desire to provide new coordinates for collective and global mobilization by troubling the politics of "decolonizing solidarity." I do this by offering Indigeneity as an international category and as a coordinate for decolonizing (and) antiracist work. I bring Indigeneity forward to strengthen, restore and galvanize our alignment with each other in the project of resisting and eliminating colonialism(s). I intend not more than alignment since I do not want to erase our difference(s) and the knowledges that embed them. I conclude thereafter with an acknowledgement of the limitations of my position and an invitation for us to continue to deepen our understandings of the position that I offer here.

Although Lawrence and Dua's work dates back to 2005, this debate is ongoing both in academic spaces and in community and activist politics. The critique leveraged in the article continues to impact not only how many Black and other racialized peoples feel about their presence in Canada, but perhaps more importantly, how we frame or unfortunately limit a politics of solidarity between Indigenous and non-Indigenous communities in Canada. The critique of anti-racism is especially potent, given that anti-racism developed out of necessity for survival for Black scholars in the academy and Black communities in Canada more broadly. Such necessity, of course, arises from the same White supremacist, capitalist and colonial structures that Indigenous communities have been and are working against in order to survive. Furthermore, anti-racism, both as a community practice and scholarly focus, has always contested the ongoing practices and effects of colonialism.

I develop this response as a counter to Lawrence and Dua's (2005) claim. I see our way forward as necessary and important. Make no mistake; I credit their work for sparking a conversation that requires careful engagement, humility, and a willingness to learn. I deeply respect their critical scholarship. I admit that although I was hurt by their critiques, and sometimes angered by it as well, I realize it must have come from their own need to make decolonization a highly visible imperative. An imperative that, I agree, must be taken with the seriousness and attention it deserves.

Prior to beginning this discussion it is important to say that Lawrence and Dua's position has shifted since 2005. I am truly glad this shift has occurred; however, this does not change the fact that their critique remains present within the literature, fully armed and aimed at antiracist scholarship, antiracist practice, and Black/Africans living on Turtle Island—whether Canadian citizens, some variation of this, or not citizens at all. This critique can easily be deployed to serve undesirable, unjust, racist and colonial aims and ends. For this reason, I disassemble it. I am aware this has been done by other scholars, yet I proceed anyway knowing that I risk this essay's dismissal as "resurrecting a dead horse." To me it is not a dead horse—far from it. I come at it from the troubling sense that every day in my graduate classes at the University of Toronto, I encounter even some Black students who speak of "Black complicity" and our "settler status" without being critical of White supremacy and divide-and-conquer politics. I write this chapter from the multiple converging perspectives that I embody as a Black/African living on Turtle Island, a Black/African with Canadian citizenship, an anti-racist scholar working in (and beyond) Canada, as a member of an Indigenous community and of the Indigeneity scholarship community, and as a Ghanaian man. I also write this response as a Black body, a body that works in both academic and community spaces, a body which has a voice that can speak to the ways my experiences can inform and contribute to our resistance practices.

My deep contention with Lawrence and Dua's call to "decolonize antiracism" is clarified through the many statements presented in building their critique. I offer a few of these statements here to frame the emphasis of this chapter: "rather than challenging the ongoing colonization of Indigenous peoples, Canadian antiracism is furthering contemporary colonial agendas" (Lawrence and Dua 2005, p. 123); "people of color are settlers" (Lawrence and Dua 2005, p. 134); and "people of color, as settlers, participate in, or are complicit in, the ongoing colonization of Indigenous peoples" (Lawrence and Dua 2005, p. 134). This essay challenges Lawrence and Dua's critique and, as importantly, it seeks to arrest the weakening of antiracism scholarship and activism that their work threatens. I do this by making an impassioned claim of my difference from the colored body that Lawrence and Dua point to. Their critique names me *settler* and they write me as *complicit with colonialist agendas*. These claims not only diminish me, bodies like me, and the communities we are connected to but they also severely delegitimize the work of anti-racism. I am, however, grateful for their critiques, for they have stirred a charged awakeness in me, an awakeness familiar to the Black body. There exists a need and desire for greater and more authentic forms of collaboration amongst our practice communities, which necessitates our collective attention and care. It is untenable because colonialisms strategically fill and complicate spaces between racialized peoples.

Colonial logics resonate here and distort our relationships further, and through this distortion, thwart our antiracist and decolonizing work. Collaboration is essential.

My work is aided by many who add complexity and nuance to decolonizing (and) anti-racist scholarship and praxis. Lawrence and Dua's initial incursion into this area continues to be opened up by different scholars in direct and indirect ways that add immensely to our understandings and to our always developing collaborations. For example, I draw on the work of Jodi Byrd which offers the concept of "arrivants" (2011). Tuck and Yang (2012) also add to this scholarship through their framing of settler and immigrant dynamics. Tiffany King's (2013) thesis regarding plantation colonialism and settler colonialism offers another level of complexity as do the works of Walia (2012) and Taylor (2011). Jared Sexton, Melissa Phung, Ann Smith, and Harshe Walia also add to this work. And unsurprisingly, a rereading of Franz Fanon's "*Wretched of the Earth*" continues to provide valuable insights. The different elements and concepts developed through these works, and others, resonate with and support the work I do in this essay. Their insights, each different and all valuable, signal new trajectories not present in Lawrence and Dua's critique. Categorically naming people of color—especially Black Africans as settler on Turtle Island—and charging such bodies with the appropriation of Indigenous peoples Land is problematic. It is riddled with undertones of anti-Blackness that the colonial project requires.

I ask: How can we read complexity into our social existence so as to recognize our collective and differential responsibilities to each other and be able to affirm intellectual and political stances without claims of innocence (Fellows and Razack 1998)? I pose this question in particular because of my social location on Turtle Island and work in anti-racism where relatively recently, the question of decolonization of anti-racist scholarship was presented. I admit that in Canada, all non-Indigenous peoples are implicated in ongoing colonization of Indigenous communities and their Lands. I would argue for a more complicated reading of the "settler" notion, to recognize White supremacy and how the positionality of bodies of color in the colonial state can contribute to their mobilization in solidarity with Indigenous sovereignty movements (see also Sandhu 2014). Complicating the notion of the "settler" is not to deny responsibility and implications. Rather, it is more a recognition that White supremacy is "a key pillar of the settler colonial state which can be mobilized as common ground for solidarity among [colonized] people, while simultaneously exposing the substantive ways in which [non-Indigenous colonized bodies] continue to contribute to the ongoing colonization of Indigenous communities and Land across Turtle Island" (Sandhu 2014, p. 18).

While it is important to be critical of solidarity claims that fail to recognize the unique histories and different contexts of oppressed and colonized groups (Lawrence and Dua 2005), I would equally contest and complicate a partial reading that the "historic and contemporary evocations of solidarity can contribute to ongoing colonization and erasure of complicities, thus failing to rearrange social and structural conditions for ethical relationship-building" (Sandhu 2014, p. 18 referencing works of Tuck and Yang 2012, Gaztambide-Fernández 2012 and Lawrence and Dua 2005). As argued elsewhere (Dei 2015), the charge of complicity of immigrant and colonized populations in the White colonial state appropriation of Indigenous peoples Lands cannot be laid lightly, particularly when settlerhood is about violence, genocide, theft and Land dispossession.

It is important to consider how global inequities and poverty extend colonialism and subject Black/African migrants to racialization in new ways. Although experiences of individual and systemic racism by African and other racialized immigrants in the Global North have long, complex and ongoing histories, new and adapted processes of racialization and colonialism emerge through neo-liberal policies and practices (Jensen and Howard Wagner 2014). Globally, neo-liberalism compels migration from the Global South under increasingly vulnerable conditions, and also largely shapes the experiences many Black/African people endure as precarious workers in the Global North, where we are excluded from full membership in society even in the case of legal citizenship. Canadian immigration laws work with neo-liberal policies at international and nation-state levels to uphold dominant social and political relations that coerce migration yet exclude and marginalize us in Canada.

In some cases, the bodies and labor of racialized immigrants become instrumental in maintaining structures of imperialism—the economic structures which perpetuate under-development of the South and a hierarchy of nation-states. This hierarchy of developed vs. less developed nations contributes to our racialization as an expendable labor pool that is inferior to Canadian-born (White) workers (Stasiulus and Bakan 2005). This racialization manifests as Canada's federal immigration policies and occupational gatekeepers restrict or exclude immigrant populations within Canada and in many occupations under unequal conditions of fewer rights and through shifting occupational accreditation requirements (just a few examples are nursing, teaching, and the medical field). Such unequal conditions render racialized immigrants more susceptible to mistreatment and exploitation than White Canadian citizens even before starting a work position, and also during actual employment. Immigrant de-skilling is common in Canada and well-known by many of us who have come here from our ancestral Lands. It may be especially true for Black/African migrants, because our degrees and various accreditations are often devalued and not recognized by Canada. There are African diaspora earning a second Ph.D. in Canada, for example, because White supremacist ideology rejects their degrees, claiming they do not hold the same status as Canadian degrees and those granted in other Western nations.

This de-skilling occurs before Black immigrants even enter Canada, and then anti-Black racism can be seen in every aspect of Canadian society, not least of which is the labor market. One recent example is when neo-liberal policies at the provincial level downsized and privatized Ontario's public health services in the 1990s, racist ideas already shaping many aspects of Canada's nursing profession were amplified through disciplinary and exclusionary techniques that targeted Black nurses, justifying their demotions, terminations, and disqualifications over other groups when labor reductions were made (see Stasiulus and Bakan 2005). Federal immigration policies were also used to discriminate racially (of course through formally race-neutral terms), as nurses with temporary work permits, the majority of whom were Black, were the first to face lay-offs during re-structuring. In line with neo-liberal aims, the downsizing and limiting of Ontario's nursing pool took place regardless of a growing need for nurses—a health care crisis which is superseded and largely amplified by neo-liberal public sector cuts and the resulting labor substitutions and privatization within many areas of health care. It was not only new or intensified stereotypes that (re)racialized Black nurses, it was the activation of these stereotypes within a network of laws and neo-liberal institutions, policies and practices that produced new forms of marginalization and exclusion that continue to impact Black/African communities in Canada today.

Not merely restrictive, neo-liberalism works to include African/Black immigrants in the global economy through protracted states of vulnerability which foreground the rights and logic of capitalism (Jensen 2016). While neoliberalism exacerbates impoverishing conditions in sending countries, it also creates more precarious working conditions in receiving nations such as Canada (Stasiulus and Bakan 2005). De-regulation of private industry and stripping of worker protections in order to free up the market lead to fewer stable employment options and more pervasive worker abuse, in particular for Black immigrants and citizens who are already de-skilled, exploited and criminalized in Canada. The ways in which global governing institutions, such as the IMF and World Bank and Canada perpetuate and benefit from these inequities are obscured, as forced or semi-forced migration becomes de-historicized and de-contextualized through the racial logic of a compassionate nation offering generous opportunities to less advanced people who are in poverty due to financial reasons rather than as a result of colonialism and racism.

White supremacy in the Canadian settler colonial state thus greatly disempowers racialized communities, and it is unclear how these communities become complicit in the ongoing dispossession of Indigenous communities and Land through investments in assimilation and citizenship. We are implicated but not complicit. It is not enough simply to unpack the differences between "White settlers" and "settlers of color" (Phung 2011) as a way to achieve greater solidarity among Indigenous and racialized communities in Canada. The designation of racialized groups as "settlers of color" places us on the same footing as White colonial settlers and the empire builders. As Sandhu (2014) notes in her examination of the work of Phung (2011) and Sehdev (2011), the approach to complicating and differentiating between "White colonial settlers" and "settlers of color' is "more focused on supporting Indigenous activism against the settler state, rather than creating a framework that engages both Indigenous and non-Indigenous communities (as well as progressive White bodies) to challenge the logics of White supremacy and the settler state together" (p. 47). This is the larger struggle to engage, such that the role of the colonial dominant in settler colonialism and ongoing colonization of Indigenous Lands is not minimized. An awareness of the positionality of racialized communities *vis a vis* Indigenous peoples of Turtle Island is significant for building solidarity, particularly in assessing how the investments of these communities in Canadian nationalism, immigration, and citizenship implicate and thwart Indigenous sovereignty while furthering the White settler colonial state project. Any theoretical analysis and rethinking of the relations of Indigenous peoples and racialized communities in

Canada need to shift beyond the narrow focus on "complicities and differences across experiences of racism" and find ways "to bridge these issues so as to work together [Indigenous, racialized, and non-Indigenous groups including White bodies] to challenge the colonial dominant" and the logics of White supremacy (Sandhu 2014, p. 49).

Resisting the designation as "settlers of color" and working instead with the notion of shared collectivities and solidarities among racialized, colonized, Indigenous populations is not an attempt to run away from implications and responsibilities. Such resistance does not recreate and sustain hegemonic and imperial relationships between Indigenous and non-Indigenous peoples. A politics of decolonized solidarity embracing Indigeneity of many peoples must be informed by colonial histories and our collective implications. While Canada promotes neo-colonialism abroad and presents a false benevolence of helping African/Black immigrants, it simultaneously denies its own ongoing settler colonialism. A claim to Canadian statehood allegedly opened up to immigrants must refuse recognition of Indigenous nations. This shows how the Canadian-nation state engages in colonialism both domestically and in the global context, and underscores the crucial need for Indigenous solidarity within Canada and internationally for decolonization efforts. A project of decolonization can only succeed when the solidarity of all peoples with shared histories of colonial oppressions is recognized as grounds for political and social collective action. This includes those who have been colonized as well as the colonizers. Decolonization is not possible in the context of claims of complicities to, and hierarchies of, oppressions and/or when peoples who are themselves resisting ongoing colonization and oppressions are deemed as "settlers" dispossessing Indigenous Lands. Similarly, any attempt at decolonization is incomplete when dominant groups are not engaged or left off the hook.

Let me clarify in a bit more detail the discursive position that makes White supremacy the main focus of solidarity politics. It is important to make a distinction with wealth of critical Indigenous scholarship on the subject of solidarity politics in settler colonial contexts. In her thoughtful essay "Heteropatriarchy and the Three Pillars of White Supremacy: Rethinking Women of Color Organizing," Smith (2006) problematizes a political organizing framework of oppressed and colonized peoples that is built on the presumption, "our communities have been impacted by white supremacy in the same way" (p. 67). A prevailing subaltern framework has assumed that "racism and white supremacy [are] enacted in a singular fashion," rather than understanding that "white supremacy is constituted by separate and distinct, but still interrelated, logics" (p. 67). While I agree with Smith, I would argue that both the recognition of and insistence upon shared histories of oppressions and colonization in solidarity politics should not be interpreted as if we speak of singular or similar oppressions and histories of colonization. Colonialisms have been varied both in approach and impacts on Indigenous and colonized populations worldwide.

Also, I would reiterate that for colonized, racialized immigrant groups in Euro-American contexts, our respective engagements with White colonial settler states such as Canada does not necessarily make us "complicit" and "settlers," although we are certainly implicated in colonial settlerhood. I would draw a conceptual distinction between "complicit" and "implicated." I also enthuse that we view the reality of "settlerhood" as about genocide, extinction, dispossession of Lands, outright theft of Indigenous property, material exclusions, forced assimilation, and the despiriting of Indigenous peoples (see Dei 2015). This reading is necessary to avoid dilution of the meaning of "settlers." Settlers are more than "strangers" to a Land. In Canadian contexts I do not believe we, as Black bodies, have positioned ourselves as "the rightful inheritors of all that was Indigenous—Land, resources, Indigenous spirituality, or culture" (Smith 2006, p. 68). Relevant questions that follow this argument are: What do we mean by "complicity"? How do we become "complicit in the victimization of Indigenous peoples"? (Smith 2006, p. 69). When Indigenous and/or Indigenous bodies seek employment, housing, and health care through the Canadian nation-state in order to survive the harsh realities of inhumane capitalism, are they then complicit in the atrocities of the colonial nation-state? I still struggle with what makes us complicit, not because I am denying our involvement and partaking in the benefits of colonial Land dispossession, but because of the very complex histories that bring us to this Land. The idea that we come here on our free will is false. The very structures we are critiquing—colonialism, capitalism, enslavement, globalization—bring us here.

These are important issues to consider. I do think that one is complicit in the process of settler colonialism if one wittingly engages in acts of Land and property dispossession, violence and genocide. Also clearly, the forced migrations make us implicated and point out responsibilities for us. But it is an incomplete reading to think that racialized/colonized bodies who emigrate from their homelands, given the harsh realities of ongoing colonizations and global capitalism, are simply willing participants in the Euro-colonial project of the nation state. Black bodies in Canada have not all fully (or willingly) joined "the colonial project of settling [on] Indigenous Lands and neither have those who have complied with the state project escaped from the 'bottom of the racial hierarchy' (Smith 2006, p. 69).

Clearly, Smith's (2006) analytical framework in "Three Pillars of White Supremacy": Slavery/Capitalism, Genocide/Colonialism, and Orientalism/War, is very useful to work in solidarity politics of oppressed populations. It is precisely through the connections of these three pillars identified by Smith that I seek an invigorated politics of collective solidarity for all colonized, racialized, Indigenous and non-Indigenous peoples (including progressive anti-racist Whites). It is the connections and inseparability of slavery, genocide, Orientalism and Eurocentrism that make for the urgency of solidarity politics among Indigenous, Black, racialized and non-Indigenous peoples including Whites. For oppressed, colonized, racialized and Indigenous groups, our solidarity politics, while recognizing the asymmetrical relations of power within groups, must be premised on collective responsibilities, accountability and social ethics. The ethicality of our politics requires that we maintain the gaze on the oppressor and oppressive practices. We are best able to devise resistance strategies that can upend the White supremacist structure if the focus is on our collective implications, responsibilities and ethicality of our politics.

4.1   Euro-Colonialism and Settler-Colonialism

Let me be clear about how Euro-colonialism and settler colonialism concepts are to be understood in this essay (see also excellent scholarship of Cannon (2012); Cannon and Sunseri (2011) among many others). Euro-colonialism and settler colonialism are taken up as different by some scholars. Lawrence and Dua's critique emphasizes settler colonialism and they describe it as distinct from Eurocolonialism. In contrast, I view Euro-colonialism and settler colonialism as being cut from the same cloth. They share more similarities than differences. I turn to Jared Sexton's (2014) article *The Vel of Slavery: Tracking the Figure of the Unsovereign* to support my position. In this article, Sexton states, "Surely, colonialism and settler colonialism can and often do coexist within the same social formation, and even the same agent or agency with a particular order can issue colonial and settler colonial demands at once or in turn" (2014, p. 3). Sexton acknowledges both the ongoing presence of these two forms of colonialism within each other, as well as the value of their analytic clarity. This dual recognition is valuable, while to emphasize setter colonialism as distinct from Euro-colonialism is clearly a red herring.

The issue of inadequate access to water is just one that demonstrates the persistence of such dual colonialisms. When Global South populations cannot access water or adequate Land to grow food in their home countries because it has been privatized by Western companies, and their currency rate is set so low by the IMF that they cannot afford to purchase water or sufficient food, migration to the Global North may be one response. Water is (typically) free in Global North nations, and although immigrants, in particular racialized immigrants, are notably de-skilled and exploited, higher currency rates offer greater resources. This example of Western neo-colonialism that compels Global South migration can be related to the lack of clean drinking water on two-thirds of Indigenous reservations in Canada. Like the continued exploitation of Global South Land, labor and resources (including water) through neo-colonial forms of rule, Indigenous Land remains under the purview of the Canadian government and the imperatives of capitalism, even when Indigenous nations are recognized through the state (Coulthard 2014). Similarly, the imposition of Western interventions in Global South nations through programs such as UN Development and Peacekeeping, and the limited self-determination of many Global South citizens due to neo-colonialism and its economic and political consequences, resembles the settler-colonial logic that denies Indigenous populations the right to self-govern in Canada (Jensen 2017). In both cases, Black/African peoples and Indigenous peoples in Canada are denied access to basic survival (clean water), and both face continued colonization. While Black/African migrants leave the neo-colonial context of their homeland, their conditions of inclusion in Canada, much like the inclusion of Indigenous peoples, is far from complete and takes place under continued racial governance.

Let me return to the cloth metaphor to make my position of Euro-colonialism and settler colonialisms clear in a different way. The cloth from which both Euro-colonialism and settler colonialism are cut is racism and slavery—Andrea Smith's first pillar of logic of White supremacy (Smith 2006, p. 67). Sexton explains that "the racial logic of colonialism tends to insist on permanent or unbridgeable differences" (Sexton 2014, p. 3) between dominant and Othered. Utopia for the dominant/colonizer is often somewhere other than the place of invasion or colonization, although of course it can also be the place of colonization (Hardy 2012). The place of invasion provides material resources for this utopia, and/or becomes a consumer market for products and goods made from the stolen resources, that the invader assumes for himself through the laws of Terra Nullius. To serve the colonial desires of the more distant utopia, there is deep entrenching of hierarchies, systems of segregation, and militarization of the colonial territory. This allows for the usurpation of resources and property, for example human bodies, Land, knowledge, and medicines. Massacre, dispossession, disappearance/cultural genocide and slavery function simultaneously and also at different times to develop, maintain and justify colonialisms.

Settler colonialism is fuelled by a different utopian logic. This logic, Sexton explains, eliminates "the categories of colonizer and colonized through a process by which the former replaces the latter completely, usurping the claim to Indigenous residence" (2014, p. 3). Utopia for the settler-invader is the place of invasion; the settler invader imaginary is one of settler nativity and settler indigenization. This makes the disappearance and massacre of those native or Indigenous people to the Land the ultimate focus of their colonial work. So yes indeed there are differences, but racism and slavery made Euro-colonialism possible and Euro-colonialism made settler colonialism possible. The deepest logic of each and all colonialisms is racism and slavery, and this is what makes them capable of emerging in and out of one another. Of course other logics and pillars of White supremacy (Smith 2006) can be added to create unique colonial landscape with particular geopolitical and historical manifestations. And this explains the necessity of different emphases, at times, in antiracism and decolonization work. This different emphasis does not mean that the colonialism of another people is not properly attended to or studied, and it is unfair to assume it as such. The point I wish emphasize here is that racism and slavery are fundamental to settler colonialism and to all colonialisms. To dismiss or ignore racism and slavery in decolonization scholarship is to engage in anti-Black invisibilization and dehistoricization. Racism and slavery are fully present in the histories and contemporary contexts shaping settler colonialism. Failure to acknowledge racism in settler colonialism is gross omission that undermines the memories of oppression and suffering of many racialized people. 1. The two forms of colonialism are clearly relational (see Tuck and Yang 2012; Jackson 2006, 2012, 2014). We do not have Euro-colonialism that is disconnected from settler colonialism, and neither has a settler colonialism been pursued by colonized populations. Racialized populations have always been marginalized in the realm of White colonialism—whether in Euro-colonial or settler colonial contexts.

4.2 Black/African: Canadian and the Settler Concept

Because Black/African-Canadians experience violent, enduring embodiments of enslavement, Land displacement and forced migration, the idea of being called "settler" is thoroughly untenable. This idea is, however, central to Lawrence and Dua's critique. Lawrence and Dua (2005) among other scholars like Waldrof and Philipullia (2011) have asked the question: How do Black/African-Canadians benefit from the existing colonial and imperial system? While this question is important to reflect on, the line of inquiry leads down a path that detracts from our potential to organize, making this a move that is riddled with ontic and conceptual errors (King, 2013). The coupling of "settler" with Black/African-Canadians is flawed and I ask that we decouple them. I begin to effect this decoupling by asking what "settler" means.

What is and who is a "settler"? A settler is a person who embodies and enacts the colonial regime and is fully complicit in its work. This body claims citizenship on a seized Land through Land grab and dispossession. The "settler", acting in the service of a settler imaginary, overdetermines their (false) rights of ownership, presence on stolen Land, and citizenship through laws and governments that privilege them and their ongoing occupation of treaty and non-treaty Land and the work of resource extraction. To ensure an ownership, the "settler" also uses laws and governments to discipline, regulate, punish, imprison, emplace, evict, and colonize *Others* who might interfere with what they claim ownership and what they steal from *Others*. This is acutely felt by Indigenous peoples of Turtle Island whose diminished and ignored nations are forced to make Land claims through the tedium of colonial municipalization with unfair colonial pressure and laws to accept less or even nothing. This process of overdetermination allows generations of "settlers" to assert the materially enstructured privilege of ownership of place and space over all *Others,* particularly Original people. These "settlers" fully benefit from colonization and remain relationally engaged with it in all aspects of their daily life through a process of co-constitution (see also Ritskes 2012).

Many scholars contend that borders of Western nations themselves merely serve an ideological purpose, as both legal and undocumented immigrants are a structural necessity for capitalism's survival (see Sharma 2009). While businesses and products cross borders freely under neoliberal policy, humans are allowed movement based on their capitalist utility. Neoliberalism has exponentiated what has been a historical commodification of immigrant laborers (Jensen 2013). When the economy has changed and certain occupations have fewer vacancies, Canada (and other northern nations) have returned to more restrictive immigration and temporary work permit policies. Refusing to grant citizenship to unauthorized immigrant workers guarantees the material benefits of cheap labor while avoiding many of the costs associated with recognition of worker rights (Sharma 2009). Despite Canada's

Multicultural Policy, its immigration system reifies, alters and creates racialized subjectivities through inconsistent inclusions and intrinsic exclusions. Abuse of non-citizens by government officials, employers, or citizens and the strengthening of a racist culture occur when racialized immigrants and refugees are "rightfully" denied the rights, entitlements and dignity expected of full "members of society." Basic needs such as health care, housing and food may be denied based on a person's national origin (Sharma 2009). With the professed elimination of legal forms of racism, this racialization of space becomes an effective dividing practice, a mode of practicing racism that is enhanced through neo-liberalism. DeGenova (2002) posits that "illegality" is an erasure of legal personhood designed not to physically exclude people, but to socially include them under imposed conditions of compulsory and protracted vulnerability.

A critical look at immigration laws in Canada illuminates the logic of race organizing society, rather than simply national origin. Sharma (2009) posits that within "national space," the racial or ethnic "Other" remains an object. In White settler societies, rights, privileges and social relations may be organized in such a way as to justify and legitimate discrimination against anyone defined as an outsider, including citizens. African/Black people are construed as outsiders in Canada, regardless of citizenship status. According to Canada's Constitution, citizens of color ostensibly occupy the same rights and privileges enjoyed by White citizens. When race *is* explicitly addressed in law or policy, racial equality remains either the professed norm or goal. However, through implementation of law as well through the structure of law itself, the state employs race in classifying outsiders, eliminating and proscribing equal rights under the law. Far from a new phenomenon, state deployment of race in the legal and bureaucratic structuring of society has not changed; rather the techniques and racial subjectivities have been modified throughout time to uphold and mask the underlying structure of White supremacy. While nation-building *is* entrenched in the notion of the citizen, *racialized* citizens have never been fully embraced in White settler nations—politically or socially.

Blacks do not and will not have full permanent claim to citizenship in Canada. This is reserved for the White settler. Blacks are, as Sexton (2014) aptly argues, experiencing social life as social death. The portrayal and waste of Black lives in settler colonial contexts suggest that Black/African-Canadians clearly cannot be settlers, and the idea of coupling of settler and Black/African is very heavy and contentious. This coupling writes again on our already deeply inscribed bodies and places huge and unexpected burden and on Black bodies. If we are going to engage a question about how Black/African-Canadians and other people of color benefit, we must be equally willing to ask this question: Who benefits from naming Black/African-Canadians as "settler"? Who benefits from a divide that has not existed, and I strongly assert still does not exist, between Blacks and Indigenous peoples? This division is the work of binary colonial logics and it does not exist, but it can very dangerously be manufactured. This is my concern. I also want to ask why this division came forward when it did through Lawrence and Dua's critique. What is happening that might fuel their analysis or generate the conditions for such an interpretation?

I want not to engage in conversations and scholarship that focus on division. I want us to see this work as collective, as many of you already see, and attend to the meaningful pursuit of decolonization through our respective locations. It is in all non-settler and Indigenous Peoples' interests to refuse the capture of divisive critiques offered by coupling one or another of us with "settler". We must approach such work with an embodied skepticism and intelligence to expose the binary logics that carry and defend them. In doing so, we strengthen our resolve and our coalition building efforts that support and surround all who have suffered and continue to suffer colonialisms. This is how we protect ourselves from division and strengthen each other's differences, both within and across our various groups. I ask that we break from binary colonial logics that threaten and condition division, through the erasure of difference, and return to Indigeneity. Indigeneity offers a holism that Indigenous peoples share and understand through their different Indigenous knowledges. These knowledges offer protection, healing, restoration and a meeting place for numerous groups. A return to Indigeneity will protect us from the compelling and seductive binary logics of colonialism and will allow us to approach each other from a place of shared understanding. Strong coalitions cannot be built through our relations to the "settler" nor through colonial logics. They can, however, be built through the knowledge that we embody and the holism that we share.

I offer a more intimate perspective by stating that I find myself present in the texts provided by the decolonizing critique. I read and experience these texts as speaking to me and asking me to think through my experience and my scholarship. This, both troubling and necessary, brings me to a place of agreement with particular elements of Lawrence and Dua's criticism. I agree fully with their position regarding implication: those who come to or arrive on Indigenous soil and seek citizenship are implicated in the colonial project. They reach toward or are pushed through colonial systems that sort and determine them. It is the same system that overdetermines and constitutes the settler which by in turn *also* overdetermines and constitutes all others who are not settlers. These "not settlers" are, through colonial binary logics, differently placed and differently peripheralized as "kinds of citizens". I say this to unsteady the notion of implication that I both agree with and also trouble. I trouble it because implication, despite my agreement with it, must not erase the particularities and distinctions between differentially colonized peoples and the different colonial moments that condition when, how, why, and by what means and mechanisms, these different peoples came to or arrived in colonial states.

Different colonial moments capture different colonized peoples and inscribe on them the story of that particular moment. These different stories at different moments not only generate different colonial lines between peoples, but also different forms and expressions of anti-racist and decolonizing work. In order to avoid erasing these differences, I offer some conceptual distinctions between "complicity," "implication" and "responsibility." While I first want to acknowledge their connectedness and the links shared between them, I advance both these connections and their distinctions later on in the essay and move now to Indigeneity.

Clearly, I "resurrect a dead horse": that being Lawrence and Dua's coupling of the Black/African with the settler, again in this section. I de-couple them this time, not through the concept of "settler", but through Indigeneity. The Indigeneity I refer to here is conceptualized broadly as an international category within anti-racism and anti-colonial work. I bring this conceptualization of Indigeneity forward because of its capacity to undo and overcome a politic of separation and division. Indigeneity is a site of multiple convergences and divergences and it is one axis, not the only axis that Black/African-Canadians and Indigenous Peoples share with each other and with myriad communities and peoples impacted by colonialisms. With this in mind I invite us together as a community of scholars to critically examine these questions: Is there or should there be one model of anti-racism in light of the different experiences and trajectories of colonialisms? Does anti-racism uphold the colonial project by not foregrounding Indigenous sovereignty/nationhood? What anti-racist purpose is served when Black bodies doing anti-racist work see themselves as "settlers" and beneficiaries of the White colonial project? I begin to ground these questions by providing the following analyses: It is true that Black/African-Canadians occupy Canada and have different degrees of citizenship and even full citizenship. It is also true that our bodies and our citizenship are always suspect, always changeable, and too often and too easily denied. This does not fit with the concept of "settler" that I offered earlier. In contrast, we are a colonized, racialized and peripheralized body and citizen. We are not welcomed into the circle of rights, nor do we secure the privileges of space, place, protection, voice, expression, movement, health, participation and development of the settler. The concept of "settler" cannot be paired with Black/African-Canadian without losing its meaning. It becomes imprecise and loses its conceptual specificity. It also effaces without eliminating the racisms and colonialisms that Black/African-Canadians continue to experience, allowing them to be more effectively denied. Black/African-Canadians are not "settlers" but they are indeed occupants of the appropriated, stolen and contested Lands of the deeply colonized and racialized Indigenous peoples of Turtle Island. Based on what we know of settlerhood as associated with violent dispossession of Land and genocide, we as Black/African scholars cannot simply accept the status of "settlers" accorded us in Canadian settler colonial discourse.

To extend my position further, one can be complicit with settler-hood while being denied or not securing full state benefits and protections. Said differently, one cannot be complicit in settlerhood and colonialism without being a settler. I say this to highlight the very important point that complicity is not determined by citizenship, although implication is. The example of Canada's Multicultural policy enacted in 1971 clarifies this point. As a ploy, multiculturalism entices African immigrants who are not (full) citizens to participate in settler colonialism's celebration of its colonial lines. The colonial bounds (re)asserted through multiculturalism provide a new mechanism for the titration and performance of tolerance of racialized Others. This aside, I return to the core of my argument.

Some anti-racist scholars, including myself, enter discussions such as this through the theoretical lens of anti-Black racism. From this entry point I ask the following: How does reading of anti-Black scholarship and practice engage colonial theories of nationalism and collude in the erasure of Indigenous sovereignty and Indigenous Land right claims? How are anti-Black racism theories and theorists complicit in the project of European colonization in ways that justify being named 'settler'? How exactly are Black/African-Canadians privileged in the colonial setting? And how, when, and where do Black/African-Canadians gain settler privilege, if they in fact do? I ask these questions to engage scholars, myself included, in a frank and critical analysis of this curious coupling of settler and Black/African-Canadians. I have shown how settlerhood and citizenship do not cohere for the Black body, nor for other colonial bodies. The forces that constitute the "settler" and allow their safe passage to and through Canada are secured through a settler government and settler laws that "crown" them as citizen. As "crowned" citizens they secure rights, freedoms, prosperity, health, security and livelihoods on the backs of Indigenous bodies and through the ongoing usurpation of Indigenous Lands and resources. Simply put, the "settler" is constituted through the racism that underpins colonialism and its sorting, segmenting and peripheralizing practices. The practices are sanctioned and overdetermined through settler governments and laws and their relations with other settler and Euro-colonial states. "Settler" and citizen are neither interchangeable nor are they approximate. They are conceptually different. Black/Africans assume Canadian citizenship but do not qualify as "settlers", and because of acquisition of citizenship they are implicated in the colonial project and not complicit.

This chapter, as I stated earlier, is purposely provocative for I am, after all, a Black/African scholar living on Turtle Island. It is also intended to be provocative because the Black/African who figures in Lawrence and Dua's critique is not one that I recognize as myself nor as other Black/Africans living in Canada. I admit to pain and shock when reading this work, and to an anger which came later. Although there has been some level of softening with regards to coupling settler and Black/African, this has sown a powerful seed of discontent which could be potentially be deployed to serve particular interests despite these authors' change in position. This work could be used tactically to serve divisive interests and we have seen this happen again and again. We need to understand what sources influence the debate that Lawrence and Dua's critique generates, and what sources inform the Black/African figure they expose in their text. This cannot be ignored. I ask then that we problematize and interrogate this debate and the figure it constitutes through the broader discourse of Indigeneity and Indigenous theorizing. I say this because I sense a danger in the collapse of one Indigenous and colonized peoples experience, in this case my experience as Black/African, into the [White] colonial-settler discourse and its colonial relations by another Indigenous and colonized peoples. This broader discourse and theorizing will help us strengthen our relationships and also weaken the division this critique compels. This does not change the fact that some very important things are brought forward by Lawrence and Dua. I have made this clear. Their critique demands acknowledgement of our relation to "settler", to colonialisms, to Indigenous peoples, and to Canada as a nation-state. I answer these demands through this essay. Black/Africans living in Canada are implicated in colonialisms through citizenship and we need to take responsibility as individuals and as collectives of Indigenous Peoples to participate more fully in Indigenous Peoples' struggle for self-determination and sovereignty. This is very important.

I, as a Black/African person, and as a scholar, feel a deep commitment to Indigenous Peoples' struggles because I have been so graciously welcomed onto Turtle Island. Indigenous and colonized peoples across the world share struggles through different colonialisms. This is where my scholarship comes in. I write, teach and engage in research about African Indigenous knowledge, and I do this to engage African peoples and myself in reclaiming our knowledges as well as to raise broader questions about Indigeneity. Through this work and through my own indigenizing experiences, I have come to conceptualize Indigeneity and decolonization as international categories. This international scale does not collapse my experience into the [White] colonial-settler discourse and relations however. To my mind it does the opposite, and this is why it is part of my scholarship and why I bring it forward here. Let me begin by saying that conceptualizing Black/African Canadians as settlers, and therefore existing only through this naming within the colonial web of relations, does something to Whiteness—and what it does is important. It dilutes Whiteness, which works to elide critiques of Whiteness that foreground the profoundly violent production of racialized, colonized and Indigenous bodies through it. This I am certain is harmful to all Indigenous and colonized peoples in our world, not simply for those occupying Turtle Island. I will not unpack the subject of Whiteness further here because I choose to privilege my experience as an African, as a Black-African in Canada, and as an Indigenous person within a collective of Indigenous Peoples. I do this because the Black-African is attacked more than any other colonized peoples in critiques of anti-racism, and because the critiques I highlight here constitute a Black/African figure who is alien to me, to Black/Africans living in Canada, and I suggest to Black/Africans in other colonial and settler nations.

Through this essay I offer my reflections and my own rethinking of anti-racism and anti-colonial within the present global imperial context. I take the frank discursive position that Black/African-Canadians are not settlers and that Black/African-Canadians are not complicit in Canada's colonialisms. Globally, neo-liberalism as a form of Western governance has intensified conditions which induce vulnerable groups to migrate, notably Black/African people from the Global South, and in many cases under greater precarity. Free trade agreements, structural adjustment programs and the global currency system are some of the major governing technologies that facilitate widening disparities between the Global North and Global South. In addition, Stasiulus and Bakan (2005) contend that globalization has exacerbated an imperialistic hierarchy of states, with exceptional amounts of pressure exerted upon developing nations by multinational and transnational corporations based in the interests of advanced nations. Growing poverty, unemployment and underemployment, as well as continued Land displacement are some of the outcomes of neo-liberal, imperial, and neo-colonial practices in the South, forcing many to migrate in order to advance or in some cases, simply to survive. With escalating poverty, many Black/African peoples from the Global South have few options except to migrate in an increased desperation for work—regardless of the terms of employment.

While the realities of coerced migration are severe, they do not absolve us of our responsibilities. These responsibilities emerge directly from our presence on stolen Land, our awareness of the persistence of colonialisms, and not least from our experience as Indigenous and Euro-colonized peoples. Complicity must be acknowledged by those who are complicit. It cannot be lifted out of one body or community and poured onto another. Nor can it be owned by one who is not complicit. Each of these cases generates a thick smoke that arrests and confuses processes of social change. They are destructive. As Black-Africans and as anti-Black racism scholars we do have responsibilities which arise through our implication in colonialisms. We live on stolen Indigenous Land and we know that racisms and multiple colonialisms make this possible. We also know from our Indigenous friends, fellow Indigenous scholars, and Indigenous movements how this impacts the daily lives of Indigenous Peoples and Indigenous communities' strivings. We take these experiences very seriously as Black/African scholars and it is important for us to find new ways to act on and mobilize around our responsibilities.

4.3   Theorizing the Indigenous as an International Category

I view Indigeneity as providing this way. It allows us to mobilize as an international category and as an international collective of multiple anti-racist communities that can build solidarities with Indigenous Peoples and their decolonizing work. I join others in this work knowing our differences are many. Difference is our strength and it must be protected. We must use and also advance our differences to enhance our collective strength. Erasing and diluting differences, the colonial directive, does the opposite. Indigeneity values difference and solidarities along its axis, which extends the reach of our resistance well beyond any one peoples' colonization, racialization and imperialization. We converge along the Indigeneity axis through our differences and with the shared understandings and embodied knowing that Whiteness centers colonialisms and is constituted through the binary logics of White supremacy.

The question as to whether re-imagining coalitions between Indigenous, racialized and colonized groups on White colonial settler contexts is desirable is not just cynical but very apolitical in the face of the glaring cultural power of neo-liberal capitalism to design futures for oppressed groups and communities in a global sphere. Frankly, I do not see how productive it is to ask whether the re-imagined coalition among the colonized/oppressed is desirable. While it may be argued that such discussions should move from an exercise in academic spatiality, it can also be insisted that we need to theorize these relationships in order to organize the political practice we wish to pursue on the ground. In the reimagining of new futures, the colonization of Euro-global capitalist modernity and the dictates of decolonization cannot be approached from the confines of spatial, collective and self-referential politics.

The Indigenous must be defined broadly to include Indigenous, the Native Americas, Australian, Hawaiian, Caribbean, and African conceptions. In taking

Indigeneity as an international category we stake different positionalities. We should be concerned with the ways contemporary community politics can proliferate the discourse and practice of Indigenous resurgences and disempower Indigenous peoples everywhere to re-imagine a collective future together. We must begin to conceptualize Indigenousness broadly in ways that simultaneously encompass Land dispossession through settler colonialism, as well as loss of Land, stolen peoples and mobility of peoples through the history of enslavement and human trafficking. Such focus will bring to the fore the "international" vs. "global." Articulations of national boundaries and nation-state continue to ground claims to sovereignty and reify periphery-center politics and conceptualizations of belonging. So how do we move beyond Indigeneity as strictly a genealogical representation of relationship to Land? The question of Indigeneity as a knowledge base is key. This latter understanding allows us to connect with works in Indigenous and Afro-futurisms, for example, that conceptualize Land and space very differently, and envision decolonization and anti-colonial politics as different yet converging. We need the anti-colonial stance to challenge the mainstreaming of decolonization as an interim measure which while resisting colonialism, decolonization also risks re-centering colonialism in many of the same "White-coded terms" (Henay 2016).

We also seek new imagined and imaginary futures working with a critical understanding of Indigeneity as a politics and a process of reclaiming identity, culture and memory while simultaneously engaging race and the Land in multiple and complex ways. We take race and Land as social, cultural and political constructs with far reaching consequences for decolonial and anti-racist politics. Race, anti-racism, anti-colonial and decolonization are intertwined politics. Any outwardly manifested tensions or conflicts between these result more from misinformed and misplaced politics. Colonialism has had and continues to possess wide global reach touching all bodies and spaces. We invoke the body not because particular bodies are the sole markers of oppression or colonialism, but because the body is a signifier that colonial difference situates within the social structure that colonialism, racisms and oppressions attain their full effects. The body is significant to understand Indigeneity and while one can only be Indigenous to a place, i.e., the Land it is through politics that we insist on our Indigeneity. The Land is not simply a fixed and naturalized physical space/place, nor is the body a fixed identity. The Land as a place called home also has come to mean a social space. Furthermore, the dispossession of Lands was not an event that has happened here and there and we have gone past it. In every colonized territory the dispossession of Indigenous Lands continues both metaphorically and in real concrete terms. There is an ongoing struggle by local peoples/communities to [re]claim [i.e., not a physical wanting back] their Lands from occupiers/colonialists. There are ongoing struggles to upend the colonial narrative of the nation state as the sovereign body. We see this, for example in Africa, where tensions between the contemporary nation state and local peoples are rising everyday centered on the question of Indigenous claims to Land and local governance. The politics of the body is significant. Land is the Earth and we politically reclaim the Land for its knowledge, teachings and spiritual guidance, and for pursuing resistance for an alternative to an imperial, hostile, consumer capitalist world of the modern nation state.

All Indigenous peoples and communities are implicated [albeit differentially] in the colonial project of the contemporary globalized nation state. We should not always be reading the racialized immigrant from a colonized space claiming his Indigeneity, as a body seeking to achieve her or his identity at the expense of another Indigenous population. As many have long noted the processes of our respective incorporation into the colonial project of the nation [settler] state are different for colonized, oppressed and Indigenous groups. For many of us our colonial entanglements, investments and insertions cannot simply be understood nor explained as simply "matters of choice."

In this re-articulation of the "Indigenous" as an international category, I also argue strongly that colonized bodies who move into new spaces, usually settler colonial contexts [e.g., racialized immigrants in White settler communities] do not automatically lose their Indigeneity or Indigenousness. Euro-colonialism challenges and subverted local people's Indigeneity, including supplanting colonial state structures, but the colonial encounter does not remove the knowledge base from mind, memory and soul. Such knowledges are being reclaimed everywhere and it is the basis for global Indigenous resurgence. Our Indigenousness resides in the body, history and in cultural memories. As already alluded to, the fact that the body becomes a signifier of colonial difference with important consequences cannot be lost in decolonial and anti-colonial politics. Clearly, there are multiple responsibilities for Indigenous and colonized bodies [inclusive of so-called racialized immigrants] in terms of becoming part of the political struggles wherever we are located to resist colonial and imperial domination, as well as identifying with Indigenous sovereignty rights globally. Neither settlement in a place nor claims to an Indigenous Land on our own soils can absolve us of such responsibility. What is important, however, is that the understanding of Indigenous of an international category and the resulting politics of claiming Indigeneity through decolonial and anti-colonial resistance must espouse a futuristic worldview constructed as constitutive of Indigenous cosmological values, belief systems and correlational understandings of the world, including the relations between the human and non-human, the socio-cultural, physical, material and the metaphysical realms of existence.

It is important for us as colonized/racialized bodies to engage the deeper structures that undergird our coloniality in order to understand how we are inserted in the colonizing structures and imperial relations. We must ask how we are implicated in colonialisms' power and imperial discourses and practices while claiming decolonization and resistance. To address this question we must understand the terms and concepts evoked, the context, and the intents and purposes of this evocation. I address four concepts or conceptual themes in this section: settlerhood and settler, White-colonial discourse and settler colonialism, complicity and implication, and lastly, responsibility.

4.3.1 Settlerhood and the Settler

Settlerhood is a very loaded term that must be read in the context of specific colonial histories. Within colonial histories, settlerhood denotes occupation on Stolen Lands through acts of violence, Land dispossession, displacement of original/Indigenous inhabitants, genocide, and theft. A "settler" furthers this by assuming legitimate entitlements and installing and deploying legal and governing systems and structures that legitimize colonial "settler" occupation. Colonial settlements invisibilize and dispossess Indigenous Peoples who become separated from their Land as well as their indigeneity. The colonial settlers' unabashed entitlement estranges original peoples strangers from their Land, their nationhood, their leaders, their communities, their families and themselves. Land dispossession deeply and abrasively eviscerates the material and psycho-cultural worlds of Indigenous Peoples to immobilize whole societies. This is what is intended by colonial Land dispossession. The original violence is recapitulated over and over again through legal statutes that transfer property and Land rights to colonial occupiers. The colonial occupier bludgeons Indigenous Peoples and their Indigeneity by stealing and illegally occupying their Land which they claim to own and then use to maintain, enhance and assert their power over others. The colonial occupier does this by (over)determining, and entrenching this overdetermination in laws and government. The settler is continuously reconstituted through these laws and government structures that become increasingly refined with each new colonialism. This is Whiteness at work. This work determines who enters and (eventually) inhabits the colonial nation and who does not; who becomes a citizen and for how long, and who does not; who has access to valued goods and services and who does not; who has a home and who does not; who can engage in and benefit from resource extraction and who cannot; who lives and who does not. The colonial occupier: the settler, overdetermines these privileges for themselves through coercion, genocide, Land dispossession and violence. These become installed structurally through laws and governments, and need not be acted out in their original way. This secures and enhances privileges through repetition and depends on the absence of and/or uneven respect for the rights of non-settlers through time.

I ask again: How do Black/African-Canadians embody the "settler"? To answer this more thoroughly than I have so far, I think it is best to center the settler discourse. I ask two questions to facilitate this discursive move: (1) What geographies, bodies, spaces and times constitute the settler?, and (2) What relationship exists between the "settler" and the nation-state? This move facilitated through these questions place colonization within its historical trajectory and aim to expose the different configurations of supremacized Whiteness inherent in settler humanism. Historically, the settler was about the (re)production of a preferred and very particular body upon whom humanness was granted, and to whom citizenship could then be granted. This was a very active and deliberate process of rejection/selection and (de)valuation of the humanness of bodies, persons, communities, nations and entire continents. This totalizing process of inclusion and exclusion within "humanity" was sourced by the binary logics of White supremacist thought, and continues to be. These logics produced and reproduced the intractable colonial forms that secured and legitimized space, place, resources, humanness and ultimately life, wealth and health for White-European bodies over all others. "Settler" then emerges from the discursive and material production of Whiteness by dominant White-European bodies. These bodies and their production generated a powerful and inexhaustible racist imaginary that characterized the "settlement" of White-European bodies in distant Lands. Upon reaching distant Lands, the well-practiced racist imaginary interpreted clearly occupied Lands as empty; the peoples on these Lands as not (fully) human; their communities and societies as unsophisticated, savage, and having neither law, culture, religion, knowledge nor order. This interpretation made these Lands home for the "settler" and no longer home for the original inhabitants. The colonial apparatus was installed to ensure this remained so and it clearly, yet unfortunately, has largely succeeded.

Whiteness invited Black bodies into settler projects, and although promising benefits, denied them and much more. To understand this complex relationship between Whiteness, Black bodies and settler projects, an appreciation of the intricate relations between anti-Blackness and settler colonialism is required, particularly their expression in genocide and enslavement (see Smith 2012). Historically, "settler" was discursively and materially produced to realize the preferred body. The preferred body was the only fully human body, which of course was the White body. Now how did this happen? This occurred by bringing Blackness into relief. Blackness gave Whiteness its meaning, its value, its superior status, and its central location. Blackness, through the logics of Whiteness and White supremacy, provided the comparator, the other half of the binary, the reference point in essence that upheld and constituted Whiteness. Blackness became the abject and was constituted as biologically, spiritually, intellectually and civilizationally inferior. This placed Black bodies nearer to animals (and to earth) than to human White bodies (and to the sky or God?). Enslavement of Black bodies was easily overdetermined through this and other binary logics that informed "White/settler common sense". They were, through "White common sense", destined to field and plantation labor that served White bodies on Lands obtained by dispossession and genocide. Whiteness then was maintained and materially constituted through Black labor and Red Land. This was a thoroughly organized violence that depended for its success on the different and particular racializations and abjections of the Black and Red body.

Historically, settlerhood was endowed and materially produced through two colonial procedures: African-enslavement, dislocation, displacement, and transmigration; and Indigenous genocide, displacement and illegal Land usurpation. Frantz Fanon provides us with many insights in terms of unpacking the historical discursive layers that constitute the "settler". He reminds us that Whiteness and the settler were constituted by and through Blackness. Whiteness and settler were over-valued for particular physical features, particular claims regarding their essentially pure, pristine, beautiful, intelligent and civil nature, and claims of their unique ontological endowments. Blackness was constituted to uphold these qualities, features and claims, and hence the inscription of barbaric, uncivilized, underdeveloped, more animal than human, and requiring domestication (see Fanon 1963, 1967a, b). This was laid on top of another process where Whiteness and settler were constituted through the devaluation of Red bodies as savage. Indigenous Lands were legally framed then as empty, satisfying the colonial logic of "finders- keepers" which was entrenched as a legal concept by the "civilized societies" through a white imaginary of the terra nullius—or empty, uninhabited Lands (Razack 2002) (discovery of Land). This deepened and strengthened the constitution of Whiteness, of settler, and their simultaneity in the White body through and against the constitution of Black and Red bodies.

I say more here about how "settler" is constituted against the Red body. The Red body, the Indigenous figure, is the original Land owner and is present and alive despite the original colonial claims of empty Lands. Settler in this case remains an active colonial agent who engages in the ongoing denial of rights to owners and first inhabitants. Settler illegitimately, although legally through its own government policies, occupies the Land owned by Indigenous Peoples. Colonialism, I think it is fair to say, is a thoroughly ongoing and very active project of disruption. Its disruption has been continuous since first contact and this continues today. For instance, let us look at Indigenous Peoples' relationship to Land. First, we know as Indigenous Peoples that the Indigenous worldview is based on a holism. The colonial binary and reductive logic of the Euro-colonial mapping project involved the drawing of arbitrary property lines. These lines confined a holistic People to topographical boxes. This disruption thwarted their capacity for stewardship, their engagement with the Land as spirit and mother, and their capacity to teach and learn from the Land. This was alien to Indigenous Peoples and bludgeoned their worldview. This is true for Indigenous Peoples the world over. Many Indigenous Peoples share a view of the earth and Land as indivisible, interconnected, and as sacred; it is bearer of knowledge and profound in its teachings; and it is the responsibility of peoples to deeply respect and protect the earth and Land for all of time. Indigenous relationship to Land creates problems of incommensurability in regards to colonial ideas of Land ownership and Land rights. The force of the colonial view of Land and property rights continues to undermine Indigenous rights and relationship to their Land and to disrupt and undermine their worldviews.

Not everyone who lives in a colonial context, and is not Indigenous to the Land, is a settler. In other words, settlerhood is not simply about occupying a place; one does not become a settler because they have an abode. A person can be "settled" in a place (as in residing in a place),

While remaining a "foreigner"/"stranger" with the ongoing threat of impermanence and eviction built into the colonial apparatus of laws and governments. In the relations between immigrants and settlers in Canada, we must ask whose laws are followed and whose laws are enforced (see Tuck and Yang 2012). We know the answer to this since first contact: Canadian law privileges the settler. The violent re-inscription processes of emplacement, exclusion, peripheralization, and eviction enacted through policy and law by the White supremacist nation-state are deployed to serve Whiteness and to grant White bodies the privilege and power of settlerhood.

4.3.2   White Colonial-Settler Discourse and Settler Colonialism

Why do I bring White colonial-settler discourse and settler colonialism together here? To begin, each reflects different colonial moments and interactions between Indigenous Peoples and European Colonizers. This distinction is important and makes clear the position that I take in regards to settlerhood, which is constituted through the violence of genocide and followed by the forced dispossession of Indigenous Peoples from Indigenous Lands. White colonial-settler discourse is a discourse about the colonial/European dominant. The discourse speaks to the ways European colonizers carried out colonization through violent genocidal practices with the active intent to seize and settle on Land or territory in order to maintain their dominance over colonized subjects. It is a discourse about the European colonizer's relation to the colonial subject and how power is used and to what degree by the dominant colonizer to subordinate the subject (for instance killing or marginalizing). In White colonial-settler discourse, the power relations between the colonial dominant and Indigenous peoples are not complicated by migration of bodies into Indigenous spaces. This discourse is about the abrogation of power by the European colonizer who can choose to recognize and not recognize whose Land has been appropriated and stolen and whose has not and cannot.

Settler colonialism follows the White colonial-settler discourse. It is conditioned and maintained by the structures this discourse imagines and then materializes and emplaces. It is the resolution of the tension between the dominant body of the European colonizer and the colonial subject and the fixing of this resolution through institutions and law. This resolution and fixing of this tension does not serve the interests of the colonial subject; rather it allows the colonizer to absolve themselves of violence, exploitation, and illegal Land occupation and to falsely arrive at a place of good conscience. When settler colonialism is operative, the violence of the colonial encounter is organized through institutions and laws and need no longer be enacted by the colonizer directly. Perhaps more simply put, the colonizer makes permanent the rules for the colonial game to ensure he always wins; and when he does not or is threatened by a call for justice by the colonized subject, he can fall back onto processes of deception that are embedded in the government, institutions and law. The violence of the encounter is enacted continuously and becomes normalized and normative through the formal structures of tension resolution for the colonizer and the colonial society through the apparatus of state.

Settler colonialism has always been part of colonialism (even in Africa), and is evident once the colonial dominant is fully installed and secured as settler. This occurs when the legal and institutional systems and structures begin to operate and to privilege indefinitely the settlers' occupation of Indigenous Land. These institutional structures and frames govern over and discipline the Indigenous body directly and indirectly. The Indigenous body must be in a constant state of disrepair and brokenness for the state apparatus to function fluidly. This apparatus secures and centers Whiteness through the unjust occupation of Indigenous Land which violently separates Indigenous People from their knowledge, culture, language, community, governing and justice systems, health, and spirituality which is embedded in all of their society and their relationship to their surroundings. This destructively separates the Indigenous person from themselves. This is the power of settler colonialism: its capacity to violate not only the material world of the Indigenous person and their society, but also the spiritual and psychic dimensions as well. These processes of separation through colonial logics violently disrupt the holism of Indigenous Peoples and Indigeneity. Colonialism, practiced on many Indigenous Peoples, does its work through binary logics and these logics explain and make permissible violent separation. The opportunity to practice and refine colonialism at different colonial moments on different peoples and Lands augmented its capacity for concealment and denial. The thorough disruption and fragmentation of Indigeneity was and continues to be a mark of colonialism's success. While the colonial logics confirmed by this success continue to persist, seeming almost unchallengeable, resistance continues and is powerful. The Idle No More movement is an expression of resistance.

It remains clear however that settler colonialism in Canada serves the preferred body, the White body. Only the preferred White body can be a settler, and this settler depends on Land for its survival and dominance. The "settler" is constituted through the separation of Indigenous Peoples from Indigenous Land and as we have seen, this constitution depends on separations for other Indigenous Peoples from their Lands also: Africans. This works because the holism that is foundational to Indigenous Peoples and to Indigeneity is paradigmatically incommensurate with the binary logics that inform colonialism and its constitution of settler and settler nations. Indigenous spirit and bodies are broken and Indigenous Lands taken, and each is necessary for settler constitution. Indigenous Peoples are not and cannot be settlers. They are used and constructed as the raw materials deployed for the settler's production.

Clearly, Whiteness is produced against and through different Indigenous bodies which are essential to its maintenance. It is also true that settler colonialism exists in Canada now. All non-Indigenous people who live in Canada are implicated in the project of settler colonialism. Migrating peoples and persons, independent of the conditions and histories of their arrival and citizenship, cannot live in Canada unless they uphold the state structures of settler colonialism that keep Indigenous Peoples separated from their Lands and their Indigeneity. This is important. Separation founded on colonial racism embeds Canadian law and infuses colonial structures as I have explained earlier. This informs systems of governments and is revealed thoroughly in citizenship and immigration practices and policies. The settler continues to be constituted through these laws, government entities, and the practices and the structures of each. I focus on citizenship and immigration practices here. Citizenship and immigration policies and practices actively select and then "properly" constitute and domesticate New Canadians. They also determine degrees of citizenship and lengths and conditions of stay for migrants, immigrants, refugees, and temporary workers. Their laws and practices (over)determine who is an illegal alien, who is suspicious, who is monitored, and who can be denied entry. When denial of entry, eviction, or genocide are unsuccessful there are other forms of punishment and discipline. Foucault provides us with these understandings. Prison is one for example, whether immediate or eventual. Limited access to goods, services and jobs is another. Impoverishment, deprivation and conditioning unfreedom is another. Each of these (and more) is embedded in settler colonialism and maintains Whiteness through the settler. Many of these social conditions also cause harm and death and maintains separations that directly impact Indigenous peoples. Settler is exclusive and is reserved for those who can fulfill the conditions and ideals of Whiteness alluded to earlier in this book and secure the full benefits of the colonial settler regimes that stabilize and fortify Whiteness. All others, non-settlers, are expected to support Whiteness by not interfering with its work. The foreigner, the stranger, the brown, yellow or Black body all live in Canada conditionally. The conditions of security and citizenship change as geopolitical relations change within Canada and the global world. Geopolitical relationships, alliances and tensions can amplify the settler colonial apparatus to target different bodies at different times. This apparatus's primary function is not to ensure the wellbeing of those who live in Canada, but to ensure the survival, protection, and continued dominance of the settler which depends fundamentally on racism and then on Land. Moreover, Black/Africans, even when full citizens for many generations and for whom Canada has been a home (chosen or otherwise), far in advance of many waves of settlers (for example Birch Town in Nova Scotia), they remain suspect—not just as Canadians, but as people and humans.

I move now to migration. Migration, in light of all the aforementioned, requires a critical awareness of place, space and state. It is important to engage in processes of inquiry regarding how a Land is organized and occupied, for whom. There must be inquiry into the processes that secure Land, health and resources for some and not others. Inquiry regarding who can live, move, pass through, work and own Land is also important. One must ask: Who was the original owner? Where are they? What are the conditions of their life? And how are different bodies impacted positively and/or negatively by this? What I mean by this is that "inhabitants", racialized and immigrant bodies generally, may not recognize the ways our presence upholds settler colonialism and its racism towards Indigenous Peoples. Although many ask these questions before coming to Canada, these questions may not be welcome. They must be asked again however, to ensure that migrants become aware of Canada's colonial race work. This may not be possible for some migrants for myriad legitimate reasons at first, but it is important and will explain some of their own experiences as non-settlers on settler occupied Land in a settler state complex. It will also allow migrants to trouble the political discourse and social practices regarding Indigenous Peoples and Indigenous Lands. It will be more clear then what their responsibilities entail, and how they can support the work of Indigenous Peoples and engage critically in processes of social change.

Here I offer my thoughts on what I believe must happen as a Black/African-Canadian, an anti-racist scholar and practitioner, and as an Indigenous person and community Leader. I suggest that we develop and deepen our processes of inquiry through the following questions: How can we, as non-European immigrant bodies, have access to Land through law when this is not the case for Indigenous Peoples?

How can nation-to-nation treaties be so easily and repeatedly violated even when exposed? How can whole nationhoods be ignored repeatedly when the international human rights review process exposes these violations and implores Canada to engage in specific and progressive processes of change in regards to Indigenous Peoples? These questions are simply a beginning. They are not exhaustive, nor will they be taken up fully here as they require more depth than I am able to provide here. I do, however, respond to them broadly as follows. Non-European immigrant bodies who live in Canada benefit from the racism that marginalizes and denies Land rights to Indigenous Peoples. This as I have said is clear and true. Citizenship, even though suspect and conditional, implicates us in settler colonial discourses and colonial racist work. We must interrogate our citizenship and ask what work it does for the colonial apparatus and its racisms. How does our inclusion as Black/African Peoples, as non-European immigrants, and as non-settlers impact Indigenous peoples' decolonizing and anti-racism work and the colonial settler discourse? What work does our citizenship do for the settler and for settler colonialism and can it be traced in settler colonialism discourses and through the colonial apparatus? I want us to think critically about the resistance work of Indigenous peoples and how it is impacted by our presence in Canada. We must interrogate how our presence here impacts Indigenous peoples' struggle for recognition, Land and treaty rights, and their rights as persons and as peoples broadly. I want us to think about the transformations of colonialisms and neo-colonialisms and ask: Whose sources are these transformations from and for whom?, and What bodies can be used to augment the neo-colonial project, well-concealed by the veil of economics? Also how does the neo-colonial express itself through the settler, through the Indigenous body, and through the non-European immigrant body, and how do their interdependencies work to serve the settler, to serve Whiteness, and to serve the White colonial project? I say again: we are here, so we are implicated. However, I believe it naive to think that Black/Africans are here because they made this choice freely. Yet, although Black/Africans are here without choice, this does not absolve them of implication and responsibilities. We are implicated not only in settler colonialism but also in neo-colonialism and other global colonial mutations. We have responsibilities here also and we must continue and strengthen our solidarity building work with Indigenous Peoples in Canada and around the world. These solidarities can resist and push against how colonialisms center Whiteness and in Canada center the settler. I make one last point here: the distinction between settler colonialism and neo-colonialism is not semantic; it is consequential. And our solidarity as Indigenous Peoples is urgent for each.

4.3.3 Complicity vs. Implicated

The foregoing calls for a clear understanding and distinction between complicity and implication. This distinction is also not simply semantic; it is deeply consequential (see also Jafri 2013). I begin with complicity. *Complicity* is defined as "the act of helping to commit a crime or do wrong in some way" (Online Merriam Webster Dictionary, 2017). Such denotation implies illegality. With this in mind, let us turn to Black/African Canadians. Let us imagine for a moment that Black/African-Canadians did participate in settler colonialism and shared settler privileges, and through those privileges, were able to steal Land from Indigenous Peoples. If this were so, Black/Africans would clearly be complicit and could rightly be considered accomplices in this crime. Lawrence and Dua's assertions would be correct. Let us return now to our understandings of material reality—our experience of it. Imagine again that a Black/African decides to steal Land—this time not as accomplice to the settler, but for them-selves. This Black/African steals this Land in the same way that the colonizer steals Land, she steals it for herself—for her own protection, or livelihood, family and future. Now what happens to this woman? It is clear what happens to her and the sce-nario rings with absurdity. How did she think she could ever get away with it? You see the rule of law applies to her, she is a non-settler, and further to this she is a Black/African and the rule of law will be vigorously applied to her. This Black/African woman is a criminal. The settler however, is not. The settler is protected and privi-leged through colonial law and also international law. I say this because only White bodies have ever succeeded in deploying Terra Nullius. This law exists for colonial purposes only. The rule of law overall interestingly and tragically succeeds even when there is no illegal act committed by Black/African-Canadians. The opposite is too often true for the settler and for Whiteness broadly. Because of this she does not ben-efit from the colonial apparatus in a fair and equal way. It was not designed for her advancement, protection or pursuit of justice. She is always suspect, her citizenship changeable; and where her citizenship cannot be revoked, there are other ways to disempower and thwart her that were mentioned earlier. Black/African male youths provide a disturbing example of the settler colonial apparatus at work. The racism that sources and infuses this apparatus and the discourse that constitutes and surrounds it makes injustice towards Black/African male youth appear as justice despite that [which is being asserted] facts which point to the contrary. Facts matter only when the colonial apparatus decides it is in their interests to make them matter. These youth and their communities are consequentially pinned in place despite their strivings and their potential. They are not preferred and are held in place to continue their work of con-stituting Whiteness. Prisons clearly reflect the embedded preference of certain bodies over others, with Indigenous bodies being the most numerous in prisons and Black bodies close behind in Canada.[1] The settler colonial project was a White project driven by White colonial settler discourses and White bodies who installed the law but did not have to abide by it. Stealing Land from Indigenous People by White settlers is not a crime in Canada. Attempting to take back Land that White settlers have stolen by applying the colonial rule of law is considered criminal by Canadians. The law is severe with both Indigenous Peoples and with Black/African Peoples, yet there are differences between the two. The law is flexible for White settlers and for capitalist

---

[1] http://www.cbc.ca/news/canada-s-prison-population-at-all-time-high-1.2440039

http://news.nationalpost.com/2013/11/26/covert-racism-behind-increased-numbers-of-aboriginals-and-other-visible-minorities-in-prisons-watchdog-says/

projects which strengthen the settler colonial apparatus. The law supports market logic, which reifies settler colonialism by deepening the polarization along the class, color, culture, ethnicity, religion, gender and ability lines. This does not generate dissonance for the settler nor for the colonial settler apparatus. Their binary logics and their racisms render them immune to feelings of discomfort and ensure their protection. Black/African Canadians cannot be in Canada unless they adhere tightly to the rule of law once they have passed the filtering processes of citizenship and immigration. They enter Canada and become Canadian through the legal apparatus. Any violation—imagined or real, would quickly abort their entry and their capacity to secure citizenship. Those who enter are chosen or permitted entry through the settler colonial and neocolonial apparatuses of the Canadian state. This apparatus has in some ways made permissible and possible the entry of certain Black/Africans at particular times under particular geopolitical conditions and in particular moments of Canadian consciousness. Black/Africans enter legally and live under the law; they have no other choice.

Black/Africans do come and live here, and I say this without examining the different sets of conditions and processes that have enabled and/or forced this migration in past and current contexts. Our presence on Indigenous Land, although legal, fully implicates us in the settler colonial and the neo-colonial project. We are not equal to the settler, to the preferred White body, and so we do not share their power, privilege, space, or centrality—and we do not share their participation in the colonial/imperial and heterocapitalist system. We also do not share their capacity to engage in illegal activity in full view without repercussion. Nor do Black/African-Canadians share the settler colonial desires that drive the settler colonial and neo-colonial apparatus. This is important. We are present however, on Indigenous Land, and know that the settler colonial and neo-colonial forms of government actively violate Indigenous treaty and Land laws and actively interfere with Indigenous desires for health, sovereignty and self-determination. Black/African-Canadians are implicated and have responsibilities in the processes of Indigenous Peoples' decolonization and to their decolonization discourses.

I reiterate, holding Canadian citizenship in the historical context of Indigenous Land dispossession and cultural genocide by Europe does not make one complicit in colonial settlerhood, nor does it make one a colonial settler. One is complicit when one knowingly engages in an act of Land dispossession through conquest. Black/African-Canadians are not complicit in this colonial Land dispossession through acts of violence and genocide, hence my use of the word implicated. Being implicated means that a person is involved in something—they partake in it. Being implicated is involvement that, unlike being complicit, is not outside of law. Implication *is* joining in, however, and Black/African-Canadians do join in the settler project by becoming citizens and having a life here. We do not claim innocence and believe that our engagement in de-colonizing and anti-racism processes, practices, and discourses is an active step. As stated earlier, I agree with Lawrence and Dua in regards to becoming more active in strengthening and supporting Indigenous decolonizing and anti-racist work. I have already suggested that we develop solidarities along the Indigeneity axis and mobilize collectively to do this. Solidarities will serve Indigenous and other decolonizing Indigenous work and desires well. Under the umbrella of Indigeneity, our diversity and different knowledges and embodiments of colonialisms allow us to mobilize a more effective challenge of colonialisms.

It is implied that we unknowingly engage and become active in projects of exclusion—but not necessarily through genocide or colonial violence. Because Black bodies are denied Canadian citizenship in the true sense of who belongs and can legitimately lay claim to valued goods and services accrued on stolen Lands, I insist that caution be exercised in claiming we are complicit in past and ongoing Indigenous peoples' colonization and genocide.

A mere admission of implication is not enough. We have seen the settler colonial apparatus make admissions over and over again. Critical awareness of how we are implicated through the structures of the state and how we are deployed in its service is important and requires revitalized effort and interrogation. I encourage us to pursue a deeper understanding of the structures and processes that seed our implication in "settler colonialism". I also encourage a deeper process of decolonization for Black/African-Canadian and racialized bodies. As non-settlers implicated in the settler regime, Black/African Canadians and racialized bodies have a twofold process of decolonization and reclaiming of identity. First, decolonizing the colonized self must occur through acts of recognition, reclaiming, and decolonizing the mind. Second, there must be critical engagement with Whiteness. We must interrogate and problematize its production and reproduction and how it is constituted through particular racialized bodies during particular geopolitical and economic moments within colonial settler states like Canada and the United States of America. Importantly, this must include a thorough interrogation of Whiteness with particular reference to its capacity to aggressively marginalize and thwart Indigenous Peoples despite, degrees of change in the racism experienced by other racialized bodies at different geopolitical and historical junctures!

In this reproduction of Whiteness, it can be (and has been) argued that we occupy and assume some levels/degrees of Whiteness. These concepts of decolonization are not applicable only to the Indigenous nations of North America; they also extend to Indigenous populations globally. They are not limited and can be transferred to other places of Indigeneity. Problems arise when there is a failure to admit implication in colonial projects, and also in the failure to address the structures of Whiteness that simultaneously reify racialized bodies and assimilate them into their projects. A complete rejection of implication or a justification to absolve implication of racialized bodies in the colonial project, or superficial lip acceptance of involvement, and a failure to address those structures that reinforce colonialism, has been and would be thoroughly problematic and would entrap all racialized bodies. I say again that racialized bodies must address the processes of how they are and become implicated in the colonial project. We must deepen the analysis in regards to how we gain power and privilege through the marginalization of specific racialized bodies and importantly, what conditions such dynamics. Engaging in these discourses is not a singular action. Rather, it is an ongoing process of continuous critical engagement within a continuously changing world. Our aim is to confront racisms; overcome binary logics that generate them, ignore them, and also pit them against one another; and to restore our Indigeneity. This work requires that Whiteness be de-centered through solidarity work. Surely this will be hard work with much to do, but I ask that we begin to mobilize through Indigeneity now.

4.3.4   Collective Responsibility

Responsibility is important in terms of the work this essay aspires to do and the work I do through it at a more personal level. I offer an Indigenous understanding of responsibility first.

Responsibility as I have learned is reciprocal, dialectic, relational and holistic. I apply this understanding of responsibility to the issues presented in this essay. When a person has rights in a place and within a community, they also have responsibilities. Rights do not exceed responsibilities. Responsibility from the Indigenous perspective I offer here is not coerced, co-opted or forced; it emerges from a clear acknowledgement and certain understanding of our shared humanness and humanity. It also emerges from an understanding that there is a deep interconnection between people who member a system or a community, and that no one can ever be "off the hook", a bystander, absolved, or innocent. All share responsibility, although differently, in the group's welfare, in its harms, and in its healing. This is not so for the capitalist and neoliberal theories that inform (neo)colonial discourses and the colonial apparatuses of settler states. They privilege the individual not the community. And the individual that is privileged, the settler, is White, male, able-bodied, "intelligent", and most importantly, "rational". Responsibility is most important then in terms of how it serves the individual. This is well understood by racialized peoples as harmful and this is not how I frame responsibility here. I rely on Indigenous understandings of responsibility that come before this.

I view humanity as a sea of people who interdepend and this view animates my conception of responsibility. An Ubuntu saying explains this well: "I am because we are, and because we are, therefore I am." This saying attempts to make clear the Indigenous understanding that people equally share both rights and responsibilities. Accusations and the hurling of blame is unuseful and does not make sense from an Indigenous perspective. An Indigenous perspective speaks to an ethic and a morality that go beyond the individual and which emerge from our shared humanity. We have both rights and responsibilities to others, to ourselves, to our communities, and to the earth. These rights and responsibilities demand that we collectively serve the interests of our interdependent communities and of the earth itself. Where harm occurs, it is all of our work to stop it and to facilitate healing. This Indigenous conception of responsibility is again borne out in the African saying that "It is not what one is called that is most important, but rather what one responds to." Responsibility is about responding at a scale that far exceeds the individual and moves toward communities, and from there to larger and larger clusters of communities to include the whole planet. Responsibility means in the Indigenous sense that we create healthy, sustainable, viable communities and we do so through holistic relationships with each other and with the Land and the earth more broadly. We have responsibilities to our Lands and to the earth, and this is also an important element of our healing and to processes of decolonization and Indigeneity.

I have often argued that equity and social justice work flows from spirituality. Responsibility infuses our inner most being and is where our sense of justice emerges from. It is this same responsibility that stewards over life and makes room for healing. Responsibility is critical to life, health, justice and sustainability. Responsibility is activated intensely when we experience or see injustice, harm, and inequity. This makes us human and it makes us human to one another. Colonialism is and has been a violent encounter. It has served to perpetuate inequities in human society and extreme conditions of suffering. Colonizing relations are, through their logics, always necessarily oppressive, unjust and violent. We can only address such oppressive relations and the violence they incur by looking frankly at how we engage with the (neo)colonial apparatus and the expression of its White desires. Responsibility is not enacted through words in the way I bring forth here; it is action-oriented. African-Canadians welcomed onto Indigenous Lands through the Canadian state apparatus have a responsibility to bring critical awareness to the ongoing colonization of Indigenous people and Indigenous Lands. This responsibility will help us to connect our struggles and to reclaim our humanity through the broader community of Indigenous peoples.

References

Anzaldúa, G., & Moraga, C. (Eds.). (1981). *This bridge called my back: Writings by radical women of color*. New York: Kitchen Table.

Cannon, M. J. (2012). Changing the subject in teacher education: Centering Indigenous, disasporic and settler colonial relations. *Cultural and Pedagogical Inquiry, 4*(2), 21–37.

Cannon, M. J., & Sunseri, L. (Eds.). (2011). *Racism, colonialism, and indigeneity in Canada: A reader*. Toronto: Oxford University Press.

Coulthard, G. (2014). *Red skin, white masks: Rejecting the colonial politics of recognition*. Minneapolis: University of Minnesota Press.

DeGenova, N. (2002). Migrant "illegality" and deportability in everyday life. *Annual Review of Anthropology, 31*, 419–447.

Dei, G. J. S. (2012). Suahunu: The trialectic space. *Journal of Black Studies, 43*(8), 823–846.

Dei, G. J. S. (2015). Race and anti-racist practice: The challenge of decolonization. In L. Drakeford (Ed.), *The race controversy in American education*. New York: Praeger Publishing.

Fanon, F. (1963). *The wretched of the earth*. New York: Grove Press.

Fanon, F. (1967). *Black skin, white masks*. New York: Grove Press.

Fellows, M., & Razack, S. (1998). The race to innocence: Confronting hierarchical relations among women. *The Journal of Gender, Race & Justice, 1*, 335–352.

Gaztambide-Fernández, R. (2012). Decolonization and the pedagogy of solidarity. *Decolonization: Indigeneity, Education & Society, 1*(1), 41–67. Retrieved from http://decolonization.org/index.php/des/article/view/18633/15557.

Hardy, K. (2012). Unsetting hope: Contemporary indigenous politics, settler-colonialism, and Utopianism. *Spaces of Utopia, 2*(1), 123–136.

Henay, C. (2016). *Personal Communication*. Toronto, Canada: Department of Social Justice Education, Ontario Institute for Studies in Education of the University of Toronto.

Howes, D. (1996). Cultural appropriation and resistance in the American southwest: Decommodifying indianness. In D. Howes (Ed.), *Cross-cultural consumption: Global markets local realities* (pp. 138–160). London and New York: Routledge.

Jackson, S. N. (2006). Guyana, Cuba, Venezuela and the "routes" to cultural reconciliation between Latin America and the Caribbean. *Small Axe, 19*(10), 28–58.

Jackson, S. N. (2012). *Creole indigeneity: Between meth and nation in the Caribbean*. Minneapolis: University of Minnesota Press.

Jackson, S. N. (2014). Risk, blackness, and postcolonial studies: An introduction. *Collaloo, 37*(1), 63–68.

Jensen, B. (2013). Race erased? Arizona's ethnic studies ban. In G. Dei & M. Lordan (Eds.), *Contemporary issues in the sociology of race and ethnicity: A critical reader*. New York: Peter Lang.

Jensen, B. (2016). *UN Human Rights for Women: How race becomes an organizing principle. Unpublished term paper*. Department of Social Justice Education, Ontario Institute for Studies in Education of the University of Toronto, Toronto, Canada.

Jensen, B. (2017). *UN Human Rights for Women: How race becomes an organizing principle*. Unpublished paper, Department of Social Justice Education, Ontario institute for Studies in education of the University of Toronto.

Jensen, B., & Howard-Wagner, D. (2014). Arizona 2010. In D. Howard-Wagner, L. Spanierman, & V. Watson (Eds.), *Unveiling whiteness in the 21st century: Global manifestations, transdisciplinary intervention* (pp. 143–169). Lexington: Lexington Books.

Kerr, J. (2013). *Pedagogical thoughts on knowing bodies: The teacher educator encounters the elder and the phronimos*. PhD dissertation. University of British Columbia, Vancouver, BC.

Kerr, J. (2014). Western Epistemic Dominance and Colonial Structures: Considerations for thought and practice in programs of teacher education. *Decolonization: Indigeneity, Education & Society, 3*(2).

King, T. (2013). *In the clearing: Black female bodies, space and settler colonial landscapes*. Unpublished Ph.D. dissertation, Department of American Studies.

Lawrence, B., & Dua, E. (2005). Decolonizing antiracism. *Social Justice, 32*(4), 120–143.

Mignolo, W. (2000). *Local histories/global designs: Coloniality, subaltern knowledges, and border thinking*. Princeton, NJ: Princeton University Press.

Mignolo, W. (2008). The geopolitics of knowledge and the colonial difference'. In M. Morana, E. Dussel, & C. Jaurengui (Eds.), *Coloniality at large Latin America and the postcolonial debate* (pp. 225–258). Durham, NC: Duke University.

Nyamnjoh, F. (2012). Potted plants in greenhouses': A critical reflection on the resilience of colonial education in Africa. *Journal of Asian and African Studies, 47*(2), 1–26. Retrieved from http://jas.sagepub.com/content/early/2012/02/14/0021909611417240.

Phung, M. (2011). People of colour in treaty. In A. Mathur, J. Dewar, & M. DeGagne (Eds.), *Cultivating Canada: Reconciliation through the lens of cultural diversity* (pp. 291–298). Ottawa, ON: Aboriginal Healing Foundation.

Ritskes, E. (2012). Comprehensive exams essay. Toronto: Department of Social Justice Education, Ontario Institute for studies in Education of the University of Toronto (OISE).

Sandhu, D. (2014). *Theorizing brown identity*. Unpublished M.A. thesis, Department of Social Justice Education, Ontario Institute for Studies in Education of the University of Toronto (OISE/UT), Toronto.

Sehdev, R. K. (2011). People of colour in treaty. In A. Mathur, J. Dewar, & M. DeGagne (Eds.), *Cultivating Canada: Reconciliation through the lens of cultural diversity* (pp. 264–274). Ottawa, Ontario: Aboriginal Healing Foundation.

Sexton, J. (2014). The vel of slavery: Tracking the figure in the unsovereign. *Critical Sociology*, 1–15. doi:10.1177/086920514552535.

Sharma, N. (2009). The racialization of space and the spatialization of belonging. In A. Itwaru (Ed.), *The white supremacist state: Ethnocentrism, imperialism, colonialism, racism* (pp. 221–242). Toronto: Other Eye.

Smith, A. (2006). Heteropatriarchy and the three pillars of White supremacy. In *Color of violence: INCITE! Women of color against violence* (pp. 66–73). Cambridge, MA: South End Press.

Smith, A. (2012). Indigeneity, settler colonialism and white supremacy. In D. H. Martinez, O. LaBennett, & L. Pulido (Eds.), *Racial formation in the twenty-first century* (pp. 66–90). Berkeley: University of California Press.

Stasiulus, D., & Bakan, A. (2005). *Negotiating citizenship: Migrant women in Canada and the global system*. Toronto: University of Toronto Press.

Taylor, M. B. (2011). *Reconstructing the native south: American Indian literature and the lost cause*. Athens: University of Georgia Press.

Tuck, E., & Yang, K. W. (2012). Decolonization is not a metaphor. *Decolonization: Indigeneity, Education & Society, 1*(1), 1–40. Retrieved from http://decolonization.org/index.php/des/article/view/18630.

Waldorf, S., & Gillian, P. (2011). *Review essay: "Decolonizing Antiracism" by Bonita Lawrence and Enakshi Dua*. Ontario: Department of Sociology and Equity Studies in Education, Institute for Studies in Education of the University of Toronto.

Walia, H. (2012). Decolonizing together: Moving beyond a politics of solidarity toward a practice of decolonization. *Briarpatch Magazine*. Retrieved from http://briarpatchmagazine.com/articles/view/decolonizing-together.

Yankah, K. (2004). *Globalization and the African scholar* [Monograph]. Faculty of Arts, University of Ghana.

Chapter 5
So why Do that Dance?

Abstract This chapter responds to the perceived tensions between Race and Indigeneity. It locates its arguments on unsettling the competing essence of Indigenous and anticolonialism. There are many valid entry points for anti-colonial intellectualism, each dependent on the body and the particular politics, conversant of the saliency of different histories and identities, the situational and contextual variations in intensities of oppressions, and the knowledge that as scholars we each engage/enter discourses from either our privileged or oppressed positions, etc. (see Dei 1996). So a question like "how do we engage the anticolonial from a privileged stance?" is relevant. As scholars, activists, and students, we acknowledge and work with the "historicity of race" as over-determining of life chances for Black bodies. In addition, we must hang on to the possibilities and limits of a "radical inseparability" of race and Indigeneity. Blackness works with a reinvention of Africanness (even in a Diasporic context), a consciousness of the saliency of skin color and what it means to be Black in the global world. This recognizes the question of race as a key/salient factor and a central organizing principle of society. Race cannot be subsumed under any other identity (e.g., class), notwithstanding the intersections of gender, class, sexuality, ability, and other identities. A poetic treatise (discourse) about colonialism must bring a historical materialist approach and interpretation to European colonization (see Cesaire 1972). We must connect colonization and civilization in anticolonial and decolonial conversations. The re-articulation of Blackness is part of a desire to mount a counter intellectual attack (a sort of "why write back"), which responds to the deliberate anti-Blackness and de-compartmentalization of Black lives and African histories, such as the excising of Egypt from Africa, and devaluations of Indigenous African inventions and Black peoples' contributions to science, mathematics, and global knowledge as a whole. The correlation between Indigenous communities and Indigenous subjects, particularly the falseness of separating race and Indigeneity.

Anticolonial intellectualism about race, class, gender, disability, lesbian, bisexual, gay, trans, two-spirited and queer studies and the body, far from eroding scholarship, is re-inserting the "ontological marginality" of identity as significant to all discourses and body politics. It is also relevant to the ways we create spaces to bring

© Springer International Publishing AG 2017   119
G.J.S. Dei, *Reframing Blackness and Black Solidarities through Anti-colonial and Decolonial Prisms*, Critical Studies of Education 4,
DOI 10.1007/978-3-319-53079-6_5

the historical specificities and particularities in relation to the "universal." Suleri (1992) asked how plural are our constructions of singularity, and how singular are what we have presented as plural? I suggest an answer lies more with the politics we pursue to achieve particular ends. The anticolonial is both about historical specificities as well as the places and spaces in which those historical specificities occur. The discursivities of "race" and Indigeneity are interdependent and intertwined, which calls for an interrogation of our discursivity and discursive proclivities in ways that complicate the margins and marginal discourses, while at the same time affirming their legitimacies as radical spaces from which to lodge counter intellectual and political struggles. These are not monolithic spaces and voices and they are continually being theorized as part of anticolonial intellectuality to help shed our colonial investments.

I share Suleri's (1992) exasperation of the universalization of the postcolonial, where every space is a hybrid space, and such spaces become "so amorphous as to repudiate any locality for cultural thinkness" (p. 759). This becomes a postcolonial devoid of historical specificity, where the postcolonial margins and its identities such as the racially male or female voice are always viewed as good. I also ask where is the space for the Indigenous body in the postcolonial and how do we ensure that the spaces we create also allow "other epistemological possibilities as much as it opens" (Suleri 1992; p. 759)? Anytime we open a space we must also be asking what other possibilities and limitations are created.

However, I am not interested as to which comes first, Indigeneity or race? This is not "the question". There are many valid entry points for anticolonial intellectualism, each dependent on the body and the particular politics, conversant of the saliency of different histories and identities, the situational and contextual variations in intensities of oppressions, and the knowledge that as scholars we each engage/enter discourses from either our privileged or oppressed positions, etc. (see Dei 1996). So a question like "how do we engage the anticolonial from a privileged stance?" is more relevant to me instead. I urge that as scholars, activists, and students, we acknowledge and work with the "historicity of race" as over-determining of life chances for Black bodies. In addition, we must hang on to the possibilities and limits of a "radical inseparability" of race and Indigeneity.

We must also be able to articulate fitting intellectual responses to how, when and what is this "race" and "Indigeneity" and their particular place in both postcolonial and in anticolonial discourses. Therefore, the difference of "anti" and "post" must be clear. Postcolonial theorists examine the legacy of colonialism without addressing race and the focus on the central issue of Land and Indigenous sovereignty; for anti-colonial theorists, the project of colonialism is ongoing. For anticolonial theorists, race and Indigeneity are central to the subversive prism—the colonial question is a race and Land question. Anticolonial makes race and Land as central planks in their thesis and theorizations. It is not a biological reading of race that equates or anchors body politics to biologism. It is rather about "embodiment" of knowledge, i.e., the body is a site of knowing, to be understood as how the body is read, discursively produced, acted upon, and also engaged in both oppressive and resistant politics. As noted in an earlier chapter, "embodiment" is the particular experiencing of the body and how it is acted upon in a given socio-historical and political context. The notion of "embodied knowing" is about coming to know, i.e., a perspective that can be attained by developing an attachment or a particular connection to knowledge. "Body politics" in anticolonial pursuits, as the particular ways the body is understood in a White supremacist context, calls for acknowledging that knowledge and experience reside in bodies and cultural memories.

The Black body is a reality that cannot be ignored when it comes to questions of lived experiences and oppressions. Thus, it is not the colonized/oppressed/Indigene/Black who chooses to exoticize our bodies. In other words, neither the anticolonial nor the postcolonial critic seeks to write "alterity into the ambiguous shape of the exotic body" (Suleri 1992, p. 763). We do not promote the "compartmentalization of Otherness" (Suleri 1992, p. 765). When the anti- or even postcolonial intellectual writes and speaks about Otherness and alterity, we are simply gesturing to what already exists.

So who creates the space of "Otherness"? Writing from the space of the "Other" is a necessity from the context of how discursive authority and authorial representations have always been assigned to the dominant to speak on behalf of others. We must be critical of dominant voices speaking for the "other" particularly in academia, where the dominant White bodies are presented as "experts" on the history of the "other". Claiming subjectivities and identities as entry points to knowledge creation is political. Claiming, naming, and representations of identities are vital, but what do we do with our subject positions and identities is more crucial.

The preoccupation with "facts" and "reality" as emerging from objectivity and objective stances with no idealism, emotions, speculation, or sentimentalism is very problematic. We come to know through both objective and subjective facts. The objectivity of the dominant is the subjectivity of the minority. The reality of the oppressed can never be understood by the dominant or through dominant prisms. Thus, we must understand "real" and the "objective' as equally constitutive of oppositional/counter voices from the margins and subordinate/marginalized lived experiences and local voices. This reading is vital for a disruption of what counts as "real[ism]".

Narrating and focusing on lived experiences of Black lives and identities as stories is about theorizing social existence (see Collins 1990). Counter, oppositional. and anti-oppression discourses on anti-Blackness, anti-Black racism, Indigeneity, etc., are not about "proprietary rights" (ownership, entitlements, property) [see Suleri, p. 764]. The insistence on asserting/claiming one's voice and telling one's stories should not be understood in the Eurocentric sense of "rights" as [individual] property, ownership, and entitlements. Nor can it be read as an attempt to seek legitimacy, validation, and acceptance from the dominant. Yet the anticolonial subversion or disruption of Whiteness is not a mere obsession with Whiteness and the race/pigmentation discourse. It is a realization of the body as always as political, consequential, and meaningful in a White supremacist state.

History has become a tool and a greatest weapon of colonization, a reality we must counter by situating colonialism and racism in theorizing Black lived experiences and oppressions. In this chapter, I offer a reading of Blackness through an anticolonial discourse as historical prose poetry on the realities, possibilities, consequences, and implications of the colonial encounter, and the necessity for a revolt/insurrection. We must see Blackness as something to yearn for and to be achieved through an intellectual and political reimagining, re-visioning, and revelation to

change the existing social order. Blackness must evoke possibilities of the known
and unknown, conscious and unconscious, implicating the mental, spiritual, and
metaphysical. In rethinking Blackness, I am reflecting on what can be/ought to be
and what might have been, and how Europe changed the course of human history
even if Europe is not the advent of human history.

I reclaim Blackness in this sense of alienation from a foreign Land and homeland, the problem of the African or the Black body's alienation from her/his culture,
history and labor (our humanity), which in itself creates a need for "disalienation"
as a politics of reclaiming culture and history and for survival. Blackness then
becomes a return to culture, roots and the authentic self, space, sense of place, and
history. It is about reclaiming authentic culture and the African and Indigenous heritage and rich intellectual traditions. It is also a process of unlearning, a call for critical anticolonial education that helps emancipates one's consciousness eschewing
the need for politics and action.

This reclamation is not dissimilar from the Negritude movement, which was
never a matter of race essentialism contrary to what its critics have assumed.
Negritude was a resistance to avoiding the race question in anticolonial struggles,
and an attempt to resurface and downplay the class question and political economy
of the global capitalism. Speaking about race does not make the discourse race
essentialist. It is essentialist if race is all we talk about. Like Negritude, which was
synonymous with Africa, Blackness is about solidarities of all racially colonized
populations. There is also a futuristic [and contemporary] component of going
beyond what Blackness has been in the past, to what is possible with this new and
counter re-affirmation and thus can be achieved in the future. It is about moving
from an abstract and coming to consciousness, to a concrete reality and sense of
being Black. This Blackness seeks to resurrect (rather than reject) Black/African
identity and the making of the African humanity through a positive, solution-
oriented reclamation of Black and African cultures and traditions, creativity,
resourcefulness, and independence.

To reiterate Blackness works with a reinvention of Africanness (even in a
Diasporic context), a consciousness of the saliency of skin color and what it means
to be Black in the global world. In effect, this recognizes the question of race as a
key/salient factor and a central organizing principle of society, and that race cannot
be subsumed under any other identity (e.g., class), notwithstanding the intersections
of gender, class, sexuality, ability, and other identities. We know that colonization is
based on psychology and the use of brute technological force. It devalues the civilization of the colonized, but it also works to dehumanize and de-civilize the colonizers. Colonialism destroyed human lives as well as the science, architecture,
knowledge systems, culture, economies, political systems, aesthetics, languages,
security, and education of the colonized peoples through genocide, theft, and violence. Through colonialism Europe came to historically annex the history, science
and ethics of Black and other colonized and Indigenous peoples. Colonialism also
espoused the colonial project as hypocritical and deeply flawed—ethically and
intellectually. Colonization was not about the spread of humane values of social
justice, fairness, and equity. It was about domination and control. Thus we cannot
understand the "tragedy of Black bodies" today outside the discourse of Euro-

colonization. European colonization disrupted the course of African and Black peoples' histories.

Black/African peoples have been denied their humanity. This denial has been materially, psychologically, spiritually, emotionally, and politically consequential for Black bodies. Asante (2005) contends that, "Anti-blackness represents the highest form of pessimism toward humanity since Blackness has been posited as the post-Western trope best qualified to serve as an ethical measure for our social universe" (p. 215). One finds "Blackness" disproportionately among people who are phenotypically Black because Black people have been at the most violent edges of White supremacy (p. 213). As already alluded to, the denial of Black humanity continues today in the insidious anti-Blackness and anti-Black racism that masquerades sometimes under the guise of disturbing an "oppression olympics" and totalizing, essentialist narratives. There is the sense that "we have heard too much of Black suffering"—enough for us to begin to talk about other oppressions and issues. But nowhere has an articulation of and the insistence that we address Black suffering been posited to discount other forms of oppressions facing other groups. Similarly, anti-racism is not just about Black peoples' causes. It is about all racisms and the links with other forms of oppression. The fact that anti-racism was pioneered by Black scholars should not be interpreted to mean it does not speak of "other issues". Anti-racism speaks of all issues of oppression including indigeneity and Land dispossession because racism underlie the colonialism and seizure of Lands in America and elsewhere.

A poetic treatise (discourse) about colonialism must bring a historical materialist approach and interpretation to European colonization (see Cesaire 1972). The colonial nation building project has been a White imperialistic enterprise, powerfully revealing the interconnections of racism, slavery, genocide, patriarchy, and Euro-colonial conquest. This was at the heart of the colonial project, leading early anticolonial theorists like Cesaire and Fanon to argue that Europe and the West is morally, spiritually indefensible and must continually be held responsible for the "highest heap of corpses in history" (Cesaire 1972, p. 8).

Thus we must connect colonization and civilization in anticolonial and decolonial conversations. Colonization is about relations of domination and subordination, about a "thingification" that denies African/Black human subjectivity and makes the colonizer into objects, a thing—something without humanity. This process of making human bodies into objects proceed along several fronts culminating in the loss of pride and the development of an inferiority and dependency complex in the colonized. There is contempt for the Indigene, the Black body, and in particular, there is no ascription of humanity to the Black/African body. The "idea of the barbaric Negro [African/Black] as a European invention" (p. 11) has continued to serve certain hegemonic interests. The linking of Black bodies with violence continues to have severe ramifications on Black bodies; this colonial construct continues to impact the lived experience of Black people.

The re-articulation of Blackness is part of a desire to mount a counter intellectual attack (a sort of "why write back"), which responds to the deliberate anti-Blackness and de-compartmentalization of Black lives and African histories, such as the excising of Egypt from Africa, and devaluations of Indigenous African inventions and

Black peoples' contributions to science, mathematics, and global knowledge as a whole. While Europe has continued to sow the seeds of its own destruction, it has also demonstrated a remarkable capacity to reinvent itself. It has resuscitated itself from terminal collapse through education, legal statutes, economics, the deployment of technology and militarism and an uncanny ability to define/design futures for others through its control of capital and knowledge.

Europe and the US have maintained this dominance perhaps most effectively through the use of governance. The UN is a key institution in the West's persistence in defining the realities and futures of racialized Others. As Western nations and discourses inform how the UN operates, all nations are ranked according to various indicators with "developing" nations cited as those in need of intervention and regulation. The discourse of development works to define and re-define a relationship of inequity and violence, establishing new goals for developing nations along with programs and policies for their implementation. Disciplinary systems such as the UN's Sustainable Development Goals (SDGs) not only rank nations, they always create excess—that which cannot be assimilated (Foucault 1975). Discipline then creates new programs and protocols to correct and manage these identified outliers. When operating in a biopolitical rather than necropolitical mode, liberal and neoliberal regimes use disciplinary systems to establish a relation. Punishment works to correct rather than eliminate subjects (or nations), and it generates new disciplinary techniques and regulatory regimes. Therefore, even with attainment of the UN's SDGs, the racial and colonial underpinnings of liberal governance obviate "inclusion" of developing nations as disciplinary subjects.

In addition to the work of the UN, new indicators, policies, and programs are also continuously developed and supported by the IMF, World Bank, and other international governing bodies which perpetuate a racial order. The alignment (or subjection) of developing nations within Western imperatives of free trade, privatization of economies, Land ownership, and other free market objectives helps conceal a racial relationship through the discourse of economics. Achievement of the SDGs will not result in self-determination, shared power, or equal legitimacy in the international arena. Ultimately, such achievement reinforces a colonial relationship. These international organizations disguise their self-interests under world peace and "education for all"; meanwhile they continue to govern "developing nations".

Moreover, Africa and sub-Saharan Africa are often homogenized in UN discourse and singled out as the areas of greatest concern and deficiency. These International Organizations force African economies into complete dependency for foreign aid which fosters this unequal power imbalance. Mbembe (2001) describes how contemporary discourses render the African human experience as one that can only be understood through negative interpretation. Attributes of Africa are produced as those of less value and inferior quality. The United Nations Development Programme (UNDP) praises African people's productivity, yet notes that bringing out of the "shadow economy" is noted as a key indicator of progress. In fact, people in Africa must not only work in the formal economy in order to have value in the world order, their development and progress depends upon whether they have recently taken out a loan from a financial institution. The work of people in Africa and African economic systems is inferior (undeveloped) when they operate outside of Western norms and the global capitalist system, including debt. This reflects just one example of many, and Africa's depiction as lagging behind in contemporary UN documents builds on this same theme of the Millennium Development Goals that ended in 2015. Follow-up reports of the MDGs note Africa's failure to meet the goals and flag it as a key area for further attention in the post-2015 Development Agenda of which the Sustainable Development Goals are a part (www.undp.org).

Identified as the poorest and most deficient region globally by the UN, IMF, and World Bank, Africa is taken out of context with other parts of the world. This means that questions of power are not relational, but rather become from the concern of Africa (or developing nations in other cases). Africa is allegedly empowered through UN Development Programmes, and its success hinges upon its individual ability/willingness to then empower (discipline) itself in alignment. The developing nation (or Africa) becomes both the subject and object of Western governmentality.

Neo-liberalism's focus on the individual helps the West construct itself in opposition to Africa—to backwardness, lack of progress, and by association—Blackness. The problem of poverty and the vast ills of which Africa is said to suffer become intrinsic to this pre-modern place and people—located in an individually identified place (Africa) and by association, race (Blacks). Although referring to individual subjects, Foucault's (1997) indication that the individual is not power's opposite number resonates here. The move to individualize Africa requires and allows the West to occlude its own brutality and erase its own history (Mbembe 2001, p. 2).

For example, when acknowledged, colonialism is consigned to history, the effects of which development has sought to improve. The UNDP website states, "The decolonization of Africa was a priority for the UN during the middle of the twentieth century. Since then, the development of the continent has become the priority." Importantly, such discourses reflect the UN's failure to address not only the residual effects of colonial history that shape contemporary issues identified by the UNDP, but also how its own liberal and neoliberal ontologies and governmentalities are inseparable from colonialism and work to sustain it through new discourses and practices. Foucault (1972) clarifies this relationship between mentalities, discourses, and practices:

> to speak is to do something—something other than to express what one thinks, to translate what one knows…to add a statement to a pre-existing series of statements is to perform a complicated and costly gesture, which involves conditions (and not only a situation, a context and motives) and rules (not the logical and linguistic rules of construction); to show that a change in the order of discourse does not presuppose 'new ideas', a little invention and creativity, a different mentality, but transformations in practice, perhaps also in neighbouring practices, and in their common articulation. (209)

Foucault's indication that a change in the order of discourse presupposes not a change in mentality, but a change "in practice…and in their common articulation," explains how Western mentalities that informed colonial rule persist through contemporary UN poverty reduction efforts—despite, and more importantly *through*, changes in certain practices. In fact, Escobar (1995) asserts that representations of the developing world are no less pervasive and effective than their colonial predecessors as they inform and authorize UN development today (p. 15). As UN discourse consigns colonialism to the past, it naturalizes the violence inflicted through biopolitical and necropolitical management of racialized populations inherent to capitalist systems and (neo)liberal regimes (Mbembe 2003).

With colonialism declared officially over, the history of Africa becomes reduced to a number of setbacks it continues to face in its quest for humankind (Mbembe 2001). These "natural and inevitable" setbacks surface throughout UNDP documents as poverty, disease, famine, and other calamities. Caught in a relation of pure immediacy to the world and to themselves, societies such as those within Africa are incapable of uttering the universal (Mbembe 2001, p. 4). Western framed and driven solutions to Africa's problems proceed from this point, allowing "the West to accede to its own subconscious and give a public account of its subjectivity" (Mbembe 2001, p. 3). The prominent public promotions of UN Development Programmes, reports, and policies are apropos. Western discourse on Africa is about both self-deception and perversion. Africa and African people become necessary inventions in the world that the West constitutes for itself and in its apologetic "concerns" and outright brutality toward others (Mbembe 2001, p. 2).

In contrast to the West, Africa is depicted as full of death, disease, and threat by the UNDP. Mbembe (2001) identifies this discursive context as part of a meta-text of animality through which notions of Africa are deployed (p. 1). Associations with monstrosity and strangeness appear as Africa represents an appealing depth that nevertheless constantly eludes and evades our capture. Africa (and sub-Saharan Africa) remain outside of the UN's (Western) capture through persistently failing to meet UNDP goals. Also, the continual narrative that African governments are 'corrupt' and 'unfit to rule' is fueling this need for International organizations to govern, which threatens and undermines the sovereignty of African nations.

These reports exemplify how "Africa is the utmost target of Western discourses of 'absence' and 'lack', identity and difference" (Mbembe 2001, p. 4). Consistently, UNDP discourses on Africa reference high fertility rates, unintended pregnancies, undemocratic institutions, high infant and maternal mortality rates, low life expectancy, high malnutrition, high unemployment, inadequate health care, and the list continues. Such assessments necessitate an abandonment of our world of meaning to conceptualize Africa as a place distinguished by absolute brutality, sexual promiscuity, and death (Mbembe 2001, p. 1–2).

Giving a broader account of contemporary discourse on Africa, Mbembe (2001) states:

> It is in relation to Africa that the notion of "absolute otherness" has been taken furthest.
> ....Africa as an idea, a concept, has historically serves, and continues to serve, as a polemical argument for the West's desperate desire to assert its difference from the rest of the world. Africa still constitutes one of the metaphors through which the West represents the origin of its own norms, develops a self-image, and integrates this image into the set of signifiers asserting what it supposes to be its identity. (p. 2)

Re-articulating Blackness is about colonized peoples needing to reclaim our histories, cultures, knowledge, and humanity on our own intellectual, economic, and political terms. It is important for us to ask, for example, why is it that time and time again, Europe has succeeded in inserting/imposing itself upon the world (e.g., Africa and colonized communities)? How and why have "we" allowed it or contributed to make this possible?

Looking at Black lives through history and in contemporary times, we can speak to the violence of colonial modernity through an understanding of "necropolitics" (see Mbembe 2003), i.e., death politics or a politics devoid of life. Violence and sovereignty are intertwined and stem from a "divine" foundation of the colonial dominant interpretation of their "manifest destiny" and social power. Black lives reveal how terror, death, life, and freedom are also "irrevocably interwoven." Sovereignty has traditionally been about the state's conception of reason, death and life, and the right to kill, control and dominate others as a natural right. In the late eighteenth century, sovereignty came to be complemented by "biopower" (Foucault 1980), described by Dreyfus and Rabinow (1982) as "the increasing organization of population and welfare for the sake of increased force and productivity" (p. 81). Through a "politics of biopower" as a particular body politics, the control of bodies by state organs and political structures through technologies of power has success-fully ensured that some bodies can be deemed "disposable." When discussing bio-power and biopolitics, Foucault (1978) clarified that what gives modern racism its specificity "is not bound up with mentalities, ideologies, or the lies of power. It is bound up with the technique of power, with the technology of power…" (p. 258). Race serves as the precondition which makes killing acceptable within normalizing (biopolitical) societies. Foucault (1978) asserted that, "… racism justifies the death-function in the economy of biopower by appealing to the principle that the death of others makes one biologically stronger insofar as one is a member of a race or a population…" (p. 258). Bringing these ideas together, Foucault noted, "…racism is bound up with the workings of a State that is obliged to use race, the elimination of races and the purification of the race, to exercise its sovereign power" (p. 258). Once a State engages in biopolitics, and it is important to note that all liberal states are biopolitical states, "racism alone can justify the murderous functions of the State" (Foucault 1978, p. 256).

Biopower and neoliberalism work together in Canada's economy: Racialized bodies are fit into an economic model as exploitable laborers; as profit-generators and job creators through increased policing and incarceration; and as those who perform crucial Canadian labor but are denied the full benefits of society even as legal citizens. There is a two-tiered structure of law that racialized people from Whites—regardless of citizenship status (Razack 2008, 2002). In regards to the death function of biopower, Foucault (1978) stated, "When I say killing, I obviously do not mean simply murder as such, but also every form of indirect murder: the fact of exposing someone to death, increasing the risk of death for some people, or, quite simply, political death, expulsion, rejection, and so on" (p. 256).

The grave endangerment of the health and lives of Black/African people in Canada, through unsafe work environments, poverty and sub-standard housing, and hyper-surveillance, policing, and incarceration, is not at all uncommon. State poli-cies show how Black lives are deemed unworthy of protecting and enabling; their popular acceptance belies the pervasive and insidious extent of anti-Blackness. Foucault's insight applies, "When you have a normalizing society, you have a power which is …in the first line a biopower, and racism is the indispensable precondition that allows someone to be killed, that allows others to be killed. Once the State functions in biopower mode, racism alone can justify the murderous functions of the State" (2003, p. 256).

Thus, the colony and modern state is primarily a state of terror. The terror of colonial occupation must be read in terms of designations of "savages," "animality" and "sub-humanity" and the consequences of such designations for Black peoples. Following Mbembe's (2003) analysis, I argue that the colonial occupation of Black lives and experiences in Euro-American contexts is characterized by the three components: (a) disciplinary measures (e.g., control, surveillance, separation, and seclusion of bodies); (b) biopolitics—the wasting of Black bodies; and (c) necropolitics—the death politics of spatialization of colonial occupation (e.g., ghettoization of Black neighborhoods and the regulation of national citizenship). But we must be able to read resistance in this existence of Black lives and experiences. In other words, we should see through this existence the possibilities of social transformation from anticolonial politics around Blackness.

Clearly, no discourses are immune to criticisms. Sunseri (2000) notes that "nationalism and nation are associated with movements for independence, liberation and revolution" (p. 144) and have been the reference points for anticolonial struggles and theorizing primarily in Africa and the Caribbean. But traditional anticolonial liberation struggles have been criticized for exclusionary claims of the nation, weak attention to women's rights, and fostering gender oppression. Such criticisms have been leveled notwithstanding clear examples of women in leadership roles in anticolonial resistance struggles, for example in Algeria.

Fanon's work has been criticized for lack of attention to questions of gender and sexuality. Postcolonial claims of hybridity, in-betweeness/third space, a space of ambivalences, contingencies, and contradictions have also been articulated to counter the anticolonial spaces of certainty and belongingness articulated through notions of the past, history, memory, culture, and/or nation.

But it is important for us to distinguish between earlier anticolonial nationalist struggles and contemporary anticolonial claims of Indigenous sovereignty based on community building, collective solidarities, and self-determination of the Indigenous destiny. We must also understand the source and nature of the ensuing tension. As Chatterjee (1986) notes in the context of anticolonial independence struggles, "the national question .....[was] historically fused with a colonial question," and the assertion of national identity was necessarily "a struggle against colonial exploitation" (p. 16). This necessitated positing a collective national identity outside of that constructed within Euro-colonial hegemonies. This is because colonialism did its dirty job around the identity, culture, and history of colonized bodies. There are implications for why we reclaim Blackness today for politics. While clearly we need to complicate claims of identity that foreclosed differences within nationalist struggles or even swept differences under the carpet (thereby becoming oppressive), we must also understand the politics of dominant critiques of identity (e.g., identity politics). As hinted at earlier, such critiques have emerged as part of the resistance of the dominant to Indigenous assertions of their own identity for political purposes.

With such conceptual readings, I want to now reintroduce arguments and high-light inconsistencies, and point concretely and pragmatically to how the "settler" in particular is defined in Euro-Canadian contexts. I have intellectual musings about using necropolitics to think through and explain the current context. The construction of the national imaginary defines who is considered a part of the space and the ways they are treated within it. The removal of Black bodies cannot be reduced to individualized racism, but must be considered alongside an institutionalized erasure that presents Black people as perpetual aliens (non-citizens) to the space. When the settler claims to belong to this Land and to own this Lands, he does not consider Black people as a partner in this endeavor. When the history of Land is written through colonial discourse, Black peoples and the means under which they found themselves on this Land are omitted from the record. When migration accounts are written today, Black peoples and those affected by ongoing colonial relations are only imagined under the rubric of cosmopolitanism, as free to travel the world (like those with passports from the Global North), while instead experiencing severe limitations to their mobility given the structural and discursive barriers and borders imposed onto racialized peoples.

Regardless of claims to access to colonial goods, Black peoples remain colonial subjects whose membership is always in question. While citizenship can be read simply as the type of passport one possesses, it is pivotal to think more broadly. To be clear, Black bodies have never been included in the national imaginary; rather, they have often been considered as antithetical to the nation. Whenever the policing and silencing of Black bodies is discussed, it is quickly disregarded; the history of Black bodies in Canada is completely erased through the prism of multiculturalism.

While some may point to the fact that at times a number of Black bodies have, under the banner of the colonial state, furthered the goals of empire within Canada/America, this is insufficient proof for a claim of complicity. As we know, the seduction of membership to the state brings many rewards, and many *individuals* have been drawn to these benefits at one point or another. Yet to conflate this with complicity is a fallacy, as complicity speaks to membership to the colonizing state and as I show below, this is too large a claim to make as it invisibilizes the colonial legacies of Black bodies in this Land as well as Black people's discursive and physical removability from the national space. This brings us back to the original argument: Black bodies are implicated in the colonization of Turtle Island, but the conceptual category of "settler" is a disingenuous proposition.

Citizenship scholars have complicated the concept of citizenship to consider how membership to the nation is defined and practiced. To Bloemraad et al. (2008), the concept of citizenship can be broken down "into four dimensions: legal status, rights, political and other forms of participation, and a sense of belonging" (p. 154). While Black bodies may have the availability to claim Canadian citizenship, we know that they are not treated the same under the legal system (regardless of the legal arena). In this way, belonging is not only determined by one's claim to the collective, they must also be considered as part of the national imaginary. We can track a history of Black displacement and disenfranchisement within the nation.

These experiences can range from the banal to more significant practices. It is not uncommon in Toronto to hear people asking others "where are you from?". Given the colonial idea that Canada is a nation of [past] immigrants (read White bodies), and the ways the word "migrant" serves as proxy for person of color, it is no mistake that when racialized people respond "Toronto," "Vancouver," or "Hamilton," the subsequent response is often, "No, where are you really from?", or in less overt instances, "Where are your parents from?", or the more pointed: "What is your 'ethnic' heritage?" While this may be considered a facet of innocent curiosity, the fact of the matter is that when White people are asked where they are from and they provide a one word response: "Toronto," "Vancouver," "Hamilton," they do not receive subsequent inquiries. These experiences tell us about the national imaginary. That is, they reify who is believed to inhabit and belong to a space, who makes up the nation, and who can legitimately be questioned regarding their presence. These experiences serve as constant reminders of non-belonging.

The stripping or denial of citizenship from Black bodies is thus a historical constant even through state policies such as multiculturalism, and it carries material consequences—particularly when accompanied by police officers, judges, and politicians who can have a greater impact on the lives of said individuals. For instance, the practice of carding has become prominent in Toronto and it is no surprise that the people most often carded in the city are Black and Brown (Rankin 2014).

As Brubaker (1990) argues, "debates about citizenship, in the age of the nation-state, are debates about nationhood—what it means, and what it ought to mean, to belong to a nation-state" (p. 380). The debates regarding citizenship can thus have discursive and material effects. Black people have historically been refused citizenship in Canada. We can trace this to the presence of slavery, the razing of Africville, the idea that "tropical" people would not be able to live in Canada as a reason to refuse migration to racialized people, to the current context where Black bodies are routinely carded in Toronto, removed from educational spaces, and refused housing opportunities. To be Black in Canada means being considered a foreigner, a threat, and a criminal. One need only remember Ben Johnson and how quickly coverage about him turned from describing him as a Canadian hero to a Jamaican cheater. A more recent example occurred in 2012 when, after a shooting at a neighborhood barbeque on Danzig Street in Scarborough, then Toronto Mayor Rob Ford quickly made comments posturing to be tough on crime (Dale 2012). After walking through the area, he quickly remarked that he would speak to the Prime Minister as well as then Minister of Citizenship and Immigration Jason Kenney regarding the possibility of deporting the suspected shooters. Within this discourse, it is clear that the bodies living on Danzig Street are automatically relegated to the periphery of Canadianness, that is, they become perpetual migrants whose belonging to the nation is up for interpretation. In trying to clarify his comments, Ford admitted on a radio talk show that he had no knowledge of the alleged shooters' immigration status (precarious immigration status would have brought about the possibility of deportation under immigration law) (Alcoba 2012). Ford's Whiteness also cannot escape us, as he normalized his presence within this Land, he also reified the foreignness and precarious belonging of Black bodies. As such, without previous knowledge or proof, one can see how easily the residents of Danzig Street were stripped of citizenship. In this way, regardless of claims of access to colonial goods,

Black people remain colonial subjects whose membership is based on the ways dominant bodies read them.

Perhaps the starkest case that shows the removal of membership is happening across the U.S., where a prominent slogan has arisen as a result of police violence on Black people: Black Lives Matter. If we go back to Brubaker's (1990) quote regarding citizenship and "what it means and what it ought to mean, to belong to a nation-state," we see that Black bodies and Black lives are under a constant devaluation that do not speak to a state of differential membership as much as to an outright denial and constant dehumanization. After all, what does it mean when a slogan that resonates with so many is based on the most simple of ideas, that is, that Black lives matter? Sadly though, the prevalence of liberalizing discourses subsume the urgency and importance of the slogan "Black lives matter" being rebutted with "All lives Matter". This takes away from the understanding of the constant surveillance and disposal of Black lives under the guise of liberal, equality, and ideas of racelessness which is pivotal in anti-Black racism.

Within the Canadian context, while overt acts of police brutality have remained outside of the mass media's purview, one need only do a cursory search on police shooting and Black people to find the names of victims gunned down in places like Toronto, Vancouver, and Montreal. Hidden beneath the veneer of a "kinder" and "gentler" space, we find that race affects the daily life of Black and African peoples and the differential space they occupy within Canadian society. Violence against Black bodies completely challenges the notion of Canada's domestic values of multiculturalism and disrupts Canada's international peacekeeping national identity.

The politics of racial profiling in North America has become synonymous with Black, Indigenous, and other racialized bodies. It speaks about citizenship for these bodies in the nation state. One can grudgingly claim that there is some sort of epistemic community around racial profiling and police carding at least in Toronto. Much credit goes to community activism (e.g., Black Lives Matter movement), segments of the local news media (Toronto Star), and the many local community protests before that. There is still, however, an absence of largely organized citizenry or citizenship organizations for anti-racial profiling and other political protests. We still have to contend with the problem of the preoccupation of the dominant with the "Other", a sort of deeply ingrained primitive "Othering." For Black bodies we have no choice but to ask: what is the merit or value of Police stops? After all, police stops are about power and hierarchical relations of law and order. To my knowledge is no reliable data on the relationship between police stops and "successful hits" [i.e., making effective arrests for genuine offences]?

Race and gender are key variables determining police stops, and this is where Black bodies are at the receiving end of racial profiling. This is compounded by the fact that there is a long standing problem of police legitimacy within racialized, Indigenous, and Black communities. Yet, when we discuss police, policing, and Black communities the big elephant in the room that many dominant bodies feel uncomfortable in speaking to is the "culture of policing" and a hierarchical system that wants to be allowed to police itself and/or to reform itself. To Black bodies in particular the difficulty of, and resistance to reforming police culture is deafening. So, we continually ask how do we justify, validate, and legitimize police officers themselves studying racial profiling, carding, etc.? The merit of this question lies is in the fact of police resistance to internal scrutiny and accountability of their actions. Therefore, when community activists advocate policy changes in policing we must be aware of the limitations of such advocacy in the context of police culture and the possible consequences of any policy changes. To many in our racialized, Indigenous and, particularly, Black communities police work is not to "serve and protect." It is contended that the police are not there to fight crime in our neighborhoods, but rather, the police have become a force of surveillance on particular bodies and to look for Black transgressions. So, we must be understood for calling out the hypocritical idea that police are crime fighters (i.e., security and safety concerns foremost).

Racial profiling gestures more profoundly to the coloniality of race (i.e., how bodies are read differently—race as privilege for some and as punishment for others) and the extent to which that fact of Black disposability must register profoundly into discussions of racial profiling. In a context where the more stops a police officer makes can mean an advancement of his or her career, the incentive to make more stops of Black bodies is attractive [even if these arrests for the most part do not lead to "hits"]. The belief that the more stops an officer makes the likelihood of hits is more of a "cost–benefit analysis." Black bodies randomly stopped for searches raise no public outcry or condemnation. The situation would be different if it was White/dominant bodies being stopped most frequently. So police officers may take chances to make stops on Black bodies with the perceived likelihood of hits/making arrests because if the evidence turns out to be to the contrary there is no cost (i.e. punishment) to the officer. There is the certainty of punishment in the discourse on police profiling because particular bodies like Black bodies are being continually punished.

When thinking about the history of slavery within North America, the ways that the prison industrial complex operates in both spaces to fragment Black families, and the structural violence experienced by Black bodies at the hands of different state institutions as well as local labor markets, one can see that Blackness has and continues to be identified as antithetical to the nation and the ways in which the state, through violent methods, works to maintain this differential understanding of the value of life. While some may have materially benefited from their allegiance to the nation, it is clear that by-and-large, Black bodies remain peripheral members of North American society given the saliency of race and its effects on daily life. Thus, remarks linking Black people to "settlerhood" are not only a dissonant construct, but also dishonest when history is considered.

And a final note. While the availability of citizenship as formal status can be seen as allegiance to the nation, we must remember that in the current state of affairs, citizenship can mean protection from the state. Given the xenophobic context under which we live and the numerous deportation raids across the nation [What Donald Trump is doing in the United States is nothing new], individuals may see naturalization as a means to resist violence rather than complicity in its perpetuation. After all, Black and Indigenous solidarity remains one of the most criminalized aspects of today's society, and having citizenship may in some cases protect individuals from some of the more punitive responses the state has to offer: removal from nation-state and possible fragmentation of families and communities.

References

Alcoba, N. (2012, July 20). Rob Ford stumbles while 'clarifying' confusing immigration statements in wake of Scarborough shooting. *National Post*. Retrieved from http://news.national-post.com/posted-toronto/rob-ford-stumbles-while-clarifying-confusing-immigration-statements-in-wake-of-scarborough-shooting

Asante, M. K. (2005). Blackness as an ethical trope: Toward a post-Western assertion. In G. Y. (Ed.), *White on white/black on black* (pp. 203–216). Oxford: Rowman and Littlefield.

Bhabha, H. (1994). *The location of culture*. London: Routledge.

Bloemraad, I., et al. (2008). Citizenship and immigration: Multiculturalism, assimilation, and challenges to the nation-state. *Annual Review of Sociology, 34*, 153–179.

Brubaker, W.R. (1990). *Citizenship and nationhood in France and Germany*. Unpublished doctoral dissertation thesis, Columbia University, New York.

Cesaire, A. (1972). *Discourse on colonialism*. New York: Monthly Review Press.

Chatterjee, P. (1986). *Nationalist thought and the colonial world: A derivative discourse*. London: Zed Books.

Collins, P. H. (1990). *Black feminist thought: Knowledge, consciousness, and the politics of empowerment* (1st ed.). London: Unwin Hyman.

Dale, D. (2012, July 18). Toronto shooting: Mayor Rob Ford says gang members should leave the city. *Toronto Star*. Retrieved from https://www.thestar.com/news/city_hall/2012/07/18/toronto_shooting_mayor_rob_ford_says_gang_members_should_leave_the_city.html

Dei, G. J. S. (1996). *Anti-racism education: Theory and practice*. Halifax: Fernwood.

Dreyfus, H., & Rabinow, P. (1982). *Michel Foucault: Beyond structuralism and hermeneutics*. Chicago: University of Chicago Press.

Escobar, A. (1995). *Encountering development: The making and unmaking of the third world*. Ewing, NJ: Princeton University Press.

Foucault, M. (1972). *The archaeology of knowledge*. New York: Pantheon Books.

Foucault, M. (1975). *The history of sexuality: Vol. 1. An introduction*. London: Allen Lane.

Foucault, M. (1978). *The history of sexuality: Vol. 1. An introduction*. London: Allen Lane.

Foucault, M. (1980). Two lectures. In C. Gordon (Ed.), *Power/knowledge: Selected interviews & other writings*. New York: Pantheon Books.

Foucault, M. (1997). In M. Bertani, A. Fontana, & F. Ewald (Eds.), *Society must be defended: Lectures at the Collège de France, 1975–76 (1st)*. New York, Picador.

Gill, J.K. (2012). *Minding the gap: Understanding the experiences of racialized/minoritized bodies in special education*. Unpublished doctoral dissertation thesis, University of Toronto, Toronto, ON.

Harvey, D. (2007). *A brief history of neoliberalism*. Oxford: Oxford University Press.

Mbembe, A. (2001). *On the postcolony*. Berkeley: University of California Press.

Mbembe, A. (2003). Necropolitics. *Public Culture, 15*(1), 11–40.

Rankin, J. (2014, July 28). Police 'carding' is down in Toronto but racial patterns persist: Editorial. *Toronto Star*. Retrieved from https://www.thestar.com/opinion/editorials/2014/07/28/police_carding_is_down_in_toronto_but_racial_patterns_persist_editorial.html

Razack, S. (2002). *Race, space, and the law: Unmapping a white settler society*. Toronto, Canada: Between the Lines.

Razack, S. (2008). *Casting out: The eviction of Muslims from Western law and politics*. Toronto: University of Toronto Press.

Suleri, S. (1992). Woman skin deep: Feminism and the postcolonial condition. *Critical Inquiry, 18*(4), 756–769.

Sunseri, L. (2000). Moving beyond the feminism versus nationalism dichotomy: An anti-colonial feminist perspective on Aboriginal liberation struggles. *Canadian Woman Studies, 20*(2), 143–148.

United Nations Development Program. *Sustainable development goals*. Retrieved from https://sustainabledevelopment.un.org/sdgs

Chapter 6
A Call to a New Dance: [Re]Claiming and Implicating African Diasporic Indigeneity Through the Prism of Indigeneity as an International Category

Abstract The theme of "Decolonization and Indigeneity as International Categories" is explored in the chapter. The goal is to forge a new intellectual dance and political praxis. It is argued that taking "Indigeneity as an international category" allows us to see how Black bodies, enslaved/uprooted Black bodies and all whose Lands have been occupied by colonialism in a range of places, can draw upon and build solidarities with other colonized and oppressed populations. Before the ascendancy of Europe, there was a world that consisted of Europe itself and other communities. The prism of decolonization and Indigeneity allows us to understand the complexity of the African experience. A critical understanding and scaling up of decolonization and Indigeneity as an international category is very necessary, ethical, and responsible. It is duly noted that the Black/African experience [as attested to by presence on Turtle Island] is politically implicated in the project of capitalism/globalization not unlike (nor separate from) the settler colonial project. I think it is helpful to understand the project of capitalism and globalization better. I suggest we begin asking questions regarding our contemporary place in relation to its power and privileges that it offers, as well as the broader economic North–South relations. Yet, reducing contemporary political implications of Blackness in regards to capitalism/globalization to the colonial power and privileged experiences of settler, perpetuates procedures of violence and social injustice upon African peoples. The whole colonial project of "International Development" and the plight of the African and her presence on a colonially appropriated space is interrogated to bring home the violence of colonialism and our multiple implications.

This chapter makes a case for taking Indigeneity as an international category. When we do so we see how Black and African bodies, whose Lands have been occupied through processes of colonization in a range of places, can draw upon and build solidarities with other Indigenous populations. We do not lose our Indigeneity and Indigenousness simply through a [forced] separation from Africa. Our Indigenousness lives in cultural, spiritual and psychic memories, as well as in our bodies. Furthermore, before the ascendancy of Europe there was a world that

© Springer International Publishing AG 2017

135

G.J.S. Dei, *Reframing Blackness and Black Solidarities through Anti-colonial and Decolonial Prisms*, Critical Studies of Education 4,
DOI 10.1007/978-3-319-53079-6_6

consisted of Europe itself and other communities. The violent colonial conquest of Europe ensured that Europeans would falsely assume some superiority in the world. Yet even this false ascendancy was not without resistance. We must therefore maintain steadfast to the idea that European colonization is NOT the entry point of human history. In taking Indigeneity as an international category I also situate the African human condition within the broad parameters of global concerns, insisting on a reclamation of African cultural knowledge as learning sites and sources. Africa is also read beyond its physical boundaries into a broader social space that allows the articulation of Blackness/Africanness to connect challenges of Africa today with Black Diasporans. This latter point is significant since it is from such reading that one justifies looking at the Black and African presence in Canada.

How do we proceed on this intellectual and political task? For my part, I insist on claiming the African presence wherever I find myself and/or identify with. I refuse to conscript this African experience in the colonial history of Europe. There are academic engagements that deny this African presence in ways that interpret the African existence within European terms and the annals of European colonial history. This practice takes place in many forms. In the current project of reframing Blackness from decolonial and anti-colonial prisms, I ask that we should NOT read the African encounter strictly along the lines of the White colonial-settler history (or, as well put by some scholars of Blackness, HIS-STORY). Africa today is itself an occupied space. The encroachment of Euro ideology and hegemonic practices on Africa has intensified the African presence outside the continent itself. Africa must be theorized beyond fixed boundaries as Africa has expanded into other Lands. The issues cut across scales, space, and time and there are similarities and parallels when we come to understand African experiences in global contexts that precede the colonial encounter, the on-going aftermath of formal European colonization, and its contemporary neoliberal expressions. This development has implications for asking such questions as how do we unpack who and what is currently included/excluded in conversations on Blackness in Canadian contexts?

In fact, the link of decolonization and Indigeneity allows us to understand the complexity of the Black and African experience. A critical understanding and scaling up of decolonization and Indigeneity as an international category to my mind seems necessary, ethical, and responsible. As argued elsewhere (Dei 2016) Indigenousness is about relations to Land, place and space; whereas Indigeneity is about process, identity, resistance, and the absence of colonial imposition. Indigeneity is a consciousness of Land and one's existence (i.e., original occupancy) on the Land and the teachings of this Land. There is contestation in regards to "Indigenous" since there is not a singular notion of "Indigenous." This is true for "Indigeneity" also, which does not have a single shared conceptualization. Neither "Indigenous" nor "Indigeneity" are fixed categories or concepts; they are always changing. This seems to me as it should be. I invite us to use "Indigenous" broadly so that it encompasses but does not erase difference or the knowledge systems unique to different Indigenous Peoples, all over the world. I assert a crucial point regarding "Indigenous" to ground this politics of the current project. "Indigenous" is a project of decolonization and all projects of decolonization require claims of

"Indigeneity." As colonized peoples, Black and African peoples and their communities can lay claim to an Indigeneity through an embrace of Indigenous philosophies and epistemologies. Claims of African Indigeneity are about new "relationships" and new "subjectivities" (e.g., "Indigene," "non-Indigenous subjects," "colonial settlers," "racialized immigrants," etc.) and new meanings and interpretations for practical and political purposes. Such relationships and subjectivities are all necessary for projects of decolonization (see also Dei 2016). In effect, there is no grand narrative or meta-narrative about Indigeneity; there are many. Difference, must be reiterated as our strength. Our difference is valued and is supported by Indigenous and Indigeneity.

Smith's (2010) exposition on the three logics of White supremacy: genocide, slavery and orientalism, is very informative here. On our colonized Lands the three logics infuse social and political forces and are unrelenting in their tenacious incapacitation and killing of Black and African peoples and our shared experiences. On-going colonizations have resulted in the violent dispossession of Lands and Indigenous properties (diamonds, water, bodies, knowledge, medicines and more), and through this, enhanced the colonial wealth. The wealth I speak of refers not simply to wealth in the capitalist sense. More importantly, it is the cultural wealth of Indigenous peoples referencing our cultural knowledges and histories, local capacity and resourcefulness for celebrating our lives and for psycho-cultural healing, the health of our bodies and Lands and the sea. It also includes the wealth of our identities, creativity and heritage, and Africa's sense of membership in the human community. The effects of colonization have been thorough and extreme and colonization continues to succeed in the project of making Whiteness supreme. This compels us, through Indigenous and Indigeneity, to engage in an international and global struggle with and for all Indigenous peoples—to reclaim our cultures, heritage, history, Lands, health, natural world and our physical properties. Capitalism is masked as globalization modernity and it is intentional. The purpose is to keep Indigenous peoples disparate, disorganized and breathless in the pursuit of wealth and the promise of wellbeing so that they forget their collective struggles and histories. Globalization is scaled up colonialism and it is well fuelled by neoliberal discourse, practices and promises of prosperity. Its greatest power, however, lay in its success in convincing all persons, particularly those in the south, that they have no choice but to join the globalization project or to make space for it because there is no other alternative. Capitalism-based globalization has been extremely persuasive and because of its totalizing narrative, resistance appears inconceivable. This is not so, however. We know from our Indigenous knowledges that there are other types of wealth and economies. We need not submit to the one demanded of us which will surely destroy us. This expression of globalization, in my view, is another form of colonialism. I know am not alone in such thinking.

I recognize that the Black/African experience is politically implicated in the project of capitalism/globalization not unlike (nor separate from) the settler colonial project. I think it is helpful to understand this project of capitalism/globalization better and suggest we begin by asking questions regarding our contemporary place in relation to the power and privileges that it offers, and broader economic North–

South relations. Yet, I see reducing contemporary political implications of Blackness in regards to capitalism/globalization to the colonial power and privileged experiences of settler, perpetuates procedures of violence and social injustice upon African peoples.

Such an anti-colonial stance requires that we resurrect our Indigenous knowledges and philosophies in order to reclaim our Indigeneity. To this end, I do not see the pursuit of critical Indigenous nationalism and decolonization as contradictory. I agree with Smith's (2010) point that decolonized nationhood is very dependent on state and/or capitalist economic systems. To this end decolonized education is about interrogating the nation state and the existing economic order, in order to create new alternative economies and systems within the state that have the responsible aim of creating more just, equitable and fair societies. Decolonized education (education as broadly defined) is more about decentering Whiteness and White supremacist logics and promoting the cultural, emotional, spiritual, material, political and physical empowerment of colonized/racialized/Indigenous communities to design their own futures and to author their own destinies.

This is a collective struggle among all Indigenous and colonized peoples that can only be thwarted and interrupted by pitting oppressed groups against each other. Colonialism and capitalism, subsumed under neoliberalism, are twin pillars and always work through the colonial logic of White (European) supremacy. Colonialism came with genocide and enslavement of peoples. Genocide and enslavement are possible and rational when one operates through a racist mindset that maliciously romanticizes superiority and the assignment of others to locations of sub-humanity and animality. This racism justifies maltreatment, the dispossession of Lands and resources, exclusion, deprivation and impoverishment.

These colonial forms of power that inform development are clearly visible in Western nations. A prime example is the legal and criminal justice system of Canada, which incarcerates Indigenous/Indigenous, Latin American and African youth in mass numbers. The school system also does its bid by punishing and pushing out these youth, and mis-educating African and Indigenous learners outside of their culture, identity and histories. It is these colonial, structural, and physical violence that decolonized education must speak to and find ways to mobilize against.

In Dei (2015), I point out that we cannot diminish the severity of colonial and imperial oppressions everywhere and that we must understand that colonized bodies migrate and come to occupy stolen Lands. Colonial and imperial oppressions are embodied and they migrate when bodies do. Some oppressions consequently are hidden and/or difficult to see and reach. The colonial encounter was painful and violent. It has left huge scars on colonized peoples everywhere. Colonized communities have been dispersed in part because of the experiences of European colonization and in part because of it [as noted] is scaled up form in the capitalist neoliberal global agenda. This different expression of the colonial operates along the three pillars of White supremacy outlined by Smith, although somewhat differently. This, is a discussion that must be taken seriously another day. In colonized peoples' own Lands they call home, previously colonized peoples can and do become part of oppressive relations, although this alone does not qualify them as colonizers. This is similar to the situation that Africans find themselves in on Indigenous soil in North America, and precisely Turtle Island, or what is called Canada. As argued earlier in the previous chapter, for Blacks and African peoples our own experiences of colonization and our continuing struggles for recognition, acceptance and validation in new homes and in our first home challenges any assertion that we are settlers and complicit in European colonization. Although I have already made this clear and it has been thoroughly argued, I add a few very important points regarding the complex issues colonized, racialized and Indigenous especially from Africa groups continue to face.

6.1 Understanding the Black/African-Canadian Presence

As noted I refuse the African experience to be collapsed into White-colonial settler discourse by accepting the "complicity" language. I agree we are implicated and I also make clear that we and other racialized and colonized peoples experience particular and unique challenges. These challenges also problematize the complicity language. The colonial logic of domination is shared by the colonial settler nation. The prime objective in both cases is to subject every non-European race into colonial submission. We cannot do a dance on the turf of the White colonial settler. The colonial dynamics employed as resistance reveal unique and different strategies given our contexts and colonial relations. To define the anti-colonial discourse within the parameters of the White settler constrains the terms and boundaries of the discourse. Such an approach will define what gets in for critical discussion and what is left out. We must carve out an anti-racist and anti-colonial response to Euro-colonial domination that speaks to the uniqueness of our positions as colonial/Indigenous subjects with connected histories as colonized, Indigenous and racialized peoples.

The long history of African presence on Turtle Island has been documented (see Brathwaite and James 1996; Mensah 2010; Winks 1997; Hill 1981; Cooper 2006). African-descended communities within the United States, Latin America and the Caribbean, for example, would be considered part of the first major "migration" out of Africa. We learn through the history of the Early Descendants that as early as the seventeenth century, an African named Mathieu Da Costa was as an interpreter for the French explorer Samuel de Champlain in 1605. It is also a fact that the first known slave in Canada was a young man from Madagascar named Olivier le Jeune. Also, as Nketiah (2009) writes on the first wave of mass migration to Canada, "During the American Revolution of 1776, a significant number of Blacks, both slaves of White British Loyalists and newly freed Blacks, made their way up north, settling in small towns. For example, there were Black Loyalists who settled in Halifax, East Preston and various rural communities in Ontario and Manitoba. Lastly, a rebellious group of Blacks referred to as the Maroons were exiled from Jamaica in the late eighteenth century, also settling in Canadian townships." The second wave of migration is marked by the "Diaspora of post-Emancipation" (i.e. post-slavery), dating roughly around the late eighteenth century. During this time, many Black people attempting to escape slavery in the US sought refuge in Canada. Then in the final wave, the "Diaspora of the Neo-Colonial Period" have come to Canada, which includes those who immigrated mostly from the Caribbean and Africa after the Second World War in search of better socioeconomic and political conditions (Mensah 2010). Ironically, this is a search for better economic conditions after the political/cultural and environmental disasters that colonial powers continue to perpetuate on "developing countries".

I offer this brief historical accounting to point out that the African history of migration has been about struggles and resistance. Today, this group includes peoples forced out of their Lands through civil war, strife, the misery of globalization, climate change, and the continued encroachment of the colonial dominant on Indigenous Land. Black/African moves to other Lands such as Turtle Island have never been about Land conquest, annexation, or forced settlement and occupation. To say it more clearly, Black migration has never been to steal Land and resources from other Indigenous Peoples, nor to participate in their oppression.

Demonstrating this point in the contemporary moment, the escalation and standardization of immigration policies in the UN and Canada are further centralizing colonial power and regulating African bodies, while also rendering such bodies more exploitable and disposable. The stakes of both authorized and unauthorized immigration become higher—feeding into the state of security that now dominates many aspects of UN governance and serves as the primary focus of Western nations (Duffield 2006; Goldberg 2009). The UN and Western nations increasingly claim further control over potential migrants from the Global South—whether they remain in their home countries due to draconian immigration laws, or endure asymmetrical rights and other forms of state and social violence as immigrants. Through these restrictions, the state also monopolizes power over subjects' extra-legal actions. Border patrol and other forms of national security have bloomed into major businesses for the state and private industry in northern nations (Goldberg 2009). Growing bureaucracies of the UN and Western states specially designed to prevent, reduce, and discipline unauthorized immigration are inextricably linked with privatized security, incarceration, and military apparatuses (Duffield 2010; Jensen 2016). DeGenova (2002) claims that illegal status is designed not to physically exclude people, but to include them under protracted states of vulnerability. Whether sending remittances home, paying numerous fees associated with immigration, working as de-skilled labor, or filling unauthorized employment positions and private prisons, racialized immigrants and their regulation remain an essential component of colonial rule under neo-liberalism.

Like all populations, Black peoples, and in particular African-Canadians, have unique yet shared challenges. Currently, there is a hegemonic threat to Africanism. There is some sense of belonging to a "new country," yet clearly it is not complete. Canadian prisons incarcerate Black and Indigenous males in huge disproportion to other communities. The Child Welfare system is targeting Black mothers and children. A disturbing number of our children are in care. There are pressing issues of rights and responsibilities differential access to health, education, jobs, and housing, as well as immigration and family unification challenges. These are all part of the ways in which the African-Canadian community feels under threat. Despite some successes that we can all be proud of, the Black/African community is continually faced with the production of youth alienation, crime and violence. The problems of African-Canadian youth's disengagement from school and "push outs" are the result of low teacher expectations, lack of curricular sophistication, absence of African teachers, and language and integration issues. Of course the conditioning of all of these through racism is well-documented (see Dei et al. 1997). There are mounting challenges in the face of the nihilism, the sense of hopelessness and despair, and the feeling of living a dead end existence among a number of our youth. There is the underutilization of African knowledge and expertise (e.g., the non-recognition of African education and credentials), which is a barrier to employment and to creating the conditions for a sense of our belonging. Our communities and neighborhoods are under-resourced and this is being amplified through capitalist neoliberal regimes of the Canadian government. The growing disintegration of the African family unit is marked by unemployment and immigration woes as well as unending family reunification troubles that create loneliness and the breakdown of relationships. The nation state creates an "us"/"them" dichotomy that continues to fuel and re-ignite the racism that colonialism long ago installed and continues to at larger and larger scales. Our communities are still struggling with how we build institutions and support structures that strengthen the Black/African family unit, with a focus on families, communities, males and youth, and Black role models and authority figures.

We must be at the forefront of redefining the sense of belonging. There are pressing issues of rights and responsibilities, access to health, education, jobs, housing, and immigration and family unification for most Black/Africans in a Diasporic context. Similarly, youth alienation, violence and incarceration are pressing threats to the survival of the Black community. I will reserve the broader question of Black education for a separate chapter, as I see this as a huge problem from my expertise as an educator, researcher and community worker.

There is a need to continuously clarify, challenge and define the type of global relations we want as an Indigenous collective living on Indigenous soil, and the relations that we seek with the Canadian nation state, the African continent, and the global African Diaspora. These prospects, opportunities, and challenges must be addressed with a specific understanding of decolonization, Indigeneity and global relations. We need to generate community-centric alternatives that resist materialistic/Eurocentric ideologies. We must imagine a new paradigm and begin to create it. In addition, we need to decolonize our minds and take responsibility for sometimes fostering divisions and exploitations rather than supporting one another as colonized peoples.

There is a methodological dilemma in conflating or reducing histories of African enslavement to a singular homogenous reading of migration patterns of European peoples. To do so is to displace African histories, which is a historical erasure of the African experience. We must ask, to what extent is this historical erasure of African enslavement a form of anti-Black racism? To what extent is this historical erasure of

African enslavement a form of epistemic violence? We must ask a lot of questions to find a new way and a new paradigm that values collective mobilization, responsibility and justice. And through this we have to always contend with the historical erasure of the Black/African experience, which we counter by encouraging African peoples to write through their embodied knowledges, their ancestral memories, and their slave narratives on the plantation and the colonizers ship; to tell our stories of Blackness and resistance from our lived perspectives. To read and theorize the narratives of enslaved African peoples such as Olaudah Equiano, Frederick Douglass, Harriet Jacobs, William Wells Brown, Fanon, Cesaire, and Wynters and to conclude that these human experiences culminate in the power and privileging of settler discourse, is in itself constitutive of epistemic, psychic and spiritual violence!

6.2   The Black Presence: Contemporary Challenges

I turn now to discuss some of contemporary challenges of the Black/African presence on Turtle Island. I do so not necessarily to create a uniqueness of the Black and African presence, but to allude to how certain challenges are shared amongst groups and to emphasize the importance of working in solidarities to resolve these problems. The Black/African community (or communities) is not island unto itself. But I also believe the community must raise its voice to put certain issues on the table not as a dismissal of the legitimacy of other groups' concerns nor as an attempt to delink from the state. I shun the politics of a community that simply raises its voices because it considers itself as the only reality worth talking about. I also disavow any divisive politics that fail to see how issues are interconnected and the fact that every community issue is our collective issue. Indigenous peoples fight for Land rights and sovereignty are legitimate concerns that affect everyone. These are all our issues and we must all be part of the collective struggle. Also requires that Indigenous peoples understand the struggles of racialized immigrant groups who have been placed in the wider geo-politics given the mechanisms and processes of colonialism, on-going colonizations, and the workings of global capital modernity. We must enter politics from where we are each located in terms of identity, history and culture. We must allow people to lead with their own voices and not appropriate struggles. Such an entry point allows one to grasp the politics of inclusivity, rather than a politics with a false claim of exceptionalism.

As a Black African immigrant to Turtle Island, there are many stories to share about our presence on this Land that speak to the magnanimity of Indigenous peoples on whose Land I have come to live and work. The fact that we are all Indigenous to the planet does not take away from the fact that the Land on which I currently live belongs to Indigenous peoples. The Land has become home as well as home away from home. I am still a stranger in ways that other immigrant groups who have come to reside on this Indigenous soil, even those who came through force, will not see themselves. With dominant they see their privilege as enough to discount any claims of being "occupiers."

I can recall many stories of how I am constantly been placed outside of this Land to hammer in the point that the place I call home cannot, in fact, be my home. Sometimes these contestations are subtle, and other times, not so subtle. On the employment front, most racialized immigrants searching for jobs when they arrive in Canada can identify with what I would call "the paradox of Catch 22," when one is often asked about Canadian experience. You get to wonder, how can anyone have that Canadian experience without first being employed in Canada?

Language has always been capital and not having the "Canadian accent" (whatever that is), has been a marker of discrimination of many Black African bodies who have come from "elsewhere." I have often told the story of my coming to Canada in 1979 and enrolling at the University of Toronto for my PhD studies in the early 1980s. I can never forget the notice board at the cafeteria of the Robarts library of the University of Toronto. There was an advert for international students to enroll in "speech language classes guaranteed to change our accents" for a fee of $20! I remember also having to wake up in the early hours of some mornings as an annual ritual to line up at the Immigration Office to renew my student visa. On more than one occasion, the Immigration staff checking our documents at the counter before you see a Visa Official would speak so loud to you, even standing right in front of him that you began to wonder if you lost your sense of hearing.

But one gets accustomed to these things with time. I recall my early years in Toronto and having difficulty coming to terms with the Canadian practice of placing Elders in the nursing homes and wondering how different this was to what occurs in my birthplace in Ghana. In Ghana, elders are always among the family in old age in order to share their knowledge and wisdom till they pass onto eternity. But with time I came to understand the situation in Canada such that I later placed my elderly mother in the nursing home until she recently passed away in July 2015.

There are many challenges that afflict the Black community. For example there is the question of citizenship as belonging, not necessarily dispossessing peoples of their Lands. Despite pretense to the contrary, we are constantly being told from many sides (not just the dominant), that Black peoples do not belong here. There is a hegemonic threat to Blackness and specifically Africanism. There is a sense of belonging in a new country on paper that does not extend to being fully accepted. These are all part of the ways in which the Black race in Canada can be cut off at the knees. There is the problem of under-utilization of local cultural knowledge and Black expertise. This can be seen in the non-recognition of African education and credentials, which constitutes a major barrier in accessing employment and developing a sense of belonging. Yet Black communities in Canada possess a wealth of local cultural resources and knowledge. What is frustrating is that this abundance of highly developed skills remains largely untapped for community building. We also encounter divisions in the community that can be traced to colonial histories of divide and conquer. The welfare state, as it currently stands, makes us both protective of our resources (defining the worthy vs. the unworthy), and gives the privileged a sense of entitlement to the resources. The situation feeds off an "us"/"them" binary that breeds racism.

Many of our young learners have still not become part of the knowledge economy of the twenty-first century. On employment, there are some basic facts to share. Isolating the African-born population, Laryea and Hayfron (2005) examine Canada's labor market performance (earnings and occupational attainments) and reveal: (a) The average annual earnings for African men ($30,828.7) was lower than average annual earnings for Canadian-born men ($33,119.5), (b) Average annual earnings for African women ($25,274.8) was greater than average annual earnings for Canadian-born women ($24,471.1), (c) Without separating average annual earnings by gender, average annual earnings for Canadian-born citizens ($29,461.3) was slightly greater than average annual income for African immigrants ($28,750.5), (d) African immigrant women with any level of education (except those with post-secondary education) were likely to have lower annual earnings than their Canadian-born counterparts, (e) African immigrant women with post-secondary education were likely to have higher annual earnings (0.9%) than Canadian-born women with post-secondary education, (f) African immigrant men with a Ph.D. were 61% less likely and those with an M.A. degree were 71% less likely to be employed in a high skill occupation compared to their Canadian-born counterparts, and (g) African immigrant women with a Ph.D. were 85% less likely and African immigrant women with an M.A. degree were 37% less likely to be employed in a high skill occupation compared to their Canadian-born counterparts. These statistics show how African-born Canadian residents face not only wage discrimination, but also de-skilling and occupational segregation at alarming rates. The impact on African-Canadian communities is huge, not only in terms of material inequalities, but also in the ability of African-Canadians to lead within their communities and within Canada.

6.3   Going Forward: Black Solidarities and Empowerment

In going forward, the affirmation of Black identities for political and intellectual purposes must be backed by concrete action. First there is a need for developing a strong, vocal Black leadership to find answers to these questions: Who speaks for us and how? How are we understood in the larger realm of Canadian public policy and discourse? How does the media engage our communities and our issues? How is Black Africa and the African Diaspora registered in the Canadian public consciousness? How do we tap the available skills and resources that such communities bring to the Canadian context? We need an intellectual and social leadership to help us utilize the wide expertise and knowledge of our local communities to both understand our challenges and problems, and to develop unique and effective African solutions to them.

Such leadership is vital in helping build and develop local capacities to articulate our own issues, undertake our own research, and offer genuine home-grown solutions to our problems. There is a strong need for political involvement that seeks political representation in various levels of government. We also must intensify political advocacy to ensure the acceptance of our foreign educational backgrounds and professional credentials.

Building strong, healthy, sustainable and vibrant local Black communities is critical. Black people contribute to the valued goods and services of society, and we must have access to the goods and services of wider society. I do not interpret this as being complicit in the colonizing projects of the colonial settler state, let alone the nation state. It is a fact that we contribute to enrich this society, and we must benefit from our sacrifices. There are no two ways about that. To be a responsible community we must have access to available resources. Questions of access to housing, good health, education, immigration and integration of families must be addressed. Rising unemployment among any population stands in the way of building strong, healthy communities.

The search for Black solidarities is about building communities that are not necessarily reliant on the nation state. We do create communities, and these are "communities of differences." Our communities are about differences and sameness because shared experiences are never singular. The nation state often homogenizes "communities." But the community is also a site and place of learning and healing. Colonial violence and on-going colonial injustice have wreaked havoc on colonized populations. We must all come together and recognize that although our histories are different, they are intertwined. It serves no purposes other than those of the dominant to continue a unilateral fragmentation around difference. We witness how the dominant often conscripts the idea of a fractured community in order to deny responsibility and accountability. It is important to connect political struggles while not subsuming our differences.

We must also address the perceived tensions between the "individual" and "community." The individual needs a community and vice versa. But the African worldview makes the important necessary distinction between a competitive individual and a cooperative individual. We must reward a cooperative individual mindset that works towards the community wellbeing.

There is the perennial question of Black unity as a means to an end, i.e., Black power. Radical Black politics are often shunned for misguided fear of what Black power means. This is not about terrorism. It is about Black peoples having the power to think through solutions to problems afflicting our communities, to be able to design our own futures, and to take responsibility to uplift our communities. Black power is not about revenge, racism, White hatred, etc.; it is about community empowerment. This is where the Black middle class comes into focus, whose role and responsibility is to invest in our families and communities. It is also about the Black intelligentsia owning up to our responsibilities to take up courses in the interests of our communities, not to study our communities form a distance, to offer solutions for the internalized racisms and colonialisms that still afflict these communities, to be distinctive voices of difference, to courageously speak about race, sexism, homophobia and the other forms of social oppression from which we are all not immune (see Dei 2014). We must connect the Black Diasporas in general and we must begin to relearn and earn each other's trust.

We must also be resurrecting our African culture/s and Black identity/ies. These lessons of the past, present and future must help us reinvent our Africanness in a Diasporic context, for example, teaching about African traditional values of family, community, ethical and social responsibility, and respect for the Elderly—values our children have lost. We must be teaching our youth not to forget who they are as Black/African peoples and the sacrifices that brought us here. We must be teaching ourselves and our children not to forget our Africanness.

We must be creating self-employment opportunities, including education and retraining of skills that can help lead to employment. Generating self-employment opportunities not only releases a heavy dependence on the state, it also ensures that we build strong sustainable communities and families that support Black lives. The Black community must network as a resource sharing unit that uses the privilege of history as a service to wider community causes. Throughout our communities, we have examples of individuals starting our own businesses. To have a strong Black community, such individual initiatives require larger community support including patronage of these businesses.

There are also other ways of becoming economically self-sufficient as a community. For example, documenting the Black/African-Canadian achievements in history; and a rewriting of the Canadian participation in the Underground Railroad presents the history of Black peoples and their stories from their own perspectives. Such re-writing of history is also about group empowerment and telling from our own stories and lives. Blacks and African-Canadians in London, Ontario can work with other cities and towns to explore Canada's participation in the Underground Railroad and the achievements of African-Canadians to date. This has the potential of generating jobs and businesses for researchers, historians, artists, anthropologists, photographers and for those that see the potential in developing educational tour programs. This could help our cultures alive and also to flourish our humanness. Such re-writings can trace old families with rich histories who have all but disappeared into the landscape and capture the histories and achievements of "newer" generations of Black peoples/African-Canadians who are creating history in the present time. This work is crucial data that must not be lost for future generations.

Global citizenship needs a focus from the community—we need to rethink the global and claim any redemptive qualities it has. Moving forward, we need to focus less on the question: At what point does one move from immigrant to Canadian, and instead work to value our "global citizenship." We must begin to honor skills and consider experience gleaned from other places of origin as relevant to the varied nature of our realities and the composition of the population.

As we work to define the type of global relations we want both as a collective in Canada and in the relations of the African continent with Canada, this definition must be addressed within a specific understanding of this global relation. Alignment in a strategic global economic presence is important. Given our numbers in the

Diaspora, can we facilitate alliances (e.g., technological, economic, institutional) that allow us to serve current needs on the continent and also enable us to build our capacity over time here in Canada? How can we shape on-going social and technological transfers to ensure they are more culturally relevant and beneficial for the critical mass of Black African and Indigenous peoples (born and unborn)? How do we ensure any new emerging global relations do not perpetuate structures that suppress us and future generations of Black/African peoples?

6.4 Conclusion

I conclude with more questions: How do we move forward? How do we envision a collective resolution without illusion? Why should "we" move forward? I emphasize "we" as a collective vision and a global effort! The future of the human world has a lot to do with the prospect of a Black nation. Black peoples are an integral part of the global future. We have been told our success closely hinges on global development. To the same extent, our future is also the global future. Being able to overcome centuries-long extreme oppression and exploitation through our resilience and resistance, it is time for us to reclaim the leadership role of human civilization. "Moving forward" is therefore a global vision; we have to take leadership. We must work to shape the future of the world, and we should do our best, both locally and globally, to define the collective resolution for our future.

But how? To move forward, we need to get beyond a few common illusions. Beyond the temptation of "moving on"—lest not forget out past! Moving forward is about making progress; however, making progress does not mean we have to move on with our past and our identity.

History has to be told and those who forget our common history are destined to fail. As Confucius reminded the Chinese, "study the past if you would define the future." Beyond the success of only a few, we must move forward with no one left behind! Moving forward is a collective vision—a future that we not only dare to dream together, we work together, and more importantly, we will share the outcome together. Moving forward is not about getting the elite, the rich and the leaders to the top of the world, while leaving the people, the poor and the underprivileged behind. No one should be left behind.

For more fortunate people who are able to attain a good education, great jobs and admirable positions, do not forget to "give-back" to the community—beyond the optical illusion! We must not be seduced by the sensation of moving forward while everything remains standing still!

In Canada, like the school system in which I have personally been wholeheartedly engaged, there seems to be new policies and programs designed to address historical and current socio-economic disparity our people are subjugated to. And yet, report after report reminds us that things have not changed a bit. African Canadians are still suffering from racial profiling in policing, suspension and expulsion in schools, chronic unemployment, and extreme poverty. Let us not be misguided by those elusive political discourses, and make sure any ideas of moving forward will bring tangible results.

We must move beyond the myth of "one world, one dream"! While striving for a better future of our continent, our people and the world, we have to ask whose dream it is and in whose interests! Moving forward is a collective resolution, a call for collective efforts, a reminder of collective responsibilities. Globally, we have to insert ourselves in every platform and every forum to make sure Black/African heritage and wisdom will be there, and to rectify biases and barriers that have been silencing us. Locally, we have to make space for our women, our youth and the poor and less educated to have their voice heard. More fundamentally, moving forward involves an on-going double consciousness of who we are as Black peoples, and who we are as global citizens. As much as we love to be equal global citizens, we also have to ask why we have to dress like others, think like others, and operate our businesses and professions like those we are not. Our African heritage has as much to contribute to the world as what the world offers to us!

We need to create an environment that facilitates growth by moving from dependence on government aid to a place of self-governance and progress. We need to empower ourselves not only mentally, but also spiritually—we need to use all aspects of our "humanness." We have to work away from the materialistic/Eurocentric ideology to a more communal paradigm. We need to decolonize our minds. Black peoples are too divided! We have to see the Ghanaian, Jamaican, Haitian, Congolese, Egyptian or South African struggle as "our collective struggle." We need to take accountability and implicate ourselves in maintaining these divisions, not supporting one another and exploiting each other. We need to acknowledge, respect and empower each other to collectively actualize hopes, dreams and futures.

References

Brathwaite, K., & James, C. (Eds.). (1996). *Educating African Canadians*. Toronto, Canada: James Lorimer.

Brown, W. (2003). Neoliberalism and the end of liberal democracy. *Theory and Event, 7*(11), 38–59.

Brown, W. (2015). *Undoing the demos: Neoliberalism's stealth revolution*. Zone Books, New York.

Cooper, A. (2006). *The hanging of Angelique: The untold story of Canadian slavery and the burning of Old Montreal*. Toronto: HarperCollins. Published in French in 2007 as La Pendaison.

DeGenova, N. (2002). Migrant "illegality" and deportability in everyday life. *Annual Review of Anthropology, 31*, 419–447.

Dei, G. J. S. (2014). The African scholar in the Western academy. *Journal of Black Studies, 45*(3), 167–179.

Dei, G. J. S. (2015). Race and anti-racist practice: The challenge of decolonization. In L. Drakeford (Ed.), *The race controversy in American education*. New York: Praeger.

Dei, G. J. S. (2016). Indigenous philosophies, counter epistemologies and anti-colonial education. In W. Lehman (Ed.), *Education and society* (pp. 190–206). London: Oxford University Press.

Dei, G., Mazzuca, J., McIsaac, E., & Zine, J. (1997). *Reconstructing dropout: A critical ethnography of the dynamics of Black students' disengagement from school*. Toronto: University of Toronto Press.

Duffield, M. (2006). Racism, migration and development: The foundations of planetary order. *Progress in Development Studies, 6*(1), 68–79. doi:10.1191/1464993406ps128oa.

Duffield, M. (2010). The liberal way of development and the development-security impasse: Exploring the global life-chance divide. *Security Dialogue, 41*(1), 53–76. doi:10.1177/0967010609357042.

Goldberg, D. (1993). *Racist culture: Philosophy and the politics of meaning*. Malden: Blackwell.

Goldberg, D. (2009). *The threat of race: Reflections on racial neoliberalism*. Malden: Blackwell.

Hill, D. G. (1981). *The freedom seekers: Blacks in early Canada*. Agincourt, Ontario: Book Society of Canada.

Jensen, B. (2016). *UN Human Rights for Women: How race becomes an organizing principle*. Unpublished term paper. Department of Social Justice Education, Ontario Institute for Studies in Education of the University of Toronto, Toronto, Canada.

Laryea, S. A., & Heyfron, J. E. (2005). African immigrants & the labour market: Exploring career opportunities, earning differentials, & job satisfaction. In W. Tettey & K. Puplampu (Eds.), *The African diaspora in Canada: Negotiating identity and belonging* (pp. 94–113). Calgary: University of Calgary Press.

Mensah, J. (2010). *Black Canadians: Histories, experiences and condition*. Halifax: Fernwood.

Nketiah, R. (2009). KLM babies: First-generation Ghanaian-Canadian women and identity formation. Unpublished MA Thesis. Department of Sociology and Equity Studies, University of Toronto.

Smith, A. (2010). Indigeneity, settler colonialism, white supremacy. *Global Dialogue (Online), 12*(2), 1–13.

Winks, R. W. (1997). *The Black in Canadian: A history*. Montreal, Canada: McGill-Queen's University Press.

Additional Resources

Escobar, A. (1995). *Encountering development: The making and unmaking of the third world*. Ewing, NJ: Princeton University Press.

Foucault, M. (1972). *The archaeology of knowledge*. New York: Pantheon Books.

Foucault, M. (1978). *The history of sexuality: Vol. 1: An introduction*. London: Allen Lane.

Chapter 7
Counter-Visioning Black Education: Rhetorical Turns and Critical Discursive Shifts

Abstract This chapter looks at some rhetorical and critical discursive shifts in Canadian schooling and education as a way to counter-vision Black education. It insists on non-forgetiveness of the over-determining effects of schooling relations and experiences for different bodies. It also calls for the critical engagement on schooling experiences of learners NOT merely as "descriptive appendages to our theoretical formulations", but rather, as a clarion call for action. The discussion starts with a focus on the contemporary issues and challenges of schooling and education in the context of Ontario. The challenges of education impact disproportionately students who are Black, Indigenous and racially minoritized. In asking: what are the transformative possibilities of schooling and education today?, the chapter hopes to engage the critical reader to think and reflect on the possibilities of educational research. We stand to learn from practical strategies of radical inclusive schooling that engage learners cultures, histories, identities, and local cultural resource knowledge base. The pursuit of educational change also requires the collective interactions and involvements of teachers, students, administrators, parents, Elders, and local communities in order to create "communities of learners." We also need classroom, school, and off-school dialogues to be multiple conversations about privilege, power and oppression, validation of diverse experiences, histories, knowledges, and practices. Such dialogues could include an appreciation of the historical and cultural narratives of all peoples in our diverse communities. Critical dialogues could include breaking down labels that dominate systems and practices. Decolonizing education is changing the normal [conventional] ways we teach, learn, and administer education. Decolonizing education is by engaging colonialism, settler colonialism and colonizing relations in general. Decolonizing education is about promoting counter and oppositional voices, knowledges and histories, and bringing into focus the lived experiences of students who have traditionally been marginalized from the school system. By decolonizing education, looking critically at the structures and processes of education delivery (e.g., teaching, learning, and administration of education), we create inclusive schooling environments that would appeal to and engage the diverse group of learners.

In this chapter it is my goal to raise some unsettling questions, "slice open" the issue of Black education, and to begin "to imagine a world that is not yet imagined" for

Black educational futurity (Fine 1994, p. 30). That is, this section will begin to question the ways we have represented texts discussions of Black education as if these texts/dialogues are "constructed without [discursive/ethnographic] author[ity]" (Fine 1994, p. 16). How have we come to deny Black/African peoples "authorial subjectivities" through ventriloquism? That is to say, do those who speak on our behalf have no particular class, gender, racial, sexual and [dis]ability differences and interests? In fact, reading an earlier work of Michelle Fine (1994) helps me think through some pertinent questions: How, through education research, has violence been done to the "raw narratives" of Black/African subjects? Through our scholarship and research expertise on Africa and Black communities in general, do we simply reproduce existing knowledge rather than producing new and critical knowledge? In what ways have our academic scholarship and research helped to unseal particular social mythologies about Black and African peoples? As Black and African scholars, when we remain silent on some of these issues, how are we complicit in ceding terrain/territories? How can we demystify discourses about Black[ness], Africa and African peoples, and further trouble or complicate the "inevitable," "immutable," and "natural" (see also Fine 1994, p. 25)? How do we interrogate the particular stories we tell about Black lives, histories and experiences, the different ways these stories can be told and "how can we organize disruptively for what could be?" (see Fine 1994, p. 26).

In linking a discussion of Blackness with Black/African and minority youth education, I bring attention to the consequences and impact of education on Black and African diaspora bodies. Education has always been seen as a tool of self and collective empowerment, social liberation and mobility. But the fact is that, despite some successes, not all education has this liberatory potential. In fact, most forms of education have ended up disempowering our communities, creating a sense of youth alienation through the denial or negation of Black agency and Black intellectualism. The lack of genuine education or the "miseducation" of our young learners has contributed a loss sense of hope for bright futures. For Black bodies we cannot make light of the question: what do we mean by education and what are the goals and purposes of our education? Critical educators, including the late Roger Simon have seen education as the varied and complex ways, options and strategies options through which we [as individuals and groups] come to know, understand and interpret our worlds and to live and act responsibly within such worlds. Education does not happen solely in schools and the four-walled classrooms. Education is about everything we do—families, streets, communities, churches, workplaces, union halls, etc. There is a false separation of schooling, the local community, and the home. The link between education and social transformation is not always insisted upon. The social worth of education should not be measured by what and how many degrees or qualifications one has, but instead, by what we do with the education and learning we receive for ourselves, peers, families, communities, nation and global world and the Land on which we occupy. The inability to make this transition of education to a broader socio-political realm can lead to charges of learners simply going to school but not necessarily receiving education (see also Shujaa 1994).

There are some "fault lines" of contemporary education for Black and African bodies. Many would see problems and challenges of education in terms of questions of application and relevance, the existential realities of education. However, when education is approached this way we merely focus on the techno-fix dimensions of the education. For example, we become concerned with science and technology education, and education for employment discourses, etc. These are all good. But we need to shift the discussion to focus on what I am calling the "humanness of education"—i.e., bringing human-and social-centeredness to education— that is, how education can help reclaim our lost humanity and make us human [again]. Contemporary education has led to learner dislocations from our communities and a weak sense of understanding the idea of "community." There is something wrong when education today takes the learner away from her or his community, culture, history and language, and our ways of knowing/cultural perspectives. The trend contributes to a sense of education for community building (e.g., education that fails to resolve the daily challenges and problems of community building). Education as geared toward needs of markets, personal acquisitions rather than self and community development is very limiting. I include in such observations the exacerbation of divisions and tensions among our communities, rather than unifying us as a people. Also, education that makes us think more in hierarchies rather than circles is a problem. So is education that encourages arrogance and not humility, and fosters youth discipline rather than promoting respect for oneself, peers and Elders. Disenfranchised or misguided education has added to some Black/African youth feeling that "education sucks." There is a societal/ systemic failure to prepare youth and marginalized communities to take advantage of available opportunities. What does it really mean to say "It Takes a Village to Raise a Child"?—The village is not a given; we need to work hard to have/create the village in the first place!

Rather than education perceived as a mechanism for social advancement for all, there is also the untold story of how education can intensify social poverty and inequalities. Neoliberalism and its educational agenda have impacted our communities through rising tuition costs and privatization of education that have put education outside the reach of many bodies. Hence education is no longer a public good. Education is sold to the highest bidder. Education is driven to serve the needs of capital and the labor market, rather than being "people-centered." It is difficult to promote a sense of "become human again" amidst the corporatism, competition, and the rugged individualism. Contemporary education has failed to teach and promote critical global citizenship for the Black/African Diaspora. This is largely a failure to understand global citizenship as about individual and collective rights and responsibilities, as well as, power relations in a global citizenry. How do we ensure that all citizens are able to access the valued goods and services? We can only talk about "rights" if individuals and groups are equipped to the resources and knowledge to insist upon these rights! There is also the failure to define our communities broadly and as not bound by temporal or physical limits. (e.g., connecting Canada with parts of the world, Africa and the Diaspora) and to define our obligations to these myriad communities broadly. The failure to promote Black/African and minority education as primarily about transformation and designing new futures for our communities implicate the politics of Blackness we pursue as learners and scholars. Black education must be teaching and learning to subvert, transgress, and transform. Such education must be rooted in the African and Indigenous intellectual traditions of relationality, sharing, reciprocity, mutual interdependence, responsibility, and social accountability. This shift may require that Black [and Indigenous] peoples have control over their children's education to address the oppressive, colonial nature, and colonizing aspects of education. We need Black/African communities to build our local capacities, resources, skills, and knowledge of Indigeneity to enhance our youth learning by controlling Black education.

The critical conception of Blackness and Africanness is very useful for resistance in the direction of Black and African youth schooling and education. In picking up on Mbembé's (2003) idea of "necropolitics" we ask within our school systems, who is deemed worthy of living and/or being killed and who is deemed worthy of education? How do we re-imagine the evocation of the "new human" that disturbs the negation and creation of racial categories, erasure and performativity of racial identities for failure or punishment? What good is my scholarship as a Black/African intellectual in the general contexts of the Black struggles for social justice and equity? There are continuous issues of and struggles over Black disposability, the nation state's disregard of Black concerns, the persistent community anti-Blackness, and gregarious consumption of Blackness and Black identities. There is also the persistent surveillance, policing and punishment of racialized bodies for showing up in unwanted spaces (as constitutive of Black transgressions) (see Adjei 2013).

Many thoughts have been penned down on Black/African and minority education, specifically with the challenges, problems, and obstacles to youth education. I will focus specifically on sustaining a re-visioned Black/African education. In earlier conversations (see Dei 2008; and other works on education) I have pointed to the need for a National Council for Black/African Education in the Canadian context which is a collective initiative to establish an arms-length community-body charged with the sole responsibility of charting the course of Black/African-Canadian education. Such a Council of Elders with anti-Black racism lens must be representative of our diverse Black/African communities acting as a watchdog for the enforcement and oversight of provincial educational systems. As a community we cannot shy away from using the legal recourse if we take education as a "Human Rights" issue, and therefore a collective right. For example, having test cases using individual students who the system has failed to challenge the state of its responsibility to ensure successful education for all youth since Black subjects pay taxes as citizens.

We know that Black education and the African presence has a long history in Canada (Winks 1997; Hill 1981; Cooper 2006, 2016; Mensah 2010; Henry 1998; Brathwaite and James 1996). This history has constitutional implications extending beyond 'education as human rights'. There is a paradox for Canada to be ranked 'the top most educated nation in the world', and yet Black/African-Canadian and Indigenous peoples still struggle for educational justice and equity. Access to education is more than opportunity. There are questions about the cultural recognition for distinct groups such as Black peoples in Canada; groups and communities having the power to access educational opportunities; and responding to challenges of retention, equitable outcomes of access, etc. How do we promote pro-Black and African-Canadian education? (see discussions in Ibrahim and Abdi 2016). There is the pressing need to develop baseline demographic data (e.g., race and gender based statistics) from which to make firm determinations on the direction of Black education in Canada, disaggregating such data to account for social difference (e.g., ethnicity, gender, class, Indigenous Black, Continental Africans, Caribbean, Latin American, and other African Diasporic communities). We need to promote new visions of schooling and education that replace the troubling police presence in schools with caring adults and community Elders. This growing police presence in schools is not a healthy development and must be addressed. We must insist on mandates for faculty of education to teach anti-racism, anti-Black racism, and equity courses for faculty and student-teachers. The creation of a Black/African education unit/section within provincial Ministries of Education could be a step in the right direction. Nova Scotia has tried this. Such sector could spearhead attempts to recreate and co-create [with Black/African local communities] comprehensive curriculum for Black/African education, and also oversee implementation and accountability measures. Furthermore, we need the creation of a 'think tank' that will serve as a 'National Centre of Excellence for Black/African Education' to nurture critical scholarship and research for needed interventions (e.g., national and international exemplary practices). And, of course, the pursuit of viable new and radical educational options (e.g., Africentric schools) must remain on the table. But it is Black peoples who have to push this agenda, as no one is going to do it for us!

Throughout our history we have many examples of alternative community initiatives/educational outlets providing educational access through establishment of community resource centers, recreational facilities and "After School Program" for our youth, etc. These initiatives emerged from an understanding among Black community members that as a community, we cannot rely on the school system to address our educational needs. Hence, community-initiated alternatives have been developed to address the failings of mainstream/conventional education (e.g., Saturday schools, tutorial language classes, etc.). There are existing organizations to speak of: Canadian Alliance of Black Educators (CABE), African Heritage Association (AHA), African Heritage Network (AHEN), part of Toronto District School Board (TDSB); and the Ontario Alliance of Black School Educators (ONABSE)[1] to name a few.

Education is vital to any community's survival. Our view of education must also be broader to reach beyond the four-walled classrooms of schools (Shujaa 1994). We must see education in the strategies and approaches through which as a community we come to understand our worlds and act within such spaces to actualize dreams, hopes, and desires. Such view of education calls for making connections at several levels of education, for example by connecting educational issues at the elementary, secondary, college and university levels. Also, connecting communities

---

[1] http://onabse.org/ONABSE_VOICES_OF_BLACK_EDUCATORS_Final_Report.pdf.

in the educational pursuit is important, and acknowledging that there are similarities and differences that permeate our communities—Ghanaian, Somali, Jamaican, Guyanese, first-generation African-Canadians, Multi-generational African-Canadians etc. We can connect issues among the Black populations in different parts of North America, Europe, Africa, and the other Diasporas. Making Canada-wide connections between say what is happening in Ontario, Nova Scotia and New Brunswick, sharing and comparing notes on Black and minority educational issues, is also critical.

Among the more specific concrete suggestions for re-visioning Black education have been calls for proposals to establish Africentric schools where teaching of the Black experience, history, culture, identity, and history is central to the pursuit of curricular, instructional, and pedagogic transformations of contemporary education. Such schools, which can be situated within the context of contemporary forms of schooling (public and/or private/charter), would need to be guided by the provision of material and financial support from the Black/African community itself. We do pay taxes. But most importantly the philosophical principles of caring, compassion, co-operation, relationality, sharing, reciprocity, inter-connectedness, culture-centered, African identities and spiritualities guide the schooling and education of young learners. The Africentric School promotes a more holistic and integrated sense of the learner as human helping us move away from a Eurocentric notion of humanism that masquerade as a universal model. The school also cultivates a multi-centric/polycentric education model that recognizes the different types of learners, their knowledges and experiences, and the urgency for a critical understanding community and the role and place of notions of "spirituality" and "community" in schooling of Black and African youth. The connections between and among learners, educators and peers are emphasized, pushing the responsibility of the learner from the self to the community and thus challenging the dominant ideology of individualism (Dei and Kempf 2013; Asante 1991).

Critical examination of the social relations of schooling often reveals "contradictory and conflicting social relations" manifested in "positions of domination and subordination" (Connolly 1992, p. 146). It is important that any approach to schooling transformation must proceed by centering the voices, experiences, and struggles of Black, Indigenous and other racialized bodies [i.e., the "epistemic saliency"] of the Indigenous and racialized voice—Dei 1999; and by challenging how the dominant body/voice can "reproduce power by playing to power" (Fine 1994, p. 23). Schools can no longer be sites of containment (e.g., the limits of multicultural education).

The principle of meritocracy is intimately embedded in multicultural educational discourses, with the notion that it is irrelevant where one is from because in Canada everyone has the "equality" of opportunity and can achieve anything regardless of social location. Giroux reiterates such "neutrality" in the following excerpt: "unlike the old racism, which defined racial difference in terms of fixed biological categories organize hierarchically, the new racism operates in various guises proclaiming, among other things, race-neutrality, asserting culture as a matter of racial difference or making race a private matter" (Giroux 2005, p. 66). The color-blind educational approach removes any discussion or dialogues of history, social location and space; it fundamentally amounts to what Giroux describes as a "lack of 'critical engagement' with power and its imposition" (Giroux 2005, p. 66). Giroux's point concerning overt and covert racism is evident in multicultural education, in which covert racism is embedded in publicly funded education. Such limiting multicultural education principles are central to the "Othering" of the struggles, histories, and the identities of racialized and Indigenous bodies in schools (Abawi 2017).

There is a need to reframe citizenship and education beyond the mechanism of state control. As already discussed, this necessitates interrogating ways the nation state has come to construct "citizenship"—separating broader questions of the Land and sense of place from collective rights, Indigenous sovereignty ,and self-determination. The problem of "market citizenship" that "forces or induces individuals to enter new relations" with local, regional, national, and "global networks where economic criteria and market incentives are predominant" must also be questioned and subverted (Altamirano-Jimenez 2004, p. 95; Alfred 2009).

In line with a political and intellectual project of thinking through possibilities for the future, with the idea and goal of working toward shared complicities and responsibilities, we must assess schooling strengths and weaknesses in order to understand what might have been, and why we need to do something about the present. It is imperative to engage the identities of learners not simply as "discursive," but also as having structural and political implications. We cannot continue to speak about Black/racialized/Indigenous bodies in schools in pathologized and fetished terms of "Otherness" and "alterity" (i.e., these bodies have both intellectual and agential power, and are continually embarking upon and re-visioning local resurgence). We must also be aware of the dangers and limitations of the spurious universalization of schooling experiences for all learners. Yet, we must not forget the over-determining effects of schooling relations and experiences for different bodies and to critically engage schooling experiences of learners not merely as descriptive appendages to our theoretical formulations, but rather, as a clarion call to action. It should be noted that the context in which this chapter will focus on contemporary issues and challenges regarding schooling is within the province of Ontario. Public education systems in Canada are different. Such recognition is not simply about uniqueness but also to point to local specificities that are significant in developing counter-visions of schooling that speak to Black/African and minority education in multiple spaces because of shared histories and struggles.

Multiple challenges negatively impact disproportionately a number of students who are Black. African and racially minoritized will be outlined numerically. The first two issues or problems are interconnected and relate to the nature of government intervention in schooling and education in the form of two government legislations contributing to [in]stability in schools. I am concerned with the impact on Black students. There are two pieces of legislation that occurred around the same time in 2014: Bill 115 and Regulation 274. The first legislation is Bill 115. The main objection to Bill 115 is it allowed the government to "walk in and completely change the terms of a labor contract." Imagine if the provincial government could just "on a whim" walk in and change the contract that educators and school districts have signed—changing all of the parameters of that contract: salary, benefits, etc. The Bill also allowed the government to end any striking through parliament (without debate). It is so draconian that the unions took it to court to challenge the legality of the Bill. It was subsequently repealed. However, that move was superficial as all of the government-imposed changes to the contracts are still currently in effect. The bill has affected the younger, newer teachers the hardest who were frozen at their pay rate and not allowed to apply their acquired experience and seniority to the salary grid.

The other government decision is Regulation 274. This greatly affected (and is still affecting) all new teacher candidates because it in essence prevents boards from hiring any new teachers out of the faculties of education. This is perhaps an oversimplification but this regulation created a series of "steps" before someone would be "eligible" to apply for a contract position or permanent job. Now teacher candidates must first become Occasional Teachers, then Long Term Occasional (LTO) Teachers and then they can apply for a permanent contract position. This, in essence, means that they cannot get a job for 2 years. This has hit the candidates hard because after they were enrolled in the Faculties, the government released Regulation 274. Imagine the government saying that no one is allowed to hire you when you graduate. It also meant that LTO positions had to be given on the basis of seniority and LTO teachers had to be interviewed for any available positions. This means a school cannot give a LTO position to a competent teacher that knows the students and is good for their school. They have to interview the most "senior" people on the newly-implemented LTO roster and would have to say why they are not hiring one of them if they wish not to. School Principals have said this ties their hands and that some people have remained on the LTO list for a reason and that they are now being pressured to potentially hire less than the ideal candidate but rather the most senior. The other side of this argument is that it removes any nepotism from the process.[2]

It is a fact that marginalized schools or schools with large Black/African and marginalized populations often have greater "turn over" of administrative staff, and are often subjected to new and inexperienced administrators to a greater level, which leads to instability and further marginalization. Are marginalized schools treated simply as "training grounds" for new administrators? This lack of stability does not make for effective planning and administration that is critical for sustaining change in these schools. Top school leadership cannot develop a trusting and lasting relationship with these schools without being held accountable for lack of educational change for education success. Stability is critical to ensure long-term investment and stake in the welfare of the school. When one adds this to the problem of the reluctance of some senior administration to take up posts in such schools, one can appreciate the magnitude of the problem.

The third problem is failing or refusal to fail students at the elementary level. Avoiding the stigma of failing schools or schools with a good percentage of failing

---

[2] For additional resources to read, please see a couple of websites that might be useful.http://www.680news.com/2012/12/04/faq-bill-115-teachers-job-action-explained/http://www.etfo.ca/resources/reg274/pages/default.aspx.

youth, there is a reluctance to fail students and so simply push them through the mill instead. There are very serious consequences that are resulting from the "transferring" of elementary students from year to year when they do not meet the minimum expectations of their grade. Why are students being moved to grade 9 with a grade 3 reading level? Does that not set them up for failure at the secondary level where they will then fail for the first time? Admittedly, there is emerging research to support not holding children back as it may psychologically impact students. It is encouraging students to move with their age group. This is where special education is important. If students are behind 2 years or more, you still "transfer" them to the next grade not "pass" or "promote." Schools would put this student on an IEP. This means Individual Education Plan. The issue is many Black students are either put on too quickly or if they are on the IEP they never get off. IEP for the most part should not be permanent. However, if a student is on the autism spectrum then that is different meaning. Also, an IEP can either be both or one of modifications and accommodations. Modifications are changing the work to grade level, while accommodations are given more time for example.[3]

The fourth problem of racialized streaming has been with us for a while. There is a significant correlation between race and academic streaming. There is a long standing research that shows that students from these disadvantaged groups (e.g., Blacks, Indigenous and Portuguese, etc.) in disproportionate numbers are also enrolled in special education and non-university stream programs (see Brown et al. 1992; Brown 1993; Statistics Canada 1991, 1993; Canadian Council on Social Development 1991; Cheng and Yau 1998a).[4] Students from dominant backgrounds are more represented in the academic (university-bound) streams. The question is how are the different stakeholders participating in the institutional and "unconscious" racism leading to this effect?

The fifth problem is that of Special Education—similar to "racialized streaming," Black/African and working class youth are being pathologized as mentally and behaviorally defective and deficient. Is special education as we know it a tool used to address individualized learning styles, or has it become a tool to re-segregate racialized bodies? A study by Gill (2012) has shown that there is an over-representation of Black and racialized bodies in special education classrooms. There is also the inconsistent application of special education policies with teachers and administrators complaining about how special education policies and practices are altered based on what appears to be arbitrary factors and different interpretations of policies. Furthermore, Black and racial minority parents' knowledge base is poor with some educators noting how the appeal process is not easily understood by parents and consequently, parents were not equally informed citizens as it concerns the Individual Education Plan (IEP), challenging the decision, or the appeal process. Black and racialized parents belonging to a low socio-economic background, of a diverse culture, religion, being a lone parent, and/or being an immigrant tend to be

---

[3] http://teaching.about.com/od/pd/a/School-Retention.htm.

[4] Brown, R. S. and G. Parekh (2010). *Research Report: Special Education: Structural Overview and Student Demographics*. (Toronto: Toronto District School Board), p. 35.

marginalized in a multiplicity of ways through the process. Some educators also point to English as a Second Language or first languages being read as a disability and how this leads to problematic diagnoses. Students are tested in English, when their first language may not be English. If the student "fails" an assessment, it is determined that they are in need of an IPRC (Identification Placement Review Committee [See edu.gov.on.ca]). Clearly, it is a fact that in the Toronto District School Board (TDSB) educators do a first language assessment. The test is done in the child's native language. Based on this there is an understanding the test will reveal if the child needs more time to acclimate to their environments or if they have a delay in their learning. The problem is the perception or assumption by many that students from African countries do not speak English when in fact almost all do. Then, there is the assumption that English speaking Caribbean students' knowledge of English is below Canadian standards. They are placed in English classes to develop their "skills".

The difficulties of assessment, testing, and accountability are profound with a number of educators pointing to their own difficulties relating to assessments, testing, and accountability thereby marginalizing students further. In other words, what are these instruments/assessments measuring and is this in fact an accurate measure of what the student knows or does not know? In effect, key questions still need to be raised concerning the legitimacy of special education. Parents and educators have both expressed grave concerns about the ultimate legitimacy of special education and question whether it functions to reproduce the status the quo of labor force. Is there an unavoidable usefulness to understanding special education? Should special education placement be encouraged given the bad history for Black and other racialized [immigrant] youth? How do we bring a critical anti-racist lens to the pursuit of Special Education if at all possible?

The sixth problem is about the Provincial Literacy test. The Ontario Secondary School Literacy Test is causing teachers and schools to "teach to the test" and to spend significant amount of academic time preparing for the test. In some schools and courses, it is normal to spend 20% of the academic time available to prepare students for the test. Is this really the best use of instructional time? Is this what we want to see happening in schools? In a 2002 study of the Provincial Literacy Test [a high school graduation requirement], only 25% of students in the applied streams (college/vocational) passed the Grade 10 literacy text, compared to 80% in academic streams (university bound). Data have consistently shown that Black, Indigenous, and other racialized students are found in applied (college/vocational) streams more than in the academic (university) streams.[5]

The co-option of neo-liberalism in the current education development agenda is not simply ensuring the ascendency of corporate capital in schooling and education. A neo-liberal educational agenda has also had the effect of ensuring a sort of creeping survivalism among learners. Learners simply want an education to survive in the corporate world. They are understandably thinking foremost of having a good paying job, raising a family, and moving up the social ladder. Concerns about social

---

[5] See footnote 4.

justice, equity education, anti-racism, and oppression studies are seen as "special interest' agendas and a luxury one cannot afford. There is also a sense of complacency that if only an individual pulls themselves by the boots strap and works hard, they will be fine. There is no system holding anyone back. For all youth and particularly Black/African and Indigenous youth, the imperative of contemporary schooling and education to transform currents social conditions is critical. The failure to assist youth to address their hopes and dreams can foster youth societal alienation.

Consequently, we have not fully come to terms with such issues of Black youth disengagement from schools and why we need to think through more radical solutions and counter-initiatives to address some of the educational challenges of our times. We have only succeeded in blaming these youth, their families and communities—putting the problem in these bodies rather than on the educational system. Recently, the Peel District School Board issued a report on Black education that clearly shows the Board is attempting to do something in the wake of anti-Black racism in schools.[6]

In the final section of this chapter, I focus on what is possible, desirable, and imaginable in counter-visioning schooling to serve the needs of diverse students.[7] This is about educational futurity starting with a deep reflection and understanding of the nature and extent of the problem confronting us all, especially when it comes to Black/African, Indigenous, racialized and minority youth education. Are we really addressing the needs of these group? I am particularly reflecting on the ways disengagement in school relates to the pursuit of particular educational practices (instruction, pedagogy, and curriculum initiatives) and how counter-visioning schooling can be informed by the bodies of learners, their histories, identities, cultural memories and heritages as well as everyday experiences and expectations. I ponder over how we can begin to break down hierarchical relations of power in schooling and begin asking new questions about what is possible, how, why, and when to promote educational excellence for all? I confront some difficult issues about power, discourse, and representation of youth experiences that produce and contextualize dropping out of school. But, rather than present actual speaking voices [narratives] of the students I pursue a self-reflexive and philosophical interrogation of the possibilities of students' engagement as well as limitations of disengagement from school. In the discussion, I examine some of the conventional factors leading to students' disengagement from school and suggest ways educators and schools can support retention/success. Where feasible, I intersperse my analysis with con-

---

[6] https://www.thestar.com/yourtoronto/education/2016/10/23/peel-school-board-launches-plan-to-support-black-male-students.htmlhttp://www.cbc.ca/news/canada/toronto/black-students-in-their-own-words-1.3819829 https://www.thestar.com/yourtoronto/education/2016/11/25/peel-school-board-plans-to-collect-race-based-data-on-students.html, http://www.peelschools.org/Documents/We%20Rise%20Together%20Action%20Plan%20FINAL.pdf.

[7] A very short and condensed version of this discussion appeared in Dei, G. J. S. 2015. "Reflections on 'Dropping Out' of School: Meeting the Challenge of Youth Engagement". Education Now. May Issue. http://www.cea-ace.ca/education-canada/article/reflections-%E2%80%9Cdropping-out%E2%80%9D-school

crete real-life examples and offer practical suggestions for applying the principles for ensuring students' success at school.

What are the transformative possibilities of schooling and education today? We need to focus on the effects and outcomes of our practices (see Fine 1991). Our intentions and actions do not always match and we may be sending mixed or wrong signals to our students. Different students perceive the actions of teachers differently. Therefore, rather than dismiss students' perceptions as ill-informed, it is imperative that as educators and practitioners we take students' perceptions seriously and examine our practices and beliefs to ensure that students get to know who we truly are, that we do care about learning, teaching, and administration of education.

In the early 1990s after a longitudinal study [working with graduate students at the University of Toronto] examining Black youths and the Ontario public school system, we concluded that the term "push out" was more appropriate than "drop out" (see Dei et al. 1995, 1997). Our intent was not to convey that educators literally hold students' hands and push them out of the door. However, the messages sent by schools, what is valued and deemed legitimate knowledge and school practice, what is discussed or not discussed in everyday classrooms, what experiences and identities count or do not count, and how students are perceived by educators, lead a fair number of Black youth to feel unwelcome and, consequently, become disengaged. There is clearly something wrong when students who are supposed to be learning in school decide on their own accord to leave school prematurely. The term "on their own accord" should not obscure the underlying factors that lead some students to make this decision. It is the process of how students get to the personal determination that needs to be critically examined. It is no longer acceptable, and in fact, it becomes a convenient escape for schools, educators, administrators, and local communities to accept dropping out as simply a matter of individual responsibility. So how do we interrogate conventional knowledge?

Tuck (2011) in an excellent read discussed some of the ways schools push out students through humiliating experiences, including assaults on learners' dignities such that these students no longer want to be in school. She reasons that schools in US produce dropping out as a "dialectic of humiliating ironies and dangerous dignities" (p. 817) that stem from educational practices including the conduct of assessments, exit examinations, testing, school rule enforcements that humiliate students and/or that students find very humiliating and a confrontation of their own dignities. Clearly, when students leave school prematurely they are fully aware of their decision as the consequences in the contexts of the contemporary social values and cultural capital assigned to education. This should inform us that dropouts are making calculated decisions when faced with a feeling of being unwelcome in schools. Therefore, we must seek to understand the question of why students make these decisions and move to a discursive interplay of institutional and personal responsibilities when accounting for school dropout.

What does educational research in Ontario tell us? We have all heard the oft-repeated assertion that statistics can be notoriously unreliable. But there are other interpretations favorably to the figures. Figures do not lie we are also told. For this discussion I maintain that statistics can help us establish the nature and context of a problem. However, considering the general reluctance to engage with race, recent statistics often employ coded language to speak about the experiences of racialized students within the Toronto District School Board. For example, studies often focus on language, country of origin, length of time in Canada, or citizenship status as it relates to student disengagement. These studies can provide a glimpse into the issue, though without an honest conversation about the role of race, it remains an incomplete picture (see Brown et al. 1992; Brown 1993; Cheng and Yau 1998a, b).

As also highlighted in Dei (2008) research conducted by the TDSB on dropping out by key languages shows that Portuguese, Spanish, and Somali-speaking students leave school at the highest rates, 38%, 37.5%, and 35.1% respectively.[8] By region of birth, English-speaking Caribbean and Central/South American and Mexican students leave at the highest rates, 38% and 37% respectively. Combined with earlier statistics, these indicate issues that extend above and beyond language and place of origin and point, instead, toward a hostile learning environment for racialized students.

Educational research on the performance of Ontario high school students shows that despite successes, Black/African-Canadians, First Nations/Indigenous, and Portuguese and Spanish-speaking students are at the forefront of student disengagement from school. Disproportionate numbers of students from these groups are also enrolled in special education and non-university stream programs. Even for those students alleged to be doing well (e.g., Asian "model minority" students) we observe narrow fields of academic choices, such as the over-subscription in science/mathematics-related occupations (see Brown et al. 1992; Brown 1993; Cheng and Yau 1998a, b).

But more significantly, perhaps, pushing out is also not just the statistics and figures. The figures do not tell us about the human side of dropping out. In our early 1990s study of Ontario dropouts we noted that there is a human dimension to the story of Black and minority youth disengagement from school. These are stories of personal struggles which admittedly do not all emanate from the school. There are personal stories of family and domestic hardships, socialization and peer culture struggles, whereby youth with stolen dreams and unmet expectations develop a degree of nihilism and a fear of apprehension of living a dead-end existence. And, there are also the challenge of navigating the school system, unfriendly and unwelcoming schooling environments, low teacher expectations of minority students which can be a self-fulfilling prophecy, the differential treatment by race, gender, sexuality or class, and the lack of curricular, pedagogic and instructional sophistication (Fine 1991; Dei et al. 1995). For Black/African students, there is a trade off to

---

[8] R.S. Brown (2008). *Research Report: The Grade 9 Cohort of Fall 2002: A five year cohort study, 2002–2007.* (Toronto: Toronto District School Board), p. 16.http://www.tdsb.on.ca/Portals/0/AboutUs/Research/The%205%20Yr%20Study%2002-07.pdfSee also M. Cheng, *"Factors that Affect the Decisions of Racial/Ethnic Minorities to Enter and Stay in Teaching and their Implications for School Board's Teacher Recruitment and Retention Policies"* (Ed.D dissertation, Department of Sociology and Equity Studies, OISE/UT, 2002).

school/academic success which is one of maintaining one's identity and emotional and mental stability (Dei et al. 1997). We have situations where students may be physically present in schools but absent in mind, soul, and spirit. It is a symptom of youth disengagement. There is a process of disengagement that starts early to build up in the life of the student culminating in the learner eventually deciding to leave school prematurely. This process implicates structures and institutions in different ways.

This calls for a critical interrogation of the structures and processes of educational delivery. Such interrogation allows us to hold systems accountable while calling for community and parental responsibility at the same time. We must extend the breadth of our academic investigation beyond the conventional discourses of youth truancy and delinquency, poor parenting and socialization skills, economic hardships, etc., which often only serves to make victims the source of the problems they are contending with. Producing school success is more than an individual undertaking. It is a question implicating more than learners, parents, teachers and school administrators and a question of systemic and structural implications and accountability. Asking parents and communities to take responsibility for the education of their children should never be constructed in a way that pathologizes families, individual learners, and their communities. Such pathologies only serve to highlight constructed or false negatives of local [marginalized] communities, [working class and racialized] families and student learners. The pathologies become metanarratives that stifle counter-debates. Hence, in accounting for youth dropping out of school, we remain uninformed in some ways on the daily struggles and challenges of families, and local creative efforts, resistances and resilience to succeed against all odds. We fail to learn from these real life struggles and we do not value or appreciate counter and oppositional stances. In fact, we punish rather than reward resistance. Yet, it is these strategies of resilience and counter-stances that offer crucial lessons for re-visioning schooling and education and thereby promote change.

I put forward some philosophical contentions on youth disengagement and push out of school. As already alluded to, dropping out is a process. It is socio-structural and political conditioning of the school system as it exists in the context of the broader society. Rather than pinpoint specific causes and factors contributing to youth push out of school I want now to work with a different intellectual gaze highlighting some philosophical contentions. I see such analysis as part of a needed paradigmatic shift to understand schooling and education. A major discursive position I am taking is that we should pay attention to the collective inability or failure to look at the foundation of the Euro-Canadian/American educational system. In other words, dropping out is actually a consequence of the structure of the conventional school system. The foundation itself contributes to students dropping out. A weak foundation cannot sustain all students succeeding in school. If we are serious about addressing the problem of school dropout then we must look at the foundations on which the current school system is built. We seem to be adding stories to a weak foundation rather than building a new foundation. For example, what are schools designed for? How do we recruit and train teachers and administrators for our schools? How inclusive are our schools, our instructional, curricular and pedagogic approaches to teaching and learning? What are our students learning and what are they doing with such education? What is the final product we are expecting when students enter the school system? These questions get to the foundation of the educational system.

To be more specific the current school system cultivates individual excellence and success. Some may see nothing wrong with this; however, the emphasis has been on rights and not responsibilities. There is also a heavy play on meritocracy and merit badges which end up nurturing, promoting, and sustaining rugged individualism and competition. A discussion of transformative possibilities ought to look at the foundational base of the current school system. As McDermott (2014) notes, "questions of transforming current schools within the conditions of capitalism, colonialism, and neoliberalism are paramount for students, teachers, and communities" ...[and] we need to build community to push against and expand the bureaucratic borders of individual competitiveness, league tables, and heightened surveillance of teaching-and-learning that urge teachers to work in isolation, behind closed doors.

The values and credentials privileged by the Euro-American school system simply mask Whiteness, White power, and privilege as the norm. What is presented as "universal" is, in fact, the particularity of the dominant. The system was initially set up to cater for particular class interests and market needs. Yet, our world is changing and we need to adapt to this change in a very transformational way. The values of the dominant which undergird the educational system no longer hold for everyone if they ever did. These values are being questioned not because they are wrong or not worthy but that they are not universally tenable. These values are not inclusive and we need to cultivate values shared by all of our humanity. The implication for understanding school dropping out is the absence of a "community of learners" and "schooling community" makes some student feel alienated and disaffected. These students become disengaged. For example, while a competitive mode may help generate individual brilliance and creativity it does not necessarily create sustainable communities for everyone. Therefore, as educators and policy-makers, how can we hope to address a nagging [and unacceptable] problem of schools failing some learners when solutions envisaged have been to simply add to what already exists? We cannot simply add new floors/structures to a weak educational building with cracks in the foundation (see also Dei 2008).

The above structural critique casts a gaze on both the multicultural (Canadian) and melting pot (US) approaches, which each work with notions (albeit somewhat varied) of integration, a central culture, and an implicit notion of ascending to a Euro-American standard cultural trope. To ensure inclusive educational success, we must entertain the possibility of creating a new educational system that holds the promise of excellence for all by cultivating multi-centricity, cultural plurality, pedagogic, instructional, and epistemological diversity. As a community we have failed to acknowledge the systemic undercurrents of the dropping out challenge. There has been a silencing of talk around institutional responsibility for failing school system and how the processes of educational delivery actually produce or create educational failures. I am quite sure there is someone reading this piece saying "hogwash." This is the problem of systemic denial and refusal to hear dissenting voices. Furthermore, most of the suggestions and recommendations and policy decisions for addressing perceived challenges with the current educational system have been to tinker with existing structures while keeping the basics in place. But how can we expect educational success while reproducing the status quo? We cannot hope for success while continuing to do the same thing that is failing us. The implication of the systemic and institutional denials for understanding school dropout problem is that we are not courageous enough and instead blame the victims for the problems they encounter. Do we stop to ask: why would a student leave school prematurely if all is going well with him or her? Is it because they simply do not want to learn or they refuse to learn given the prevailing conditions. Who refuses education? For sure, learners can refuse to be miseducated. They can refuse to be abused. They can exercise their agency to leave a school system that disembodies, depersonalizes them, and makes them mere statistics.

Also, we have not all fully accepted the fact that there is no leveled playing field in the current school system. Many of us are defensive when it is claimed that the school system advantages some learners while disadvantaging others. A clear resistance to such position comes when one if confronted with such questions as: What and who does the "system" refer to? What is [White] privilege? Who is disadvantaged? To voice concern about the school system one can easily be dismissed or maligned by fault finders. When it is claimed that some Black bodies have not been served well in the school system a quick response has been others in similar situations are faring well so why can't we? No one is holding us back. But, if we are frank in acknowledging inequities in the system it goes a long way to developing a commitment to search for solutions. The denial of exclusion is a big part of the problem. The denial does not allow for us to put our collective hearts and minds together to find solutions. The denial distorts reality and corrupts our imaginations. We have not developed any explicit investment in creating a level playing field. This is because we have failed to recognize the uneven and inequitable circumstances in which education is embedded—i.e., the a priori inequality existing among students, within school cultures and educational discourse and in the Euro-American curricula given the power relations of schooling. If we are to acknowledge the inequities, it will require that we target our responses to those segments most disadvantaged, recognizing the severity of issues for different bodies. It also means that our models of social justice would have to be more than the usual let us "treat everyone the same." Ideally, we can recognize differences and meet and embrace the needs of all learners, which will work against existing inequities. The implication I am drawing here for understanding school dropouts is that any educational measures to dropping out of school, apart from being systemic, must also seek to target the most disadvantaged groups.

Furthermore, an important approach to problem solving is accepting and recognizing that we are all in a collective struggle to transform our communities for ourselves. We are each implicated in the existing inequities and "no one is off the hook." If we operate with an understanding that notwithstanding some successes, not everything is working well within the school system, then there are multiple complicities and responsibilities. As an educational response we must have all hands on deck, including the valuing of each other's knowledge, history, experience, and contribution. This includes students, educators, administrators, policy makers, private, business and public sectors, parents, guardians, community workers, and our varied communities. One implication here for understanding school dropout is that we cannot find solutions outside the contributions, experiences, and voices of the school dropouts themselves. Dropouts are part of the solution. The problem of dropping out persists because school dropouts are often dismissed as failures, troublemakers and as "problem" students. There is a hierarchy of knowledge, in terms of what and whose knowledge counts and why.

Bringing all hands on deck is about building workable partnerships. Partnerships with business and corporate capital may be critical in this endeavor. However, I would caution that a shifting of the pendulum in favor of private/business sector involvement in public education has been part of the problem of late. Arguably, neoliberalism has heavily and negatively impacted schooling and education. Frankly, any positives have been outweighed by the negative consequences. Today, many local communities face policy directives of largely fiscally conservative governments that undermine public education (see Porfilio and Malott 2008). This is not a North American or European phenomenon. In Africa, Asia and the Caribbean, faced with budget deficits, economic recession and other monetary woes, national governments are reneging on equity commitments and "education for all." They are "… favouring privatization, reduced government expenditures, user charges and difficult choices between subsectors in education" (Jones 1997, p. 373).

McDermott (2013, 2014) in an exhaustive discussion points to how an increasing neoliberal framework has shaped Euro-American educational institutions and social relationships since the 1980s (see Giroux 2008; McMahon and Portelli 2012; Harvey 2005; Davies and Bansel 2007; Gallagher and Lortie 2005a, b; Gallagher and Fusco 2006). She notes that education in the Euro-American context "has undergone significant and constant externally-imposed reforms" (see Ball 2003; Goodson 2001; Lasky 2004; Hargreaves 2005; Lingard and Mills 2000; Day 2002; Day and Smethem 2009). The problem as McDermott (2014, p. 30) argues is that these reforms are framed through "business models developed usually by non-educators, non-students and parents and are permeated with rewards and punishments for districts, schools, administrators, teachers and students who either 'meet' externally imposed 'standards' or do not" (see also Day 2002; Day and Smethem 2009; Ball 2003; Spring 2006; Darling-Hammond 2010; Essed and Goldberg 2002). There are social, spiritual, psychological, and cultural dimensions to the dilemma of school dropout that cannot be fixed solely by corporate capital encroachment in schooling and education. For example, how can we get a student who is emotionally, psychologically, and spiritually distraught about schooling to become engaged simply by infusing more capital into the system? Perhaps, another issue with corporate capital is not that it represents simply more capital, but that it comes with strings attached, earmarked for particular subjects, or is threatened to be withdrawn if we veer from the current course.

An important mission of school is helping integrate learners into society. In Canada, there is unquestioned faith in integration which is rooted in the multicultural paradigm. Integration [as we know it] has not guaranteed success for our youth. Our approach to integration is one size fits all. Those who do not fit are cast aside and/or seen as the "problem." But we must be critical of integration and begin to ask: Integration for whom, why how, and at what/whose expense? The implication I am drawing is that those who drop out, in fact, do not find a place in the school system as currently designed. One size cannot fit all. Multiple visions of schooling including educational innovations and initiatives from marginalized communities must be envisaged and encouraged. They must equally be valued, promoted, and supported. Increasingly, at the policy level it is troubling to see how a blind faith in integration continues to lead even non-dominant, immigrant, racial minority, Indigenous learners along the path of "cultural destruction." Teaching and learning should be about decolonizing minds, bodies, souls, and spirits to be more critical of ourselves and communities. Learners must be bold enough to ask difficult questions: What is the goal and purpose of education? What are the collective responsibilities of learners, educators, parents, and local communities in education? What is the place of policy in bringing about educational change? Who is making these policy decisions that affect schools? What are the particular experiences that policy makers bring to their work? And, in whose interests have conventional educational policies served? It is not unthinkable to have school dropouts input policy decision making in schools. Their views, experiences, and perceptions of schooling must count. We need to reclaim multiple and multi-centric ways of knowing for promoting effective education for all learners. Such knowledges work with the affirmation of learners' and educators' myriad identities, histories and social contexts of learning and teaching, the promotion of Indigenous cultures and language heritages, and addressing broader questions of curricular, instructional and pedagogic relevance.

Are there some concrete strategies we can think of to promote student retention in schools? Dropping out of school is fundamentally a problem of youth disengagement from and disaffection with school. While I agree that solutions to the dropout/push out issue must embrace school, off-school, home and community connections, there are also some concrete strategies that educators and administrators can undertake to retain students in schools. Schools must be made more interesting than they are currently for all students. Schooling should be about what learners can identify with in terms of their everyday cultural, social, material, and spiritual existence. I have increasingly become skeptical of the bland, liberal, and depoliticized talk of inclusion with no attention paid to issues of power, transparency, and accountability. I believe inclusion should lead to structural transformation. The traditional "add and stir" approach, and the dominant celebratory multicultural approaches must be interrogated. Inclusion should be about beginning anew. Inclusion should not simply be adding to what already exists. Often times what already exists is the source of the problem in the first place. Hence, we cannot hope for change merely by adding to what already exists. Yet I am not ready to give up on the concept of inclusion. Rather I want to work with "radical inclusion" in calling for more effective inclusive approaches in our schools to retain students. We need to recognize the space between and in between ourselves and others, where all the history, pain, trauma, resistance, and love live in order to see inclusion as about a wholeness, completeness and varied, complex communities.

There is vast literature on how to make schools inclusive and I see no need to reiterate these ideas. Suffice to say that the school curriculum must be diverse. Instructional and pedagogic practices used in classrooms must engage all learners and the different learning styles. Teaching, learning, and administration of education must work with students' lived experiences, myriad identities, histories, cultures, and knowledge base. In other words, education must be meaningful and relevant to the students themselves. Education should be holistic to encompass material, social, cultural, political, physical, psychological, spiritual, and metaphysical realms of social existence of learners. Inclusive education includes teaching about society, culture, and Nature (i.e., environments and Lands). Also all students must feel included and welcome in our schools. Identity is linked with knowledge production. Teaching must recognize the myriad identities that our learners bring to classrooms (e.g., racial, gendered, classed, sexual, [dis]abled subjects/learners). Social difference (race, class, gender, sexuality, [dis]ability) implicates schooling and is consequential for educational outcomes. Therefore, educators should teach about social difference as sites of power, strength, and identity. School teachings must engage the home and off-school [community] cultures of students in ways that break the false separation of home, community, and the school. Local and Indigenous languages of learners must be broached in schools alongside teaching in dominant languages (English and French). Students must see themselves reflected in the school culture, as well as visual and physical landscape of their schools. Students should also see a diverse physical representation of teaching and administrative staff such that they are able to identity with people in positions of power and influence as equally coming from their own communities.

Regarding the more practical strategies to retain students at school, it is important for educators to access pertinent resources for developing an inclusive curriculum. Among the practical measures could be the use of students as knowledge holders of their own experiences, guest speakers from diverse backgrounds, including finding places in our schools for parents, Elders caring adults, and community workers to come as teachers engaging in multiple conversations with students, faculty, and staff. Beyond the formal teaching schools can hold more of public conferences and seminars, community workshops, use local [including community] print media and television, community bookstores, public libraries, as well as visual aids, popular culture as resources for youth education. These resources can be employed with a discussion of their social contexts and histories as entry points of dialogues. Classroom teaching must engage learners and draw on school–community interface. For example, Nasir (2005) observes common characteristics of out-of-school learning environments that make success and a sense of belonging available to African American students. She focuses on basketball, track, and dominoes. She highlights "four aspects of teaching and learning that support this sense of belonging and identification: fostering respectful relationships, making mistakes acceptable, giving learners defined roles, and offering learners ways to participate that incorporate aspects of themselves" (p. 530). First, coaches fostered respectful relationships by disallowing negative comments and helping to coordinate informal, after-hours team activities designed to create cohesion and a sense of community. Second, making mistakes was acceptable. Nasir (2005) recounts a story of a track coach working to reframe a moment that the student felt was a failure into a moment they felt good about and could learn from. Third, students, led by their coaches in track and basketball, specialized in aspects of the sport that was conducive to their strengths. Giving learners a defined role based on their interests and strengths "reinforces an overall sense of expertise, belonging, and identification" (p. 530). Finally, coaches and teachers offered learners ways to participate that incorporate aspects of themselves. This includes acknowledging individual personalities and the uniqueness of students. Nasir provides examples from various activities where some students are jokesters, rule keepers, motivators, etc. She states, "These informal roles support a sense of belonging, for they allow students to feel that who they are matters to the success of the activity" (p. 531).

Classroom teachers can encourage students to use personal experiences and cultural stories as learning tools. Educators can rely on practical teachable moments and real life scenarios to explain complex subject matter to the students. The instructional and pedagogic strategies would call for the engagement of different learners and creating a decolonized space (i.e., spaces where there are no hierarchies of power) to make all students feel valued and welcome. This feeling helps create a "community of learners," particularly where classroom instructional and pedagogic strategies involve students, parents, Elders, community workers, and local cultural knowledges.

Educators should strengthen students' abilities to ask new and difficult questions in class. The students can begin by questioning their own selves and local communities, the school and wider society. Teaching should also emphasize learners' responsibilities to their communities, peers, and to themselves. Allowing all students to showcase their own voices and knowledges, commenting and assessing their own schooling and education are important educational strategies of inclusion. Prioritizing the voices and knowledges of students whose voices and knowledges are absent is critical to transforming schools. Also among the practical strategies for developing inclusive curriculum, educators can begin to examine their own classroom pedagogies and teaching methodologies using approaches to diversify the curriculum through infusion of multiple teaching methodologies, pedagogies, and courses. For example, as pointed out elsewhere (Dei 2016) there must be a consideration of more dialogical curriculum co-creation involving students, parents, local communities, and schools. On the evaluation and assessments, schools must work with multiple definitions of success. Schools can move away from a model of education which reserves attention and praise solely for those who fit narrow definitions of success, toward an accessible framework for student achievement which recognizes not only barriers to success for many, but also multiple paths to success for all. In other words let us define success broadly, and also to include social and academic success, and not see success as simply the flip side of failure. In other words we must reimagine evaluation. Classrooms should promote collective successes where students succeed together so that evaluations take into account how students are supporting each other. A failing class would be one that could not support all its members. We could evaluate on the basis of improvement. There could be peer reviews and grading so that the teacher is not the only one in control of grades and the hierarchies are less severe.

Again as noted in Dei (2014), educators must deal with the rigid and orthodox Euro-centered evaluation methods. A re-conceptualizing of evaluation methods and approaches in schools can be initiated in classrooms. For example, educators can consider orality as equal medium to written text. Classroom teachers can give students opportunity to submit assignments orally. This still involves articulating theory and praxis, expecting students still to be able to demonstrate integrating in-class materials and community resources. Educators must not limit text to only academic projects, but also, include community-based events as sites of learning. Students could be given opportunities to attend a community event or participate in organizing an event and then write or present reflections on it. Very often attending community cultural events provides access to Elders and other "teachers." Learners would be able to connect community work to their learning for it to be meaningful and more practical. It allows students to develop a sense of ownership of their knowledge and knowledge creation process. Furthermore, we can encourage students to present non-traditional papers (arts-based, multimedia). In this way students are not only given the opportunity to be creative and think outside the box, but educators show that they do recognize and honor multiple ways of knowing and being (see Dei 2014).

In pursuing inclusive practice in today's classrooms for social change the human interactions of teachers, students, administrators, parents, Elders, and local communities is key to the creation of "communities of learners." For example, we need classroom dialogues to be multiple conversations about privilege, power and oppression, validation of diverse experiences, histories, knowledges, and practices (see also Schick 2010). Such dialogues could include an appreciation of the historical and cultural narratives of all peoples in our diverse communities. Critical dialogues could include breaking down labels that dominate systems and practices, and appreciating that learning cannot solely be measured linearly (e.g., "standardization recipes" [Lewin, 2000]/standardized education). There must be space of sharing where we treasure Indigenous cultural knowledges, pursuing multiple pathways to educational success, working locally but thinking globally, and acknowledging both macro and micro relations and processes and the ways myriad oppressions are connected, but also, unique to different groups. Additional inclusive educational practices and strategies could include cooperative education with a lesser focus on competition, seeking diverse representation (including multiple segments of the community—not just teachers, students and administrators), addressing the question of community languages (e.g., incorporating and accepting languages other than English and or French), giving students, parents and local communities a voice in constructing the school curriculum, and broadening access through diversifying the medium of delivery for inclusive education.

Decolonizing education is changing the normal [conventional] ways we teach, learn, and administer education. Decolonizing education is about promoting counter and oppositional voices, knowledges and histories, and bringing into focus the lived experiences of students who have traditionally been marginalized from the school system. Knowledge is power and promoting multiple and oppositional knowledges help address the question of power sharing. By decolonizing education, looking critically at the structures and processes of education delivery (e.g., teaching, learning and administration of education), we create inclusive schooling environments that would appeal to and engage the diverse group of learners. Schools can be welcoming spaces and that feeling of a sense of belonging and ownership of the schooling process can help engage students and allow them to stay in school. It is difficult to understand why someone who is valued, wanted, feels a sense of belonging and is welcome will decide to leave school prematurely. When we say students do not want to learn because they have dropped out of school we also must ask why and how we see ourselves, our communities, and our institutions implicated in dropping out of school.

It is imperative for Black scholars to continuously come up with methods to decolonize the education system. For the Black scholar/leader, the challenges of Black education require that we become a distinctive voice in speaking and using our scholarship in youth education. So the question of what it means to be a Black scholar in the academy will always be relevant. I picked on this question in some detail in the next chapter. We must strive for excellence knowing that there is a constant gaze on us and our work. We must strive to define our subject positions while challenging the problem of our subjectification. As argued elsewhere (Dei 2014) there is the discomfort about Black[ness] in the academy and many of us have failed to live and love our Blackness. We need to develop the courage to resist knowing full well that our resistance is continually punished. As part of our own collective decolonization we must ask new questions, pursue multi-centric ways of knowing and challenge the universalization and hegemony of Western science as the only valid way of knowing. Our Blackness must be about an interruption and subversion. Part of the struggle to challenge our colonial investments is to resist the seduction of neo-liberalism which reifies the individual subject as about the self and how well we perform under the strict guidelines of corporate market and capital. We must eschew the elitism of studying our communities from a distance and ensure that all we do is always guided by the relevance to our communities. Such community groundedness is our intellectual, spiritual, and moral fiber as academics and learners.

Radical Black leadership is needed to fight for the schools and the educational system we want. There are different roles and responsibilities in this fight. As Black/African scholars we need to make our communities proud of us as intellectual warriors. We must help build communities and forge solidarities with other oppressed groups. We must be prepared to mentor our younger colleagues and develop the spirit of "giving back" to support others. Fighting oppression, marginalization, and exclusion also calls for "writing back." We need to take the initiatives to think out solutions to the challenges we face. For example, in the schools we must take the lead to draw up a concrete action plan about how we proceed on diversifying the academy, especially the teaching faculty and top administration. We must also be suggesting ways of infusing oppression studies into the curriculum both as integrated courses of study and also specially designed courses on race, class, gender, intersections intersectionality?, etc. We must be actively and politically involved in the struggles to retain and sustain traditionally educational outreach programs that have sought our marginalized groups into our educational institutions. Moreover, we must promote and support fully fledged African, Caribbean, and Indigenous Studies programs in our institutions. To reiterate again exist African Indigenous cultural resource knowledges working with such social values as caring reciprocity, sharing, relations, mutual interdependence, community, social responsibility, respect, acknowledgment, ethics, and accountability. These values can be tapped into in the pursuance of a new politics of educational futurity for our youth.

I see this as a project of reclaiming radical Blackness and Africanness in our education.

References

Abawi, Z. (2017). *Marginal voices: Indigenous and immigrant dialogue in education* (Graduate students symposium: Selected paper 11, pp. 35–48). Kingston, Canada: Queen's University.

Adjei, P. B. (2013). When Blackness shows up uninvited: Examining the murder of Trayvon Martin through Fanonian racial interpellation. In G. J. S. Dei & M. Lordan (Eds.), *Contemporary issues in the sociology of race and ethnicity: A critical reader*. New York: Peter Lang.

Alfred, T. (2009, November). Colonialism and state dependency. *Journal de la Sante Autochtone, 5*, 42–60.

Altamirano-Jimenez, I. (2004). North American first peoples: Slipping up into market citizenship? *Citizenship Studies, 8*(4)349–365.

Asante, M. K. (1991). The Afrocentric Idea in Education. *Journal of Negro Education, 60*(2), 170–180.

Ball, S. J. (2003). The teacher's soul and the terrors of performativity. *Journal of Educational Policy, 18*(2)215–228.

Brathwaite, K., & James, C. (Eds.). (1996). Educating African Canadians. Toronto, Canada: James Lorimer.

Brown, R. (1993). *A follow-up of the grade 9 cohort of 1987 every secondary student survey participants*. Toronto: Toronto Board of Education.

Brown, R., Cheng, M., Yau, M., & Ziegler, S. (1992). *The 1991 every secondary student survey: Initial findings*. Toronto: Toronto Board of Education.

Canadian Council on Social Development. (1991). *Stay in School Supplement: Social Development Overview.* 1:7–14.

Cheng, M & Yau, M. (1998a). *The 1997 every secondary student survey: Preliminary findings*. No. 227. Toronto: Toronto District School Board.

Cheng, M. & Yau, M. (1998b). *The 1997 grade 7/8 every student survey: Preliminary findings*. No. 228. Toronto: Toronto District School Board.

Connolly, P. (1992). Playing it by the rules: The politics of research in 'race' and education. *British Educational Research Journal, 18*(2)133–148.

Cooper, A. (2006). *The hanging of Angelique: The untold story of Canadian slavery and the burning of Old Montreal*. Toronto: HarperCollins. Published in French in 2007 as La Pendaison.

Cooper, A. (2016). Black Canada and the law: Black parents and Children in the legal battle for education in Canada West: 1851–1864. In A. Ibrahim & A. A. Abdi (Eds.), *The education of African Canadian children: Critical perspectives*. Montreal, Canada: McGill-Queens's Press.

Darling-Hammond, L. (2010). *The flat world and education: How America's commitment to equity will determine our future*. New York: Teachers College Press.

Davies, B., & Bansel, P. (2007). Neoliberalism and education. *International Journal of Qualitative Studies in Education (QSE), 20*(3)247–259.

Day, C. (2002). School reform and transition in teacher professionalism and identity. *International Journal of Educational Research, 37*(2)677–692.

Day, C., & Smethem, L. (2009). The effects of reform: Have teachers really lost their sense of professionalism? *Journal of Educational Change, 10*, 141–157.

Dei, G. J. S., Holmes, L., Mazzuca, J., McIsaac, E., & Campbell, R. (1995). *Drop out or push out? The dynamics of Black students' disengagement from school*. Report submitted to the Ontario Ministry of Education and Training.

Dei, G. J. S. (1999). Knowledge and politics of social change: The implications of anti-racism. *British Journal of Sociology of Education, 20*(3)395–409.

Dei, G. J. S. (2008). *Racists beware: Uncovering racial politics in contemporary society*. Rotterdam: Sense.

Dei, G. J. S. (2014). The Black/African scholar in the Western Academy. *Journal of Black Studies, 45*(3)167–179.

Dei, G. J. S. (2016). Decolonizing the university: The challenges and possibilities of inclusive education. *Socialist Studies//Etudes Socialistes, 11*(1), 23–61. Retrieved from www.socialist-studies.com

Dei, G. J. S., & Kempf, A. (2013). *New perspectives on Africentric schooling in Canada*. Toronto: Canadian Scholars' Press.

Dei, G. J. S., Mazzuca, M., McIsaac, E., & Zine, J. (1997). *Reconstructing 'drop-out': A critical ethnography of the dynamics of Black students' disengagement from school*. Toronto: University of Toronto Press.

Essed, P., & Goldberg, D. T. (2002). Cloning cultures: The social injustice of sameness. *Ethnic and Racial Studies, 25*(6), 1066–1082.

Fine, M. (1991). *Framing Dropouts: Notes on the Politics of an Urban Public High School*. New York: State University of New York Press.

Fine, M. (1994). Distance and other stances: Negotiations of power inside feminist research. In A. Gitlin (Ed.), *Power and method: Political activism and educational research* (pp. 13–35). New York: Routledge.

Gallagher, K., & Fusco, C. (2006). I.D. ology and the techniques of public (school) space: An ethnographic inquiry into the neo-liberal tactics of social (re)production. *Ethnography and Education, 1*(3)301–318.

Gallagher, K., & Lortie, P. (2005a). Building theories of their lives: Youth engaged in drama research. In D. Thiessen & A. Cook-Sather (Eds.), *International handbook of student experience in elementary and secondary school* (pp. 405–366). Dordrecht: Springer.

Gallagher, K., & Lortie, P. (2005b). How does 'knowing my business' make you any safer? Critical pedagogy in dangerous times. *Review of Education, Pedagogy and Cultural Studies, 27*(2), 141–158.

Gill, K. J. (2012). *Minding the gap: Understanding the experiences of racialized/minoritized bodies in special education*. Unpublished PhD dissertation. Ontario Institute for Studies in Education, University of Toronto, Toronto.

Giroux, H. A. (2005). Spectacles of race and pedagogies of denial: Anti-Black racist pedagogy under the reign of neo-liberalism. In L. Karumanchery (Ed.), *Engaging in equity: New perspectives of anti-racist education* (pp. 59–78). Edmonton: Brush Education.

Giroux, H. A. (2008). *Against the terror of neoliberalism: Politics beyond the age of greed*. Boulder: Paradigm.

Goodson, I. F. (2001). Social histories of educational change. *Journal of Educational Change,* *2*(1)45–63.

Hargreaves, A. (2005). Educational change takes ages: Life, career and generational factors in teachers' emotional responses to educational change. *Teacher and Teacher Education,* *21*(8)967–983.

Harvey, D. (2005). *A brief history of neoliberalism.* Oxford: University Press.

Henry, A. (1998). *Taking back control: Black women teachers' activism and the education of African Canadian children.* New York: State University of New York Press.

Hill, D. G. (1981). *The Freedom Seekers: Blacks in Early Canada.* Agincourt, Ont: Book Society of Canada.

Ibrahim, A & Abdi, A. A (2016). [eds.]. The Education of African Canadian Children: Critical Perspectives. Montreal: McGill-Queens's Press, Canada.

Jones, P. W. (1997). The World Bank and the literacy question: Orthodoxy, heresy and ideology. *British International Review of Education, 43*(4)367–375.

Lasky, S. G. (2004). *An exploration of teacher vulnerability in a context of large-scale government-mandated secondary school reform.* Unpublished doctoral dissertation, OISE/University of Toronto, Toronto, Ontario.

Lewin, K. M. (2000). New technologies and knowledge acquisition and use in developing countries. *Compare, 30*(3), 313–321.

Lingard, B., & Mills, M. (2000). Teachers, school reform and social justice: Challenging research and practice. *Australian Educational Researcher, 27*(3)93–109.

Mbembé, J.-A. (2003). Necropolitics (L. Meintjes, Trans.) *Public Culture, 15*(1)11–40.

McDermott, M. (2013, February 22–23). *(Re)Tracing contours of student voice, subjectivity and desire.* Paper presented at the 6th Biennial Provoking Curriculum Studies Conference: As Strong Poets. University of Ottawa.

McDermott, M. (2014). *A teacher's story of autoethnography and student voice pedagogies.* Unpublished doctoral dissertation thesis, OISE/University of Toronto, Toronto, Ontario.

McMahon, B. J., & Portelli, J. P. (2012). The challenges of neoliberalism in education: Implications for student engagement. In B. J. McMahon & J. P. Portelli (Eds.), *Student engagement in urban schools: Beyond neoliberal discourses* (pp. 1–10). Charlotte: Information Age.

Mensah, J. (2010). *Black Canadians: Histories, experiences and condition.* Halifax: Fernwood.

Nasir, N. S. (2005). Everyday pedagogy: Lessons from basketball, track, and dominoes. *Phi Delta Kappan, 89*(7)529–532.

Porfilio, B., & Malott, C. (Eds.). (2008). *International examination of urban education: The destructive path of neoliberalism* (pp. 195–210). Rotterdam: Sense.

Schick, C. (2010). Whatever happened to anti-racist education? In C. Smith (Ed.), *Anti-racism in education: Missing in action* (pp. 47–28). Alberta: Canadian Centre for Policy Alternatives.

Shujaa, M. (Ed.). (1994). *Too much schooling, too little education: A paradox of Black life in White societies* (pp. 221–244). Trenton: Africa World Press.

Statistics Canada. (1991). *School leavers survey.* Ottawa: Education Culture and Tourism Division, Statistics Canada.

Statistics Canada. (1993). *School leavers survey.* Ottawa: Education Culture and Tourism Division, Statistics Canada.

Spring, J. (2006). *American education* (12th ed.). New York: McGraw Hill.

Tuck, E. (2011). Humiliating ironies and dangerous dignities: A dialectic of school pushout. *International Journal of Qualitative Studies in Education, 24*(7)817–827.

Winks, R. W. (1997). *The Black in Canadian: A history.* Montreal, Canada: McGill-Queen's University Press.

Chapter 8
Learning from the Experiences of Being a Black Body in the Western Academy: Countering Hegemonic Thoughts

Abstract This chapter attempts to draw out/upon some of the lessons from the experiences of being a Black body in the Western academy and the challenges of countering hegemonic thoughts. Working with ideas of CLR James, the chapter stretches the discussion to the role and responsibilities of the Black scholar in general. The specific question of how we take up race and racial identity in the academy is broached. The chapter notes that the contemporary world, where class, gender, race, sexuality, and other cleavages are important dimensions of identity, it is significant for us to be critical of evocations of "community" that erase these differences. Moreover, African leadership or leadership in the Black community, broadly conceived, should not be inordinately focused on critiquing the West. While it is clear that race-based organizing has paved the way for Black intellectuals to hold positions, can such organizing be abstracted from the influence of other forces and factors which are themselves independent of the intentions of Black political practice? Some questions need to be asked. For example, in our struggles and trepidations in the Western academy, where are we going to walk next as racialized faculty? What does it mean to work with the possibilities that can be unleashed with our critical capacities? If we are into "transformative education," how do we subvert dominant readings of transformative learning that are so individualistic, focused on attitudinal changes and agency of the individual learner, while failing to name critical issues of race, racism and anti-racism, sexism, homophobia, ableism, other oppressions, colonization, and Indigeneity? How do we foster dialogic and generative forums for such critical discussions in the academy? The possibilities for personal reflection allow for my writing voice to be heard and be present within and without the text the "text." What do we do with our academy presence, specifically, our teaching and scholarly research in terms of the real world out there?

Quite recently, as a Black body/scholar, I was invited to contribute to a discussion on the experiences of racialized faculty in the academy. I took up the opportunity in a different or indirect way, that is, to reflect on my work and how the scholarship we produce either sits within conventional discourses and/or disrupts mainstream dialogues. In this chapter, I recap some of the ideas I shared with the participants. The issues of racism, social oppression, marginalization, devaluation, and

© Springer International Publishing AG 2017

G.J.S. Dei, *Reframing Blackness and Black Solidarities through Anti-colonial and Decolonial Prisms*, Critical Studies of Education 4,
DOI 10.1007/978-3-319-53079-6_8

hierarchization of knowledges are very much part of the experiences of Black and racialized bodies in the Western academy. As a Black/African, racialized minority faculty member, one always has to prove oneself to be the best they can be. There is the sense of a microscope focused on you, and you better not slip up. I have encountered many supportive colleagues and students in my academic career at the university. But one also cannot forget those colleagues and students in the larger realm of university life who at times perceive racial minority faculty as not belonging with them, that your scholarship is not to their taste, and that if they had the power, they would get rid of you. These colleagues and students, working within the hierarchy of knowing that the Western academy is notorious for, will sometimes pit you against other racialized *and* dominant colleagues in the department or university, positioning them as "scholarly," "theoretical," and "deep thinkers" all because they write and speak the language the dominant wants to hear.

To reiterate, there is a particular push back on race and equity issues and significantly from where I sit, I see Blackness as threatening as we are continually being forced to construct, enact and navigate our racialized identities in apolitical ways. The mantra is that Blackness and Black identities are complex, fluid, contested, and negotiated. This is an intellectual stance professed within rigid orthodoxies, tyrannical hegemonies such that one not dare to espouse counter stances such as "strategic essentialism" without cost, discipline, and punishment in return. Oppositional and critical discourses are not warmly embraced and even less so depending on who is articulating such discourses. Our institutions have not always been welcoming spaces for particular bodies and scholarship. Some of us have to continually fight to resist at a huge cost to our social, psychological, spiritual, and psychic well-being.

One can go very far in the academy by being silent on race, equity, and social justice issues especially if you are a racialized minority scholar. Just simply complicate race, make everyone equally complicit, see no colonial-dominant, share the blame for colonial oppression, and you will see what I mean! If you speak race and anti-racism you can be seen as the "race (wo)man," too Black and Africa conscious, and very threatening in many ways. You are loved if you are post-colonial and post-modern rather than Afrocentric and anti-colonial. [Although I now notice that even those speaking "post-colonial" are all of a sudden changing their tune to "anti-colonial" in the same breath that they utter decolonization]. Some students and faculty read this dynamic very well and play the game. Some faculty and students may push students away from your work even as much as the student tries to engage with the scholarship. Why? It is not because you have nothing to say, nor is the work without scholarly merits. It is because your work may be read as too "in your face" and disruptive of the status quo, complacent knowledge. No one wants to disturb the academic peace! These colleagues and students wonder why you appear so angry and are always critical of everything. They want to muzzle others and they say: "can't we simply get along"! You can also have another racialized colleague buying into the established reward structures of the academy because they are validated, legitimized, and valorized for being the antithesis of what you are or represent. And these racialized faculties very consciously take in this power and privilege. This is when they begin to put their own community and people under the bus. It is interesting indeed.

I agree that in the contemporary world, where class, gender, race, sexuality, and other cleavages are important dimensions of identity, it is significant for us to be critical of evocations of "community" that erase these differences. Moreover, as I insist in a forthcoming paper (Dei 2017) African leadership or leadership in the Black community, broadly conceived, should not be inordinately focused on critiquing the West. But any attempt to offer a counter discourse is a critique of the dominant/hegemonic discourse. There are no two ways around this. I agree that our analysis must center African/Black leadership in African Indigenous knowledges as a philosophy that leads us to be critical. There are some important works of Black scholars developed from the interests of the community, which are informed by a critique of Black intellectualism that has emerged from the community itself. As Black intellectuals aspiring to help pioneer new systems for understanding our communities, we need to heed existing critiques, since for many our scholarship alone is insufficient if it lacks a vision for addressing the needs of the Black community. Clearly, both the issue of "relevance" and the concept of "debt to community" arise, which I have problems with when critique extortionate and rejectionist criticisms are made of those Black scholars who do not perform a hegemonic narrative of what it means to be Black. I agree with this position. I am not interested in presenting a hegemonic discourse or prescribing what we must all do. However, I am interested in pushing an intellectual agenda. My intellectual work has a politics with no apologies. It has not forced compliance. I do not want to be silenced with postmodernist/ Eurocentric charges of "Black essentialism." I would not dispute the claims of any scholar who sees "Black community/ies." We may be a heterogeneous, complex, and competing communities, but we are still "Black community/communities." In claiming, insisting, and working with "Black community/ies," I am not being defensive; but clearly I have a political and resistant tone. Sometimes the two can be confused. I am reiterating some facts/stances a few may not want to hear! Must every single Black/African scholar devote their scholarship to the Black community, which is itself not a monolith? (See also Dei 2017) No. Yet, I would maintain that academic excellence as has been defined in the West is not enough for our Black communities. Academic excellence at one's craft as a scholar is not enough, and debates about what is enough, when is it enough, and on whose terms/standards, misses a critical point. Our work must always be in the service of the community and at the end of the day, if we feel we are accomplishing our tasks, it is enough. There are some luxuries and privileges of academic grandstanding in the West that Black scholars cannot afford.

While it is clear that race-based organizing has paved the way for Black and African intellectuals to hold the positions they do, can such organizing be abstracted from the influence of other forces and factors which are themselves independent of the intentions of Black political practice? Why is there a need for such questioning? What are we afraid of? We can never pay our debt to the community no matter what, given the histories and legacies we have been dealt with; and so even to ask, "When will our requisite 'debt' be paid?" is seriously flawed. It is not when, but how. In complicating what Pan-African leadership might look like, we must be asking the right questions. We must also address other problems. There is limited engagement with the implications for imagining gender, sexuality and class in terms of Indigenous knowledges and the politics of Black leadership. We must also access the roles African women have played as Black communities engage in reclamation and transformation.

I have always wondered why, for example, a focus on Black and or anti-racism issues becomes a "narrow" or "parochial" preoccupation? Is the study of Black youth education simply a "Black issue"? There are no universal students and so what explains this desire to go universal every time? Why is a preoccupation with White students, Whiteness, and European studies never branded this way? Under the guise of complexifying social categories we deny the intellectual agency of some scholars. We can problematize social categories all we want, but categories are meaningful notwithstanding their limitations. Through social categories we demand systemic and institutional accountability and transparency.

I could go on and on. But I chose to focus my discussion more on where I see my work going as a Black scholar in the [Western] academy. For sure some colleagues may disagree with my positions. I respect that. My intellectual politics and project are merely to undertake brief personal reflections on my years of teaching and learning in North America as a scholar of African descent. While I speak from the entry point of a racialized subject, I am not unaware of my own personal complicities and implications in the very challenges I choose to bring forward. I am hoping that I speak with other racialized bodies in the academy who share these experiences and make similar reflections. In effect, this work is not a "single-authored" essay. I work with the idea of shared collective experiences with other colleagues, faculty, staff, and students in the sojourn in academia. The micro-politics of the academy makes us complicit in dominant structures. Many times, we only insert ourselves into the logic, reasonings, and implicit stances the very things we are contesting, rather than offering counter perspectives that truly subvert what we are contesting. When this happens we are no different from what we critique. For racialized bodies, our existence in academia is about contesting and negotiating boundaries and ensuring that our sanity remains intact in the disciplinary confines and apparatus of higher education.

So I ask: In our struggles and trepidations in the Western academy, where are we going to walk next as racialized faculty? (see Dei 2014) What does it mean to work with the possibilities that can be unleashed with our critical capacities? If we are into "transformative education," how do we subvert dominant readings of transformative learning that are so individualistic, focused on attitudinal changes and agency of the individual learner, while failing to name critical issues of race, racism and anti-racism, sexism, homophobia, ableism, other oppressions, colonization, and Indigeneity? How do we foster dialogic and generative forums for such critical discussions in the academy? The possibilities for personal reflection allow for my writing voice to be heard in the "text." What do we do with our presence in the academy, specifically, our teaching and scholarly research in terms of the real world out there? For Black scholars in Canada I know that, in so far as racial profiling, high school school push rates, and a disproportionate number of our children remain in care, our work remains undone. I will not present any victory narratives because they can be seductive and may even help dilute the complexities of our work in dangerous, unkind, and less caring places.

In a recent paper (Dei 2014), I articulated what I see as the responsibilities of African scholars in the Western academy. Since then my attention has also been drawn to related discussions by James and Gorden (2013). In this chapter, I will extend this discussion looking at our scholarship and the responsibility to upend both the academic and the colonial narratives. While not wanting to prescribe a particular politics, I find it unsettling for any academic let alone the racialized scholar to claim her or his world is devoid of politics. Quite frankly for many of us, this is a luxury we cannot afford. I say this because for most racialized scholars, it is through historic community struggles that any academic spaces have been opened for us. It is interesting to me that usually those who claim this space as a place where we need to be objective, neutral, and free of detachment are so often those seen as the "scholars"!

The reader must allow me to place certain issues on the table. I do not know why, but increasingly I have developed little patience for academic grandstanding. In the academy we all know too well that proximity to Whiteness sells a lot. Whiteness has currency and yet we all fall prey. Why is there such enticement and/or seduction? Why is it that usually (but not always), the scholar who enjoys a degree of skin privilege would dismiss as political or anti-intellectual, the claims made by those of us with "dark skin" about the saliency of skin color in racism? This is what I mean by Blackness as consequential. Reflecting on my academic experiences, I would affirm without any apologies that skin color racism speaks to the profound effects of being African and Black to the core. Please note I am not interested in intellectually futile debates about who is African or not. Molefi Asante (2007) asks us to remember that when Europeans came to the continent to enslave people, they knew without question who the Africans were! Such unending questioning may serve some intellectual curiosities by complicating and making ambivalent and contradictory any easy claims. But what is the end game? To what intents and purposes is our questioning if it only ends up negating any true sense of our identities? Whose interests have been served? Are we "intellectual" simply by not succumbing to reductionism and essentialism without any politics of identity? I have no false pretenses. I know where I stand so when going to the riverside to have a drink, I usually carry my own cup.

Tomaselli and Mboti (2013), in a very critical interrogation of Cultural Studies (CS), note:

> Many African scholars, whether relocated to the North or working from the South, have tended to locate themselves in trajectories of conceptual mobility that leverage, mobilize and re-create Northern codes of conduct/doing, language and theory. These scholars re-process CS jargon within a de-territorialized discursive western conceptual space that obscures the experientiality of the local and the ordinary as lived *beyond texts* (p. 6).

They continue by asking, "Why are Africans exported to study in the North expected to study Africa rather than casting an African's eye on Europeans themselves? Why do *they* get to study us, but we don't get to study *them*?" (p. 8). Recently a colleague whom I respect very much asked me why an African student would come to North America to study Africa? Isn't Africa the best place for such studies? The question has merits. I replied pointing to the necessity to theorize Africa broadly—physically, socially, culturally, and spiritually. But, upon later reflection I think the real concern is if our scholarship, as Black/African learners living in the West, does not help us turn the gaze also on the West itself then we have not done the job of critical learning! I believe these questions are very appropriate and indeed worthy of deep intellectual reflection.

8.1   Pursuing Radical Black Scholarship as a "Return to the Source"

In this section I want to speak from the self, as a Black/African scholar in the Diaspora and what the lessons of my experiences as a teacher, learner, community worker and a racialized subject have taught me. I start by turning a gaze on the Motherland, Africa. My long standing affiliations with African educational institutions have facilitated my own professional and academic development. An important aspect of the learning that occurs in research work in North America and Africa and working with local African colleagues and students is through knowledge sharing, reciprocity, and "giving back." This requires that the "outside" researcher find time to share, assist, and mentor colleagues and students in the spirit of reciprocity. I see this as an opportunity to "give back" knowledge and expertise working with African colleagues and students. There is a need for us as African scholars in the Diaspora to develop genuine reciprocal relations and a co-relational status with local scholars and be on top of African scholarship in ways that can be mutually beneficial.

I have learned very much from my academic sojourn in North America since 1979. Among other things, I have come to appreciate that it is intellectually and politically limiting simply to read scholarly interactions as a one-way track. I do not think that Black/African scholars in the Diaspora can only assist by taking up a full-time appointment with African institutions and be based solely on the continent. While I agree we cannot study our communities "from a distance" or from the "periphery," we live in inter-related communities and what has been termed "a global village." We must think creatively about how we share knowledge. There is a need for "brain circulation." One way African scholars in the Diaspora can assist in African educational development is by making our expertise available to students and faculty colleagues on the continent.

In my own academic work, a major preoccupation is the production, interrogation, validation, and dissemination of knowledge about Africa to challenge imperial and colonizing knowledges. I have also come to realize that development concerns of Africans on the Continent and those in the Diaspora converge a great deal.

Similarly, the South and the North are inextricably linked in many ways, least of which is asymmetrical power relations. There is a broad spectrum of converging interests around social and economic development issues. This calls for collective dialogue among scholars and students in these spaces. As Zeleza (2005) long ago exhorted, we must find collective ways address and come out of the "book famine" on the continent, especially in the current climate of economic hardships and dwindling publishing outlets. This is crucial in breaking away from the entrenched relations of domination and dependency between African scholars and Euro-American publishing outlets. This is critical if we are to define our problems, articulate home-grown solutions, and direct and control the study of Africa. We must recreate won knowledge about Africa.

For Black/African scholars teaching in North America, Europe and elsewhere, we must constantly be in touch with our communities to rejuvenate our knowledge base. While my research and teaching interests span across a broad intellectual and geographical spectrum, I do supervise a number of Black/African students at the University of Toronto. I also work with non-Black/African students who are interested in studying Africa. My research has always centered on Africa although not exclusively. I look at Canadian and Global South issues too. Discussions about decolonizing research about Africa, challenging the colonial imaginary of Africa, or claiming the African intellectual space can only be meaningful if we are grounded and, particularly, if we are in touch with on-going research, teaching, and other scholarly developments on the continent. When we do so we become the best students and teachers of Africa in diasporic contexts. It is our anti-colonial intellectuality that makes our work "authentic" (i.e., not pure or uncontaminated, but remaining true to ourselves, our voices, and our identities as African scholars). We need to be informed about African development on the ground as we contextualize those academic spaces where Africa and the African experience are often erased, negated, devalued, or even misunderstood or selectively miscaptured. To me, the intellectual project of challenging the coloniality of Africa and redefining our intellectual mission in [Western] academic spaces is about the African scholar not becoming an "intellectual imposter" (Nyamnjoh 2012) in the Western academy through "colonial mimicry" (Bhabha 1994). We must ground our teaching, research and studies of Africa in the African experience, both for the sake of our own professional and scholarly development, and also in terms of the materials we teach and our abilities to supervise students who study Africa.

There is an honest, practical, and pragmatic consideration. Increasingly, it is becoming difficult to maintain links with Africa as a researcher because of the high cost of research (e.g., travel and sustaining a long academic presence as much as one wants to). African scholars may have good intentions but the reality on the ground is different. There are huge material/financial costs and logistical constraints of sustaining one's research in Africa. How can the African scholar be able to go back to assist, research, and work collaboratively with local scholars and not be over consumed by material questions or material upkeep? Having one less worry allows for intellectual imagination and scholarly creativity to flourish.

I see a potential impact in "taking up" Africa as a site of learning in my own academic and professional growth. There is much to learn by being grounded in critical African scholarship. I am always looking for possibilities to enrich my own academic training, research, teaching, and particularly my theoretical scholarship, as it pertains to scholarly engagement in Africa. There is some urgency for us to bring a personal commitment to shed any abstract intellectualism and to make our work more relevant to local communities' needs and aspirations. I think interactions with local African scholars and students bring to the table questions of the local, national, and international relevance of our work. What are the possibilities to engage in collaborative research with local African scholars and students, and to source research grants for projects jointly designed, implemented, and carried through? Africa is neither static nor frozen in time and space. New issues are emerging every day. How can we be part of the existing crop of scholars designing Africa's future research agenda? The dynamism of African cultures, historiography and scholarship can only be gained with constant and sustained research. For example, I teach graduate courses on Africa and African issues. Like many of my colleagues, I am always looking for ways to bring new knowledge into my teaching, curriculum development and classroom instruction and pedagogy. Being on the ground in Africa and in regular intellectual dialogue with faculty, colleagues, and students creates possibilities to become socially, emotionally, politically, and spiritually involved as critical praxis. This, to me, is bringing an embodied connection to studying and teaching Africa.

Increasingly, universities in the Global North are reaping the benefits of international education. But there must be institutional credibility for what we do. How do we help address the problem of institutional credibility, particularly of Global North institutions? Debates about internationalization have been shaped by markets and what external universities stand to gain through international education. The received knowledge argues that home institutions benefit from such exchanges. That is not in doubt. But I want to contribute to a more critical gaze about other potential benefits by bringing the question of the responsibility Global North institutions have to the Global South to the table. It is a question of ethical responsibility and about enhancing the scholarship of the faculty of the home institutions through the pursuit of critical, decolonizing, counter, and oppositional scholarship. In effect, these institutions gain when their faculty pursue informed, critical scholarship in the delivery of education to their students. Such local level, country by country engagement of faculty can be an entry point in global discussions by our home institutions informed by their faculty's work. We address institutional responsibility not just through the lens of asking what is in this for us, but also by ensuring that institutions meet our shared and collective obligations to local disadvantaged communities from whom we have traditionally benefitted through past and on-going colonial relations.

Global North and Global South relations implicate the African scholar in bringing issues of equity, power, and social justice to the fore for discussion. But the link also implicates the scholar to contribute to mutual sharing of knowledge and expertise. African institutions could benefit from our scholarly arrangements at both faculty and student levels (e.g., we could contribute to graduate teaching, help train local students in research methodologies, assist in graduate advising and supervision, work on student and faculty co-publications, and take on joint research endeavors). We should also search for ways to create a mutually beneficial platform or faculty–student exchanges between the home and host institutions, thereby increasing the international profile of both educational institutions.

The "brain drain" from the Global South to the North, where we are increasingly witnessing a greater recruitment of African students/researchers/scholars to institutions in the Global North, cannot be downplayed. The Global North continues to "mine" the bright minds from the Global South like others. I use "mining" as an intentional word choice; people in this system are reduced to resources which can be extracted and exploited for economic agendas. Education in the era of globalization is seen as a commodity for export, and much like how Africa is viewed as both a resource exporter and potential market for the reselling of Western goods, it is now perceived as a market for educational models, reforms, and development. I see a responsibility to assist in changing and subverting dominant intellectual mind sets by working with local African graduate students.

Since the early 1990s, equity, anti-racism, and inclusive education have become the focus of my academic research, teaching, and scholarly writing. I have been exploring new ways to ensure that learning, teaching, and administration in schools meet the needs of all students. I have always taken up Indigeneity broadly to speak to African, Latin American, and European contexts while noting significant differences and the implications of colonialisms and settler-hood (see Dei 2011). As has been noted, much of decolonization scholarship has been focused on Indigenous peoples in settler colonial contexts such as North America. How can this be enriched by discussing Fanon and other African anti-colonial Indigenous scholarship? How can these connections be complementary to each other while recognizing the differences and potential challenges in putting these into conversation with each other (see Ritskes 2012)?

My work is about the possibilities of decolonized education. I am asking such questions as: How have Indigenous forms of knowledge been taken up as alternatives to Western and conventional approaches to schooling, learning, and education? Where are the local voices in educational policy prescriptions? My academic interest in working with students in promoting Indigenous African philosophies is to assist in transforming debates about what constitutes legitimate knowledge and how such knowledges should be produced, and disseminated locally, regionally, nationally, and internationally. We must ask our students to question how we understand education. For example, what are the goals and purposes of education in a globalized context? What is the role of localized knowledges in this increasingly globalized educational environment? In what ways can education be pursued to help local communities find solutions to pressing problems? What are the prospects for the Global South for tying educational fields to local opportunities where the government/institution creates jobs and/or allocates resources to fields to reduce brain drain to the Global North?

The search for new educational futures is an on-going task. New questions to be posed in educating young learners for today's world are: How do educators provide education in ways that allow young learners to develop a strong sense of self and identity, collective respect, and empowerment for community building? How do we empower young learners to make their schools learner-friendly, healthy, working communities? How do we create "communities of learners" with responsibilities toward each other and their communities by approaching "schooling as community"? How do we reframe "education" based on counter visions of schooling and education which espouse values such as social justice, equity, fairness, resistance, and collective responsibilities? This last question is significant since traditionally there has been a dominant approach to schooling that aims to build "strong character" among learners (see Dei 2014a, b; 2015).

A critical focus on African Indigenous philosophies seeks to employ the multi-faceted ways that communities, scholars, and students can enact transformation and democratic education in schools. In this vein, our research studies should challenge the often competitive individualist and hierarchical models of learning and success that have been instituted through neoliberal value systems of productivity, efficiency, and meritocracy (Fitzgerald 2011). Many of the key works on higher education and the university as a site of teaching, learning, and the intensification of research and scholarly productivity do raise issues worthy of note as we bring a broader and more nuanced understanding to knowledge, student and faculty experiences, and the challenge of educating young learners in pluralistic contexts. In this broad area of neo-liberalism and higher education, other concerns have been raised about the meaning of the shifting discourses and practices of educational "accountability," "quality," "standards," "excellence," and "competencies" in the context of free markets, deregulation, competition, individualism, and privatization entrenched in university education (see Porfilio and Malott 2008; Andreotti et al. 2011). It is critical to explore multi-centric knowledge building and the ways we can tap into multiple knowledge sources to advance the course of education, which will be defined holistically to include the strategies, methods, and practices through which people come to know their worlds, and how they live and act within such worlds to effect lasting meaningful change.

There is another aspect of the internationalization of education that has not received proportional attention. As noted elsewhere (Dei 2013), classism is perpetuated through the lack of recognition of credentials or education obtained in Global South, such that a blue-collar workforce and lower class is maintained in the Global North. But we must also be frank in our analysis of classism. Too often what is derided as class-based privileges, especially in regards to the privileges that higher education affords, is privilege doled out because of (or because of the perception of) the proximity to Whiteness and the access that this proximity affords (Da Silva 2007).

There is also the on-going control of knowledge and what I have termed a "culture of hierarchies" in the Western academy and its colonial satellites. The commercialization and privatization of education in Africa and the Global South (like the Global North) has also led to funding the allocation of funding to certain fields (hard sciences, technology, engineering, business, and management) at the expense of the arts and humanities which foster critical thought and counter-hegemonic ways of addressing poverty, education, and notions of the common good.

For the Black scholar, it is a small revolution in itself knowing full well the costs for some of us when we engage radical thinkers in our scholarship in Western academies. I have taken the liberty with which we can engage CLR James for contemporary Black radical politics. I make no pretense to understand the complexity of James' thought and ideas. I know there are many who are steeped in his works. Nonetheless, I maintain some knowledge of this complex man—enough to help me formulate my thoughts and ideas of the struggles for Black unity, particularly in the contemporary so-called "post-modern" context. I engage James as I understand him. I am moved to raise some broader questions of the impact and meaning of CLR James for contemporary politics and the rethinking of Black solidarity across geographical spaces. I engage CLR James not specifically in Trinidad, but rather with how his later sojourns in the US, Britain, and Africa helped shape some of his ideas about the ways we can rethink Black solidarity and consciousness broadly. Specifically, I have been fascinated with CLR James in the specific area of how the "African Revolution will proceed and succeed." I am more interested in CLR James as a Black subject and the implications for Black peoples and for Africa.

My thoughts have been drawn to some of his influential work, such as his texts *The Black Jacobins, Beyond A Boundary,* and *American Civilization,* and also his manuscripts *The Rise and Fall of Nkrumah, The Revolutionary Answer to the Negro Problem in the US, From Toussaint L'Ouverture to Fidel Castro, The People of the Gold Coast, Black Power, Black People in the Urban Areas of the United States,* and *Black Studies and the Contemporary Student* (see The C.L.R. James Reader 1992).

My discussion is thus anchored in CLR James' ideas regarding liberation/revolutionary struggles in calling for a rethinking of Pan-African union in contemporary contexts. CLR James is relevant in this intellectual undertaking given the lessons of his ideas for understanding the challenges of a critical reading of race and class intersections to foster the cause of Black and African unity/solidarity in Diasporic contexts. In examining the possibilities of revolutionary politics for change today, my discussion hopes to bring a gaze on the intersection of identities, the understanding of identity as political, and what the project of decolonization entails. This assessment (discussion?) strives for a rethinking of Black/African solidarity in contemporary times through a re-examination of on-going calls for unifying causes around the lines of social identities, politics, economics, and environment, as well as emotional, cultural, and symbolic solidarity.

My three main learning objectives are as follows. First, we must reclaim and affirm African past intellectual traditions, knowledge, and contributions in world history as a necessary exercise in our decolonization and intellectual sanity. That is, an engagement with the intellectual African traditions of which CLR James was part of will help us in examining contemporary issues facing our communities, particularly the project of decolonization. Second, we must recognize the importance of reflecting on the present in order to theorize Africa/Blackness beyond its physical and natural boundaries. While this calls for engaging the Diaspora, it also calls on us to the particular troubling place of the Caribbean, as the Caribbean comes to be located through the Diaspora in the West. And third, the big question of Black consciousness must be explored. We need to examine how the pursuit of a critical reflection on our collective existence is about consciousness of our interconnected realities and social well-being as racialized groups, and how we can contest futures to set our own agenda going forward.

As a Pan-Africanist there is always the challenge to work with the intellectual traditions of our earlier African thinkers. I pose these questions: What are the challenges of a critical reading of CLR James to foster the cause of Black and African solidarity in Diasporic contexts? How do we bring a gaze on the intersection of identity and the understanding of identity as political? This discussion takes as a departure point the following: a CLR James reading that Black unity is about the quest for liberty, fraternity, and equality [the central themes of the French Revolution that Toussaint L'Ouverture appropriated for Haiti]; and also, a Frantz Fanonian affirmation that "a nation which undertakes a liberation struggle rarely condones racism" (Diawara 1996, p. 3).

It is argued that in strategizing and rethinking ways of addressing the problems and many challenges confronting us as a people, Black peoples need to heal ourselves spiritually, mentally, and materially. This calls for an affirmation of the African sense of community, social responsibility, and spiritual re-embodiment. This is a search for a new anti-colonial project that allows the Black struggle to define its own agenda for freedom and recognition and makes linkages with other peoples drawing on issues of community and responsibility.

8.2 The Political and Academic Learning Objectives

I know CLR James met Kwame Nkrumah when the latter was a student in Lincoln College in Pennsylvania, United States in 1943. In fact, we learn it was James who introduced Nkrumah to George Padmore. The latter's influence on the Conventional Peoples' Party organization among Ghanaian rural masses and the liberation struggles against British colonialism is legendary for any Ghanaian with the slightest inclinations to socialism. Nkrumah's writings acknowledge how CLR James influenced his own initial thoughts in their "politics and strategy" conversations (see Lawrence 2004). With this discussion then, I want to highlight aspects of James' ideas, in particular from his works that raise contemporary questions concerning the complexity of the Black/African dimension and revolution, such as:

(a) James' position that leadership and [small group] organization were critical to the success of any revolutionary struggle. It has been argued by others that in fact CLR James bestowed too much faith in personalities and leadership (e.g., Nkrumah and Nyerere in the African contexts), only to be disappointed.

(b) The concept that revolutionaries ought to remain true to their principles. It was this belief that later lead him to be critical of such African leaders as Nkrumah (compromising his socialist policies) and Julius Mwalima Nyerere (Pan-African Congress meeting).

(c) The view that Pan-African Socialism must be all embracing of the continent and the Caribbean, including Cuba. An important observation was James' declaration that true African socialism was the Mozambique experience and that Algeria, Libya and [Nasserite] Egypt socialism were more akin to Arab Socialism (see Lawrence 2004).

(d) As an extension of this third point, CLR James would argue for the need to theorize Africa beyond its geographical boundaries/physical spaces, that we must see the African construction of identity through a shared history being constitutive of "collective identities." Such reading has stood the test of time as a powerful challenge to Western liberal epistemology which continues to embody, espouse, and over-privilege individualism. Of course, the African shared collective is not and has never been a singular experience. As we well know, the African shared collective is heterogeneous and fecund through the myriad different experiences of the African-geo-subject.

CLR James is becoming more and more relevant today. He may be a man full of contradictions, but our task is to give some coherence—in a sense to disentangle, some of his ideas in relation to our contemporary epoch. He is essentially a materialist to be located in time and history, and hence, the importance of situating his works in historical contexts. CLR James' oeuvre has origins that come to be augured in questions concerning, if I can say, how the different forms of resistance come to be represented as national culture in the context of the Caribbean. He was also interested in the faith of the Black peoples. While CLR James was about the total reorganization of society under capitalist rule, his ideas had a particular bearing to our Black/African communities.

CLR James' intellectual and political influence spans many academic fields/terrains. Cultural theorists may read him differently than say a social anthropologist interested in the sociology of education. James was interested in the Black subject as newly located within the geography of America (see *American Civilization*). He interpreted these experiences by looking at the material existence of the Black subject through the areas of culture, aesthetics, language, and politics, to name a few. James challenges us to think of this experience as being distinct from the African continent, emphasizing the heterogeneity of the Black subject. This experience was not encapsulated in a social/cultural vacuum, and James shows that we need to think of the historical development of Blackness through a particular reading of Africa rather than a sum total, homogenous reading.

It is important for us then to situate CLR James in some contemporary questions. As I have argued in other contexts, the worth of a social theory must be measured in terms of both its philosophical grounding as well as how the theory helps us to engage concrete social political action for change. I now want to take up five interrelated areas in connection with CLR James' ideas and radical Black politics. I do not apologize for bringing a Fanonian take on the discussion because I believe ideas of Fanon and James collide and connect with each other.

First, *is the linking of the revolution and decolonization.* The question of decolonization and the implications for the revolutionary struggle are important conversations to broach when reading *The Black Jacobins.* James speaks about a revolutionary politics, and also addresses questions of decolonization for the oppressor/oppressed alike; revolution should be a total movement that involves resistance, rebellion, and more importantly, decolonization. James speaks about the myriad dynamic relations of the plantation—of how the enslaved body became organized and hierarchized through hue. James was not only speaking of revolution from an alien imposition. He very much spoke about the power mechanisms/racializing process as residing within the public sphere of the plantation, of how a particular body comes to be located within the center/margin of plantation operations. He amplifies the politics of the *mulatto/mixed-race* as being distinct from yet co-joined with the African body/experience. Despite the racial schema of plantation bodies, they were able to unite, organize, revolt, and take up an anti-colonial stance. In effect, within the racial historical schema of plantation enclaves, liberation/resistance strategies and pedagogies were not being handed down from the colonial power, but coming from within, from difference within Blackness to unite and coalesce to a sum emancipatory politics. Often enough, African unity has been touted by some scholars as being essentialist-homogenous politics, as not being heterogeneous (or not being conversant of Black heterogeneity). The dominant misreading is that such calls for African unity often succumb to "ethnic absolutism." But importantly with *The Black Jacobins,* James tells us that revolution was not going to come from Europe. Africa is not going to be liberated from the imperial West by the imperial West (not that the West is free from its responsibility, as James does well to point to a dialectic of history). Yet James is pointing to decolonization for oppressor and oppressed alike, and Africa for Africa. James reminds us that resistance and rebellion do not necessarily mean decolonization, that resistance and rebellion sometimes simply insert new forms of hierarchies. Decolonization must begin from within, from recognizing the connectedness and collectivity of experiences (not singular experience) of the oppressed/oppressor and the colonized/colonizer. Decolonization is also talking about responsibility in a way that acknowledges history and collective implications and complicities. While the search for unity is critical in this undertaking, James invites us to think of Black unity not as an end in itself. It is only a means to an end. Black power and control over its own destiny and affairs is that end. This is a question of African autonomy, i.e., genuine African Independence of the state.

Let us take an example. While in Ghana one summer not long ago I had the opportunity to listen to US President Barack Obama speak about Africa regarding its current economic situation. Obama mentioned that Africa needed to take responsibility for its economic/social perils—that Africa could not continue to blame America/the West. Much was said about what Africa needed to do, which in a sense shirked Western responsibility. I was thinking, how can James help us to disentangle these complex historic moments Obama is speaking about? What can we learn from James through his *dialectical historical material* approach to understand Obama's words in the context of decolonization? This is the Black body coming to govern the imperial rule. And how can James help with understanding these present-day questions of co-optation and the reproduction of globalized imperial relations? I am also asking, how do we begin to understand contemporary questions of decolonization/ revolution in the context of Western historical amnesia? What does it mean, in the decolonization context, when the African/Black body comes to govern the West and organizes continued imperial relations on the African continent?

James in *The Black Jacobins* tells us of how we come to know today as the revolutionary movement of *Negritude* emerged through histories of resistance in Haiti. In doing so he recalls the challenges experienced by the colonized body in Haiti. James pushes his readers to think about the certain geo-politics of what it means to be human as constructed by Euro-modernity, in particular the ensuing position of the Black body within plantation life of Haiti in relation to the colonial society of Euro-modernity as governed by France. James well noted that after the revolution, Haiti participated in a certain production of modernity that likened itself to Europe. In other words, French was everything. French was language, French was food, French was intellectual, and French was culture (see James 1989: 394). James does well to tell us that this newly formed humanism of Haiti, which likened itself to Europe, was soon enough chastised by the same said Europe. As a counterpoint Haiti had nowhere else to go but to turn toward its own, resulting in a decolonizing shift that materialized as a particular body of knowledge which we come to know as Negritude, in that, Negritude was borne out of Haiti, Negritude was borne out of resistance, Negritude revealed itself as counter to the dominant Euro-colonial reading of the African body as located within Haiti. James reveals the way in which Haitian peoples had to "resuscitate" as he puts it, their African ancestry, African culture, and African way of life (see many o his works James 1992a, b, c, d, e, f, g; 1993a, b). What I am asking is: how can James help us understand Haiti in the present-day conditions of existence as they come to be geographically compelled through the recent seismic events? Indeed James would have us note how currently in the news, global society as a whole accelerates to further humanitarian aid. We also need to note that presently we are witnessing a global race to broach the economic lacuna, one colonially governed through Western imperialism. James leaves us with a dramatic anti-colonial account of the Haitian revolution from 1791 to 1803. We know today that the anti-colonial movement of Haiti faced and continues to face economic prohibition whereby historically there exist, a particular imperial impetus from France. We know today the anti-colonial revolution culminating in 1803 continued to be dis-recognized by France until 1825, whereby France in their colonial trope decided they were owed a particular compensation for the supposed liability incurred by the Haitian liberatory movement. What James is pushing us to talk about is the question of debt and reparation. Whether ideas propel material conditions or material conditions propel ideas, the question of Black solidarity with the call for economic accountability and responsibility looms despite the colonial cloak of the *conceit of globalization*.

Second, is *Black Consciousness and the Quest for Solidarity/Unity*. In recent years, there have been calls for Black unity and solidarity in face of the many challenges afflicting our communities. There is a feeling that the community needs to think through our complex collective identities and shared histories to properly inform us of our strength, and contributions to a global community. This call for me, transcends all aspects of the New African Diaspora to engage the continent itself. But we must also engage what has been some of the intellectual responses to the quest for Black solidarity and unity? Often enough, African solidarity/unity has been touted by some scholars as being essentialist homogenous politics. The dominant misreading is that such calls for African unity often succumb to "ethnic absolutism." I would ask us to think through what have been some of the consequences of such unilateral and unfettered fragmentation around difference, and at the same time to challenge the dominant's proclivity to conscript the idea of a fractured community to deny responsibility and accountability. CLR James would have asked us to hang on to the idea of shared/collective identities. Such shared/collective identities are never singular identities.

Concerning the African body in America, James calls for us to consider/reconsider the historic material circumstances that shape their lives/consciousness, in relation to the material interests of the country. He reminds us that we cannot simply think through the question of class and politics as devoid of history. He pushes us to be mindful of the dialectic of history, and to think of particular relationships concerning the nation-state, nationalities/identity, and imperialism.

Moreover, CLR James regarding "the Negro question," invites us to think of the Civil War and the anti-colonial Haitian revolution of 1791–1803 by Toussaint L'Ouverture. To grasp the necessity for political and intellectual liberation, this in the context of Africa, and through the work of anti-colonial writers coming from the Caribbean and Africa (e.g., Marcus Garvey, Aimé Césaire, George Padmore, Stokely Carmichael, Frantz Fanon), which trumpeted solidarity and decolonization in a particular way, James reminds us, that anti-colonial writers were often enough, not understood by the people of the Caribbean and Africa. (See *American Civilization*, & "Black Power" in CLR James Reader).

My interest here is understanding the complexity of the Black subject, and the relevance of critical education that speaks to the wholeness of the human experience—the myriad intersection/interconnectedness/interwovenness of race, class, gender, sexuality, culture, and politics and how these lived movements lead to the production of a particular Black/African subjectivity. The question of humanism provides the decisive thrust of *American Civilization,* in which James was primarily interested with the interplay between human rights, the lived social experience, and the African body. He understood the given American epoch, if I could say, as the need for the human to experience/engage in a series of transmissions, interwoven/interconnected, complex subjectivities, mobility of knowledge, particular locations of capital, and the need/want to engage in some fulfillment of the socialization process.

In *American Civilization*, James took up questions of human rights, the socializing ways of displaced African peoples, and questions concerning democracy to name some. James more so took up the problems of the social, in particular the African/Black body as lived through the then contemporary epoch of America, by contesting Western metaphysical dualities as they become codetermined through the sequencing of particular categories of bourgeois/proletariat, rich/poor, art/culture, intellectual/peasantry, Black/White, beauty/ugly, civilized/barbaric as such. Grounded through a Marxist framework, James engaged in dialogue by thinking through theoretical frameworks of *dialectical materialism* and *dialectic of history,* to understand in a holistic way, the whole sense of American social ills. Here, James moved away from traditional Enlightenment epistemologies to look toward the conversation/culture of local peoples and the narratives from these organic intellectuals, in order to understand the emerging modernity/humanism that was already being counter-hegemonically lived through subaltern aesthetics. The power of place [even when transformed] is a site of knowledge transmission. This assertion is true given the lessons of Haiti as understood from CLR James' writings. James believed in the creativity/productive forces of the ordinary/local peoples: that within local peoples lies the impulse for a different modernity, for a different way of experiencing the human, for a different way of coming to know, for a different way of coming to understand one's lived experience.

How has the Euro-Canadian/American public school system helped our communities and youth to understand the complexity of the Black subject and her or his existence and to be able to connect questions of culture, politics, identity, and history to the materiality of the [Black/African] body? What knowledges are being transmitted to young learners that help them to understand the economics of schooling for racialized bodies? Are the school systems equipped to address the miseducation and under-education of Black learners? How can we address the sense of nihilism, and feelings of lost hopes some of our youth today? How can we arrive at a psychic preservation of our Africanness/re-invention of Africanness in a Diasporic context given James's opus about dialectical histories, dialectical materialisms, and historical solidarity with Africa?

In search of re-invention of Africanness in Diasporic contexts, some of us continue to argue passionately for Africentric schooling for our children. It is important to raise this issue here when speaking about our collective existence and the need for decolonization in the context of historic African solidarity. Foremost is the question of African-centered pedagogies and the interplay of everyday lived/local knowledges as they give meanings to the "social and political." In a sense, this is to affirm complex/multiple identities and subject locations as entry points to engage broader issues of learning/understanding the human as governed through this, if I could say, post/colonial/modern geographies. Second, is the need to challenge the Eurocentric gaze for interrogating the Africentric school that comes from some segments of our communities. I have heard some Black and African peoples ask: "What would dominant society think of some of our own initiatives towards uplifting ourselves and our communities?" Or, some would say the Africentric school is very controversial—I ask, "controversial to whom"? What is so controversial? Is it the school itself or the fact that we supposedly live in a multicultural society and have a mono-cultural school system? Or, someone would ask me: George are you not that concerned about balkanizing the school curriculum? My response: Why would I be concerned … especially when the current curriculum is not working for our kids or does not speak to us in terms of the complexity of our lived realities?

What we are dealing with is essentially a struggle to design our futures. For far too long others have carved out this future for us. They have designed it for us as a people. It is about time to engage in contestations to reclaim the power of the community to think out our own solutions to problems that afflict us. In order to be successful, however, we have to resist the internalized colonizing assumptions that continually divide us. As a people we have a collective sense of shared [not singular] history and identity. As I have argued repeatedly, we must challenge/resist the dominant's proclivity to conscript the idea of a fractured community to deny responsibility and accountability. Of course, we are a "community of differences." Articulations of our experiences must respond to other diversities within our communities and the differences structured along lines of race, ethnicity, class, gender, [dis]ability, sexuality, religion, and language.

Third is on *The question of the Ontological Lineage with Africa and the Caribbean.* I would venture to argue that in CLR James' thinking, within the given tapestry of Pan-Africanity, that immanent to the fluid/heterogeneous African subject/body there exists a particular *ontological primacy*, as co-determined through the temporality of Africa. James is asking us to think about, how do we work with/live by, and what are the consequences/implications of such an ontological primacy as rooted to the stasis of African temporality/historical solidarity? In other words, how do we in the Diaspora see a connection to Africa (in terms of aligning with her contemporary challenges/struggles) through a collective politics of engagement? This calls for us to think through James' *dialectical history/dialectical materialism*, and the historical solidarity with Africa; we have to begin to speak about the economic, material conditions in and through a historical solidarity and ontological lineage with Africa. For Black/African scholars of today, how do we take James up here? Do we simply negate/nullify Africa in our scholarship?

There is a powerful connection between what happens in Africa and how this is portrayed in the West and how the West relate to Africans in Diaspora. We cannot afford to decouple/separate the issues affecting Africans in the Continent, Caribbean, and the African Diaspora. The experiences of displacement, dislocation, fragmentation, sense of homelessness, and belonging all mean as African peoples everywhere must continually put ourselves "back together" through diasporas coalition building (see Massaquoi 2007:81). As a community we must examine the possibilities for "grassroots transnationalism," where small, community-based organizations in Africa can be connected to African Diaspora communities globally in building transnationally supported educational institutions at local levels for our mutual benefit. We must also understand the consequences of traditional mobility for us as a people.

The fact is "Africa" [by extension African] and even "Black" are artificial/social constructs. We must expect tensions, disputations, complexities, and differences as sites of engagement when we claim Africa[n], and least of all, the African Diaspora. But we can use this construction as a starting point for discussion on how we move forward to address our shared [not necessarily singular] community problems. The challenge is not the difference. It is how we create a community out of our differences. In other words, our approach to solidarity building among diverse African communities must be aware of the political paralysis that can result from the tendency for us to spend too much time dissecting our differences and the tensions/ambiguities. How do we articulate a new sense of Africanness, which is more inclusive of our differences, is a more appropriate focus!

History is so important to these discussions. There is a long history of African peoples and communities' struggles, and political advocacy to change their social conditions.

There is a need for us to reclaim the African-centered ideas of social responsibility, community, traditions of mutuality, mutual inter-dependence, African spirituality, and history as a totality of lived experienced, respect of/for the elderly and the youth as our future.

Re-conceptualizing the sense of belonging to a community also means addressing issues of rights and responsibilities, access to health, education, jobs, housing, immigration, and family unification in a Diasporic context. There is a vast amount of local cultural resource knowledge regarding the strengths and contributions of African communities, and the much developed and untapped skills offered for nation and community building. So how do we tap the available skills and resources that such communities bring to the transnational context? How do we build and sustain the African community in the Diaspora to be self-dependent? How do we work with Diasporic communities to maintain strong relationships with homeland communities in spirit of mutual interdependence?

The idea of solidarity with Africa brings up the challenge of unity and togetherness. It is important for us as peoples of African descent to discuss our differences as well as our shared histories. Simply accentuating our differences for its own sake is a vice not a virtue. The interconnectedness of history and a Pan-African vision means allowing our differences to be the source of strength, rather than becoming the force that divides us. African ways of knowing are relevant in the search for an ontological lineage among all peoples of African descent. As noted, the Western liberal epistemology that privileges the individual may have some strength in particular historical moments. We need to distinguish between a competitive individual and a communal individual. The Indigenous African way of knowing emphasizes that the individual only makes sense, only when she/he is harmoniously connected to the group/community to which she/he is part. This is philosophy of Ubuntu. For Black/African communities dispersed all over the globe our individual and collective successes must be anchored in a spirit of self-help that transcends geographical boundaries and a desire to make effective use of available opportunities wherever we found them to transform the wider society.

Decolonization as a starting point in a process of emancipation means teaching about our shared histories, identities, and resistances. Searching for solutions to our own problems would mean breaking the yoke of dependency. The Black/African community must harness its economic power through collective solidarity among itself and with others. There is a particular responsibility of leadership, that is, Elders, leaders of diverse communities ought to encourage collective solidarity among racial, class, gender, sexual, and [dis]ability lines.

Fourth, is the *Responsibility of the Black/African Intellectual and of Black Scholarship.*

How do we deal with the "knowledge crisis" and the "cultural crisis" in our communities?

Again, let us take James's position on Black Studies where he held his ground. His point being that it was not simply enough for the African/Black body to take up Black Studies. That our engagement of such intellectual endeavors must allow us to take up different strategic positions of power and influence in the economic/social order so as to transform our social existence. For the Black intellectual today, the necessity to re-write knowledge and our histories as a necessary exercise in our own decolonization and mental firmness (see also Du Bois 1947, 1969; Diwara 1996).

The expertise and knowledge of local communities make it imperative for us as Black intellectuals to tap local communities for an understanding of their own challenges and problems and what ought to be done to address these. There is also the opportunity for us to build local capacity to articulate their own issues, undertake their own research, and search for genuine homegrown solutions to their own problems. The African idea of community is knowledge that is embedded in us. We can retrieve it in highly individualistic context.

We need the Black intellectual and middle class to assist the wider African family and community in the areas of our collective social existence (e.g., education). For example, helping to address what I call the "Economics of Schooling," specifically, the issue of educational access. The high cost of schooling and ever-increasing tuition money requires strategic responses from the institutions of grants, scholarships, and bursaries to help struggling communities. For the Black intelligentsia this may mean owning up to our responsibilities. We must recognize the sacrifices that others made to pave the way for us. We have reached the top on the back of community struggles. We can highlight such intellectual voices such as to understand the realities of African peoples in the Diaspora. What is required is a holistic approach, one that considers the diverse social processes that each African community faces, based on their socio-economic and political positioning, nationalist affiliations, and access to state resources. African scholars everywhere have a responsibility to document the differential impact of contemporary national economic and social turmoil in our community, including highlighting the gender differences of policy impact.

Fifth, is *Breaking Out of Our Boundaries and Confinement:* How do we teach CLR James to our students? James broaches very contemporary questions in *Beyond a Boundary,* where in thinking through cricket, he spoke of the constraints/limits/possibilities as imbued through cricket that governed the local peoples within the colonial geography of Trinidad. Cricket provided a technological instrument, a colonial means through which the Black subject came to experience a piece of modernity/humanism. The Black body despite her/his successes "in the game" still functioned within the confines of the colonial boundaries as governed through the game of cricket. But James argues well that such confinement is not simply within the game of cricket. When the Black body steps outside cricket he/she is still confined within the boundaries of Euro-centric ways of knowing. The game brought the conditions of being Human onto Blackness. But as James notes, it has its limitations. In effect, what James wants us to understand from the game of cricket is that cricket offered possibilities which at the same time provided limitations for Blackness. This is why James would argue that it is not simply enough to resist/ rebel. Only through decolonization can the oppressed/oppressor alike achieve a Humanism beyond colonial boundaries. Genuine revolution materializes or lies in the decolonization process.

The question for me here is how do we reach a wider audience with our academic, political and cultural pursuits, and yet hold on to the saliency of the Black subject, subjectivity, and human condition? The idea of remaining true to the intellectual principles and dignity of our work and not succumbing to Eurocentric and colonial mimicry is key. Today, some scholars have silenced the question of revolution and emancipation. They ask, Liberation from what? Emancipation from what?

Notwithstanding our achievements and successes, I see a crisis in Black community and particularly education today. It is more than a "crisis of knowledge"; it is about the lack of political sophistication to understand and tease out our own problems in the same vein as CLR James saw the power of such education when talking about Independence and revolutionary struggles.

I would reiterate that a new Pan-African vision is only meaningful if it is thought about in the context of the concrete problems and realities of African and oppressed peoples in the struggle for political, cultural, spiritual, social, and educational liberation. This will be a Pan-Africanism that borrows from the ideas from before, but will also add new meanings and confront challenges—starting at the source, grassroots, local community organizing, and possesses a healthy ideological frame to diagnose problems and offer African solutions. This will be an approach not ashamed of our culture, histories, and identities as peoples of African descent. We need to challenge on-going adaptations of Eurocentric visions of the world as articulated through understandings of "communism," "scientific socialism," "governance," and "democracy." We need a new Pan-African ideology that shifts a centering on Marxist social thought onto African concepts and knowledge principles.

There is power in anti-colonial thought and practice. Anti-colonial thought sees "colonialism" and "imperialism" as never ending. Anti-colonialism today is about decolonization of minds, thoughts and actions and certain observations are worthy of noting: for marginalized and colonized peoples, decolonization has always been a part of our history. One would say from 1492 Indigenous peoples [in the context of North America, Indigenous peoples] have long been resisting the colonial will. In fact decolonization was a way of life for Indigenous peoples.

When we turn to CLR James (Black Jacobins) to speak about the Haitian Revolution (1791–1803) led by Toussaint L'Ouverture we also know that the decolonizing process was long engaged by enslaved and Indigenous peoples, long before decolonization became textualized within academic halls. When Frantz Fanon (1963) enthused that decolonization can only be understood as a historical process that ultimately culminates in changing the social order, the link with CLR James' thoughts are equally clear.

Decolonization is always successful but only after hard fought battles and struggles here is an end point ans as many have opined, decolonization is historical, ongoing process culminating in the establishment of a new social order. As a subversive act, decolonization meets with resistance from the colonialists who institutes very punitive measures for those who seek to decolonize. As African peoples in search of unity and solidarity we must expect resistance from the dominant as we seek to decolonize our minds and de-Europeanize our thoughts and actions. But we can be rest assured that decolonization is the surest bet to address the "cultural crisis" that afflicts our communities.

For the oppressed and marginalized communities, there is a consequence not to decolonize: there are other consequences for embarking on decolonization. For example, elites who have been "whitewashed" flee initially from such discursive engagement and political entanglements; we must expect a denigration of local Indigenous cultures, tradition, values, and histories. Fortunately, we should expect at some point a "return to source," that is, reclamation of culture, history, and tradition.

In conclusion I want to reproduce here [with the editor's permission] a modified short piece, "*Africa, Ebola and Our Imperial Saviors: Speaking Differently*" that was originally written and picked up by various international blogs.[1] I take up the case of Ebola in Africa, Ebola, and our Imperial Saviors in a discussion of Blackness, racial politics, and the question of Black solidarities to show the urgency of theorizing Black and Africanness beyond boundaries. In 2014, like everyone else, I was extremely concerned about Ebola which is making rounds on the daily news circuit. The threat of Ebola must be addressed. So, why would someone question Western assistance in fighting the scourge of Ebola in West Africa? After all, Ebola is deadly and the entire global community is at risk. Judging by what we are told, everyone in West Africa can easily get Ebola. We are at a high risk zone. So the world is panicking. After all, did not some major airlines cancel flights to selected West African countries? Even in Africa there has been a troubling discussion about cancelling the African Cup of Nations soccer tournament slated for Morocco in 2015 because of Ebola. Interestingly, a commercial plane Land in the US and a passenger on board shows symptoms of Ebola and the entire plane is quarantined. We need to check and be sure. But then Ghana has no reported cases of Ebola and yet we know there have been discussions about some Western tourists cancelling trips to the country. Curiously, we have reports of Ebola in New York. At least one medical personnel who served in the West African region had contracted the disease. In case we missed it, no one is talking about boycotting New York, and nor are commercial airlines cancelling flights to the city. Such is our world, our global village today—perhaps not so global after all. Hypocrisy is everywhere and unsurprisingly we have also learned to be cynical. Out of a genuine sense of "helping" or "saving" Africa, the

---

[1]Environmental and Community Service blog (https://ecscsite.wordpress.com/about/) and Association of African Studies blog (http://www.africanstudies.org/blog/124), American University of Paris blog (http://www.aupschool.org/apps/pages/index.jsp?uREC_ID=302105&type=d&pREC_ID=698333).

West sends troops to the continent to carry out their humanitarian accord. The West assigns itself a sense of global humanitarianism, steeped in the mindset of what it means to be a universal, altruistic human. We risk abandonment for even raising voices of critique or dissent. To reiterate Weheliye (2014) in another context, those who take up the questioning of the Western universal "human" from a situated position are often dismissed as anti-intellectual and/or are marginalized as speaking to localized, specific situations and, therefore, not sufficiently "theoretical" or transposable (McDermott 2014).

We are continually bombarded with the knowledge that responding to Ebola as a menace is an act of humanity and, therefore, rather than castigate those who offer support for Africa we must be thankful. I do not want to sound like a heartless intellectual. I congratulate and appreciate all who work hard to rid our communities of the scourge of Ebola. But, I want us to complicate matters a bit to challenge or even to upend our commonsense understandings of "humanitarian" aid as something which is always good and without blemish or concerns. When Western aid agencies do good in Africa it is not without some problematics. Usually, the understanding that shapes such interventions is about a hapless continent at the mercy of an epidemic on one hand, and the savior West on the other: indeed this narrative has been with us since the earliest colonial invasions. The conventional narratives are about Africa and Africans as victims, hapless souls who require the blessings of the imperial savior to survive. In other words, Africa deserves to be rescued from its predicament.

The discourse of development perpetuates this thinking through both discourses and practices, working to define and re-define the relationship of inequity by establishing new goals for Africa along with programs and policies for their implementation. Disciplinary systems through UN Development not only rank nations and regions, they always create those which cannot be assimilated (in particular Africa) (Foucault 1975). Discipline then creates new programs and protocols to correct and manage any identified outliers—those noted as "lagging behind." When operating in a biopolitical rather than necropolitical mode, liberal and neo-liberal regimes such as the UN use disciplinary systems to establish a relation. Punishment works to correct rather than attempt to eliminate African nations, and it generates new disciplinary techniques and regulatory regimes. Therefore, even with attainment of development goals, the racial and colonial underpinnings of UN governance obviate "inclusion" of developing nations as disciplinary subjects (Jensen 2016).

In addition to the work of the UN Development, new indicators, policies, and programs are also continuously developed and supported by the IMF, World Bank, and other international governing bodies which perpetuate a racial order. The alignment (or subjection) of African nations within Western imperatives of free trade, privatization of economies, Land ownership, and other free market objectives helps conceal a racial relationship through the discourse of economics (Jensen 2016). Achievement of the Development objectives will not result in self-determination, shared power, or equal legitimacy for Africa in the international arena. Ultimately, such achievement reinforces a colonial relationship.

In the current climate, the Ebola debate is shaped by how we contain it in Africa rather than how we eradicate it globally. It is more about the immediate quarantine of human bodies and not the extinction of the disease. The point I want to put on the table for discussion is that the West does not have all the answers nor solutions. The way we frame or make our interventions can constitute a big part of the problem. Perhaps reframing some questions may get us to the correct footing: How do we begin to look into Africa for solutions and not merely see Africa as a hub of problems or a basket case? How do we start conversations about Africa from a position that Africa is about hope, agency, resistance, creativity, and resourcefulness? How do we follow Africa's steps and initiatives in the search for answers or solutions? How do we initiate debates about African solutions to African problems? We must continually trouble this Western humanist thought and subjectivity as part of project of decolonization. Why is it that Africa's current medical system is incapable of addressing mounting health problems and challenges? How does global resource distribution implicate and complicate this emergence?

I am taking up my African voice as an articulation of agency, experience, local knowledge, and cultural memory in order to challenge the insulting idea that others know us better [as Africans] than we know ourselves (see also Prah 1997). My voice is one of many Black/African voices. But it is also part of the collective voice which is often silent and silenced in global debates. Again, to reiterate I am challenging the Kipling's Victorian colonial tutelage of Africa as "the Whiteman's burden," an ideological construct and thought process that still exists in the minds of our colonizers. Under the guise of helping Africa we are still infantilized and perceived as needing salvation and saving from our woes and by our colonial masters. Not many of us stop to think of our complicities in the making of the "woes" and "crises" in the first place. What are we saving ourselves from? The menace is still there. The big elephant is still in the room—and indeed he is still tearing the room apart. We cannot run away and we cannot hide. The imperial savior mentality gives the West a sense of comfort as contributing to solve a human problem when, in fact, the structural and systemic dimensions of the problem remains intact only to resurface time and again. "Help" as we know it through the imperial savior image is about mal-development. Certainly, "help" cannot be imposed and neither can African peoples be acted upon. African communities and peoples have shown remarkable degree of resiliency and agency that speaks to the capacity of the people to resuscitate ourselves and our communities from the doomsayers' notion of terminal collapse.

This conversation is part of a larger debate about "development practice" which as Sachs (1992) along with others noted a long time ago has been caught "in a Western perception of reality" (p. 5). In truth, much of on-going intellectual discussions on arresting the Ebola disease in West Africa are caught in the dominant paradigms of Western thinking. For example, Ebola is perceived as of African making and not a global disease. Ebola is an African outbreak that must be contained in Africa itself. We must isolate Africa rather than isolate the disease. We must build global hysteria to make our own peoples become fully aware of the dangers of Ebola and thus understand the severity of the situation and thereby justify why we need to shun any contact with [West] Africa for the time being. This thinking reinforces the ways in which the West is able to extend its disciplinary and normalizing mechanisms to dominate Africa and shape the debate about global disease (see also Escobar 1995 in another context). Lauer (2007) has observed that degrading stereotypes about African governments persists even to this day. There is the persisting idea that Africa needs foreign direction to manage her own affairs! The Ebola outbreak and the castigation of Africa and African governments is a case in point. To reiterate, the Western/West's approach to the outbreak is framed in the whole discourse of the "imperial savior" and Africa as a "basket case." Through this discourse Africa is rendered impure and satanic in the White gaze and imagination (see also Appiah 1992). In such discussions "Whiteness" and purity as racial identities and racial codes contribute to "valid" knowledge production about what is proper, human, and "development."

Clearly, social identities significantly implicate how experts and practitioners come to produce, validate and use "knowledge" about marginalized communities. Nearly two decades ago, Chabal (1996) has lamented on the "Politics of the Mirror" where Africa is held up to be what it is NOT. Sadly, many of us as Africans have also learned the language of development. By hammering on our precarious situation we hope to engender foreign sympathy and aid. Thus, we tell "our saviors" what they want to hear about our impoverishment to elicit more aid and assistance! We welcome Western assistance in fighting Ebola. But we do so not out of pity for Africa but a realization that Africa is us, we are complicit in the making of Africa and our responsibility is to redefine our terms of engagement to work with African resilience, creativity' and resourcefulness.

References

Andreotti, V., Ahenakew, C. & Cooper, G. (2011). Epistemological pluralism: Ethical and pedagogical challenges in higher education. *AlterNative: An International Journal of Indigenous Peoples, 7*(1).

Appiah, K. A. (1992). *In my father's house: Africa in the philosophy of culture*. New York: Oxford University Press.

Asante, M. K. (2007). *The history of Africa: The quest of eternal harmony*. New York: Routledge.

Bhabha, H. (1994). *The location of culture*. London: Routledge.

Chabal, P. (1996). The African crisis: Context and interpretation. In R. Werbner & T. Ranger (Eds.), *Postcolonial identities in Africa* (pp. 29–54). London: Zed Books.

Dei, G. J. S. (2011). *Indigenous philosophies and critical education*. New York: Peter Lang.

Dei, G. J. S. (2013, April 30). *The global 'economics of schooling' in the context of Africa and the Caribbean*. Keynote Address, AERA Caribbean and African Studies in Education (CASE) Special Interest Group (SIG) in San Francisco.

Dei, G. J. S. (2014). The African scholar in the Western academy. *Journal of Black Studies, 45*(3), 167–179.

Dei, G. J. S. (2014a). African indigenous proverbs and the question of youth violence: making the case for the use of the teachings of Akan proverbs for Canadian youth character and moral education. *Alberta Journal of Educational Research, 59*(3), 1–19.

Dei, G. J. S. (2014b). African indigenous proverbs and the instructional and pedagogic relevance for youth education: Lessons from the Kiembu of Kenya and Igbo of Nigeria. *Journal of Education and Training, 1*(1), 1–28.

Dei, G. J. S. (2015). Integrating African proverbs in the education of young learners: The challenge of knowledge synthesis. In P. Sillitoe (Ed.), *Indigenous studies and engaged anthropology: The Collaborative Moment* (pp. 181–200). London: Ashgate.

Dei, G. J. S. (2017). An indigenous Africentric perspective on black leadership: The African scholar today. In T. Kitossa, P. Howard, & E. Lawson (Eds.), *Re/visioning African leadership: Perspectives on change, continuity and transformation*. Toronto: University of Toronto Press [in press].

Diawara, M. (1996). Pan-Africanism and pedagogy. Retrieved from http://www.blackculturalstudies.org/m_diawar/panafr.htm1

Du Bois, W. E. B. (1947). *The world and Africa*. New York: Viking Press.

Du Bois, W. E. B. (1969). *The souls of black folk*. New York: Penguin.

Escobar, A. (1995). *Encountering development: The making and unmaking of the third world*. Princeton, NJ: Princeton University Press.

Fanon, F. (1963). *The wretched of the Earth*. New York: Grove Press.

Fitzgerald, T. (2011). Tracing the fault lines. In T. Fitzgerald, J. White, & H. Gunter (Eds.), *Hard labor? Academic work and the changing landscape of higher education* (pp. 1–22). Bingley: Emerald.

Foucault, M. (1975). *The history of sexuality (vol. 1): An introduction*. London: Allen Lane.

James, C. L. R. (1989). *The Black Jacobins: Toussaint L'Ouverture and the San Domingo Revolution*. New York: Vintage Books.

James, C. L. R. (1992a). The revolutionary answer to the negro problem in the USA. In A. Grimshaw (Ed.), *C. L. R. James Reader* (pp. 182–189). Cambridge: Blackwell.

James, C. L. R. (1992b). From Toussaint L'Ouverture to Fidel Castro. In A. Grimshaw (Ed.), *C. L. R. James Reader* (pp. 296–314). Cambridge: Blackwell.

James, C. L. R. (1992c). The people of the Gold Coast. In A. Grimshaw (Ed.), *C. L. R. James Reader* (pp. 347–353). Cambridge: Blackwell.

James, C. L. R. (1992d). The rise and fall of Nkrumah. In A. Grimshaw (Ed.), *C. L. R. James Reader* (pp. 354–361). Cambridge: Blackwell.

James, C. L. R. (1992e). Black power. In A. Grimshaw (Ed.), *C. L. R. James Reader* (pp. 362–374). Cambridge: Blackwell.

James, C. L. R. (1992f). Black people in the urban areas of the United States. In A. Grimshaw (Ed.), *C. L. R. James Reader* (pp. 375–378). Cambridge: Blackwell.

James, C. L. R. (1992g). Black studies and the contemporary student. In A. Grimshaw (Ed.), *C. L. R. James Reader* (pp. 390–404). Cambridge: Blackwell.

James, C. L. R. (1993a). *American civilization*. Cambridge: Blackwell.

James, C. L. R. (1993b). *Beyond a boundary*. Durham: Duke University Press.

James, J., & Gorden, E. T. (2013). Activist scholars or radical subjects? In J. James (Ed.), *Seeking the beloved community: A feminist race reader* (pp. 215–222). New York: State University of New York Press.

Jensen, B. (2016). *UN Human Rights for Women: How race becomes an organizing principle*. Unpublished term paper. Department of Social Justice Education, Ontario Institute for Studies in Education of the University of Toronto, Toronto, Canada.

Lauer, H. (2007). Depreciating African political culture. *Journal of Black Studies, 38*(2), 288–307.

Lawrence, K. (2004). Padmore and CLR James. Retrieved from online: www.marxmail.org/archives/February99/padmore.html

Massaquoi, N. (2007). An unsettled feminist discourse. In N. Massaquoi & N. Wane (Eds.), *Theorizing empowerment: Canadian perspective on Black feminist thought* (pp. 75–94). Toronto, Canada: Inanna/York University.

McDermott, M. (2014). A teacher's story of autoethnography and student voice pedagogies. A thesis proposal, Department of Social Justice Education, OISE, University of Toronto.

Nyamnjoh, F. (2012). Potted plants in greenhouses: A critical reflection on the resilience of colonial education in Africa. *Journal of Asian and African Studies, 47*(2), 1–26. Retrieved from http://jas.sagepub.com/content/early/2012/02/14/0021909611417240

Porfilio, B., & Malott, C. (Eds.). (2008). *International examination of urban education: The destructive path of neoliberalism* (pp. 195–210). Rotterdam: Sense.

Prah, K. (1997). Accusing the victims in my father's house: A review of Kwame Anthony Appiah's 'In My Father's House'. *CODESRIA Bulletin, 1,* 14–22.

Ritskes, E. (2012). *Comprehensive exams essay.* Toronto: Department of Social Justice Education, Ontario Institute for studies in Education of the University of Toronto (OISE).

Sachs, W. (Ed.). (1992). *The development dictionary: A guide to knowledge and power.* London: Zed Books.

Silva, D. F. (2007). *Toward a global idea of race.* Minneapolis: University of Minnesota Press.

Tomaselli, K., & Mboti, N. (2013). Doing cultural studies: What is literacy in the age of the post? *International Journal of Cultural Studies, 16*(5), 521–537.

Weheliye, A. G. (2014). *Habeas viscus: Racializing assemblages, biopolitics, and black feminist theories of the human.* Chapel Hill: Duke University Press.

Zeleza, P. T. (2005). The academic diaspora and knowledge production in and on Africa: What role for codesria? In T. Mkandawire (Ed.), *African intellectuals: Rethinking politics, language, gender and development* (pp. 209–234). Dakar and London: CODESRIA Books and Zed Books.

Chapter 9
Rethinking Blackness: Some Concluding Thoughts on Power and Knowledge

Abstract In this chapter, I share some concluding thoughts on writing the book, by highlighting particular struggles at the curious interface of skin, body, psyche, hegemonies, and politics. Re-theorizing Blackness has not been easy; given that we do have certain hegemonic understandings of Black identity and Blackness making it difficult to dispense. Bringing a sense of agency and resistance to Blackness, and not being afraid to engage in the radical politics of Blackness and Black identity, have been essential for discursive and intellectual politics. It is noted that a critical study of Blackness as an alternative to Western approaches to schooling and education cannot be pursued outside the prism of African philosophy and Indigenous cultural knowings. A study of Blackness should place local cultural knowledge and community voices in the educational discourses and practices for change. Moreover, a study of Blackness should also lead to questioning the relevance of academic scholarship for local communities (e.g., the curricular, pedagogic and instructional implications, and the scholarship's relevance to addressing social problems that afflict our myriad communities today). Such intellectual pursuits contribute to making us whole, engaged, and committed "scholars." But more important, the pursuit of community and creating "communities of learners" where Black and African scholarship is recognized and excellence mentored is also key to Black success. At the end of it all this is about a search for Black unity with an end goal of Black power (e.g., intellectual agency and power). Advancing a way forward to [re]theorizing Blackness, a framework for analyzing power relations is crucial. This is where Mbembe's conception of necropower is relevant as a critique of our institutions and in understanding anti-Black racism and the Black body in settler societies. In rethinking power in relation to Blackness and Black identity however, I want us to be working with power as not necessarily repressive, but productive in terms of self-actualization, resistance, and coming to voice. We must acknowledge that Blackness in itself is a point of self-affirmation and reclaiming.

Writing this book I have struggled at the curious interface of skin, body, psyche, hegemonies, and politics. While this internal struggle is important, it is precarious and harmful. This is especially so if what I am trying to convey simply elicits sympathy without seeping into the structures of the academy or other institutions to

G.J.S. Dei, *Reframing Blackness and Black Solidarities through Anti-colonial and Decolonial Prisms*, Critical Studies of Education 4,
DOI 10.1007/978-3-319-53079-6_9

bring about change. I do not want to see conversations in this book dropped down to a personal level that do not disturb the system enough for true change to occur.

Re-theorizing Blackness has not been easy given the White supremacist hegemonic understandings of Black and African identities and Blackness that have been difficult to dispense with. This is so especially when those understanding have permeated our own understandings of Black/African diaspora identities. Bringing a sense of agency and resistance to Blackness, and not being afraid to engage the radical politics of Blackness/Africanness and Black identity have been essential for my discursive and intellectual politics. We must seek to restore the sense of pride, honor, and respect for our myriad identities without feeling shame or fear when particular identities are evoked. Apart from the ways Black bodies have been signified in contemporary socio-political relations, certain meanings and practices have also been inscribed and written on Black bodies. Walcott (2003) notes that the Black body "is not only used as a biological mechanism, it also works as a site for the contestation of social relations as those relations relate to acts and actions of power on and through the body" (p. 97). Beyond the racialized reading of the Black body, we must offer additional readings that reveal strength, resistance, and power in order to design counter-futures.

The body is always political and must be politicized. In fact, the Black body needs to be politicized because it is lived and experienced through racist, colonial, and imperial encounters. Walcott (2003) again instructs that:

> Because bodies, actual and imagined, are at stake, it is imperative that we make representations matter beyond the discourse of merely seeing ourselves. Representational strategies have to account for something, and the politicality of any given representation can never be read as innocent or apolitical (p. 98).

Clearly, the Black body does not exist in isolation from what is happening all around us. We are in constant interactions, engagements, and [dis]entanglements with wider society and the issues and concerns that afflict humanity in general. These interactions reveal multiple sites and sources of responsibility, accountability, and implication for all of us.

Black bodies and other racialized and Indigenous peoples cannot go further to change racism unless White people are involved in deeply confronting their spaces, places, and psychic operations that uphold it. Hence, we collectively must engage in difficult dialogues with each other to decenter Whiteness in the academy and in wider society. Black, Indigenous, and other racialized minority scholars occupy peripheral spaces in the academy. In the continued existence of White hegemony, we can no longer afford to be silent when it is claimed that our current academic spaces are "different" and "new." Such claims reflect the structural and systemic denial of the embedded nature of colonialism and racism within White academic spaces, a deep dynamic that is psycho-culturally, spiritually, emotionally, politically, and materially encoded (Jesso 2014).

Any discussion of the Black racialized experiences should be mindful of the slipperiness of race, although arguably there is nothing slippery about racism. Racism is a problem of the West and Euro-modernity in the sense of its roots in Euro-colonial expansionist projects and the associated Enlightenment discourses rationalizing these projects buttressed by religion. But racism has transcended boundaries and there is a globalization of racism today that implicates all of us. Thus, anti-racism and anti-Black racism cannot be read as a strategy to find solutions to a Western problem. Racism is a global problem. All Indigenous, Black, racialized and colonized peoples, notwithstanding the historical specificities and contingencies of our colonizations, share two basic facts: first, the experiences of Euro-colonialism and, second, a deep spiritual and emotional attachment to the Land and the teachings of the Earth. As we seek to affirm the specificities of European colonialisms for our respective communities, it must be recognized that it is through a collective politics that we can embrace our connectedness. Through a politics of collectivities and relationalities, we can successfully displace the yoke of colonial oppressions in every space, including the academic space.

Wherever the Black/African body is situated, we cannot simply take up space. Black existence is about action, resistance, and survival. Let me take the academy as one of such spaces. We must learn from the lessons of history and the struggles that led us to our current situations in the first place (e.g., the Black learner in the academy). Given the glaring social inequities around us, I ask: So what do we do about social justice? How do we address our situational, locational and global injustices and inequalities? Intellectual ideas and politics must be combined to ensure the pursuit of political activism. In the academy, the space we occupy and the bodies that are present are extremely important, whether in terms of the politics of claiming space, or acknowledging the different meanings and signifiers of bodies. Pursuing academic/intellectual work for the purpose of advocating for social change and transformation is significant. We cannot decouple our intellectuality from politics. So the pursuit of academic activism must be about combining theory and practice and making our academic pursuits "action-oriented"; i.e., scholarship through advocacy. Our intellectual work is always political, as we examine what constitutes knowledge, how do we use it, in defense of what, and to what intents and purposes?

Within our institutions (including schools, colleges, universities, workplaces, churches, union halls, etc.), we must boldly place some questions at the table for discussion: What is our vision of the university or workplace that we belong to today? What is the mandate of our academic institution? What types of education should be taking place at the university or in our workplaces? The university as a site for education must be seen as a "knowledge liberation front." The same can be said of the workplace, our homes, and within our families and communities. Currently, the university has become a place for survivalism. Such survivalism is individual instinct. We must begin by re-imagining the space, to be more creative and innovative and to change futures. In reimagining such spaces, the body politic is key. What it means to occupy a place for particular bodies is significant. Black bodies cannot be complacent within the spaces/places we occupy. We must work to transform these spaces that have historically and traditionally been exclusive of others. Our spaces must be welcoming of all bodies, knowledges, and experiences.

Clearly institutions like our universities themselves have to contend some challenges. The mandate of the university as a public serving institution is being subverted by corporate capital/majority interests and those who see the public in a particular way that centers their interests and maintains the status quo. This involves an ongoing disciplinary and regulatory technology of bodies, knowledge, and scholarship through the particular forms of validating and credentialing what we teach, research on, and how we express our scholarship and writing (see Newson and Polster 2010). The university is increasingly moving away from being interconnected with community and taking up the causes of the community. There is also an ongoing de-spiriting of the body in academia. While we may cherish the academic freedom that allows us to raise difficult questions, we must also define and defend academic freedom in a broader sense by coupling our understandings of freedom with academic responsibility. We must create and sustain safe space for studying, teaching, and researching that transforms our communities. We must understand what it means to become a community worker, for example by championing the causes of the local community in the face of competing interests and desires. It is in this vein that the notion of community becomes relevant.

So I now want to highlight ways we can work with an understanding of Blackness as community, i.e., by creating learning communities in our varied institutions. Quite evidently, the thoughts and ideas I am expressing are not solely for Black bodies. These are strategies of community building we can all help achieve, which will make possible decolonial solidarities, bridging of differences, acknowledging each other's sense of self, collective worth, and contributions, and recognizing the need to share power to enable all of us to actualize our hopes, dreams, and futures.

For Black peoples, these are crucial discussions as they affect our collective survival in communities where we are often on the margins of social and public discourse. Our struggles have always been about survival and a fight to belong. The idea of community and Blackness is even more significant if one looks at the way the community has become fractured through a failure to utilize our own local, cultural knowings about community and wider family responsibility. Blackness is antithetical to individualism and I resist attempts to simply affirm our individualities without recognition of how we are connected together by history and struggle as communities. Our individualities matter, but only insofar as they are connected to the communities of which we are a part. Blackness and Black identities are about collectivities, and it is through the affirmation of a collective that we can genuinely begin to promote Black solidarities in a decolonial frame.

Consequently, as noted earlier a critical study of Blackness cannot be pursued outside the prism of African philosophy and Indigenous cultural knowings as an alternative to Western approaches to schooling and education. A study of Blackness should place local cultural knowledge and community voices in the educational discourses and practices for change. A study of Blackness should also lead to questioning the relevance of academic scholarship for local communities (e.g., the curricular, pedagogic and instructional implications, and the scholarship's relevance to addressing social problems that afflict our myriad communities today). Such intellectual pursuits contribute to making us whole, engaged, and committed "scholars."

To see Blackness as community, we must acknowledge and love our Blackness. This "loving Blackness" as bell hooks (2001) long ago noted is about collective welfare, destiny, and hope. Community emerges from reciprocity, sharing, and giving back of knowledge, cultural resources, and power. There are many ways we can talk about such community building. Given my location as an academic and community worker, I am reflecting on this creation of communities through the role and responsibilities of academic mentorship. There is the absented presence of the Black body in the academy. We are there and yet not there. We are not the majority and many times we exist on the margins. The few of us who occupy positions of power and influence are delusionary if we think we are part of the "network." The loneliness and individualism of the academy offers a challenge for Black bodies to think through collective solutions for survival. We must make Black identities count positively (as in solution oriented) in the academy (see Dei 2017 for an expanded discussion). Black learners have a responsibility to mentor each other if we want to create learning communities. Mentorship is about building community and in the academic institution the whole area of building community is vital to educational and social success. There must be a community-mindedness to our work as scholars, learners, educators, community workers, parents, guardians, etc. All members of the learning community must feel a sense of ownership, connectedness, and belonging to the place/institution where we do our work. Academic mentorship, approached as part of acknowledging and loving our Blackness, should be a learning process whereby younger and new faculty, staff, and students are shepherded/guided into the academic culture through the guidance, knowledge, and assistance of older and established faculty, staff, and students. Such tasks could include collaborative work in publications and conference presentations, networking within the academic profession, and other information sharing and tutelage to help new faculty get their foot in the door with teaching, research, writing, field dissemination, etc.

Under this mentorship, new faculty could be assisted with exemplary practices of graduate student supervision, transfer of research skills, guidance and brokering of collaborative international partnerships, teaching styles and lecture delivery, how to handle large classes, preparation of course outlines, and getting published. Seasoned scholars can take initiatives in creating support networks for younger colleagues and students. Study groups can partner different students together within faculty publication projects.

Learners can engage in joint collaborative work. Mentorship could be geared toward supporting the development of highly competent and confident young researchers who have solid research plans. Collaborative work could include putting proposals together (e.g., students doing a literature search), encouraging students to come up with viable research projects for investigation, hiring students on research projects, allowing students to use part of the research material for their dissertation, and co-publishing research findings with students. Such faculty-student research team projects help foster a climate of broader community outreach, thereby enhancing teaching and research collaborations with communities. Our research must be community-centered in the sense of involving community outreach, identifying local communities as key partners of our scholarship, confronting the major challenges and competing interests, and enhancing the student experience by creating conducive learning environments.

Teaching mentorship strategies for community building could include assisting new and younger teachers, designing and co-teaching courses, exploring ways to "manage course delivery," and maximizing classroom interactions of learners to ensure effective learning and thinking through questions. Mentors and mentees need to have discussions around questions such as: What do we want our students to acquire by the end of the course or teaching session? How do we get that knowledge across or how do we get there with our students? How do we catch the attention of our students? How do we resolve classroom tensions? What are some of successful teaching strategies?

When it comes to mentorship for academic supervision, the whole area of teamwork is equally vital. It may involve collective mentorship, a buddy-system, co-supervision strategies, and shared responsibilities among doctoral committee members. Mentors can assist mentees in graduate supervision, feedback on students' work, expectations of students and supervisors, best practices of graduate supervision, and ways to also mentor students for academic success. For beginning scholars, such questions as: what does it mean to supervise a graduate student? What are the roles and responsibilities of the supervisor? What steps must take place for the selection of committee members? And lastly, what are the stages for the continuum of advising and supervising students?, are all critical. Also discussions about ownership of knowledge and what is defensible work—when work goes forward for oral defense, helps in creating communities.

I have come to realize through the years learning and working with students that caring relationships matter. For example, the little things one does matter. Enhancing students' experience is primarily about improved support and shortening the time to completion of studies. There is thus a need to develop and understand clear student trajectories while in the program, which includes establishing procedures for monitoring students' progress (e.g., an "Annual Student Progress Review Form" to be completed and signed by both supervisor and students which identifies academic progress and challenges, and how challenges will be addressed). Also, it is important to establish some formality with supervisor/student meetings (e.g., meetings held once a month, setting expectations, and developing an agenda for such meetings), and with the maintaining of timelines (e.g., coursework, comprehensives, thesis proposal and ethics, fieldwork and data analysis, write-up, format/schedule for submission of chapters). Furthermore, providing feedback and reporting schedules is an important area to cover as a mentor to new faculty (e.g., 2–3 weeks maximum for turn-around of students' submitted works, providing written feedback along with face to face meetings, encouraging students to bring a tape recorder to their meetings, and working delicately to create a relaxing atmosphere for students during such meetings).

Similarly, the mentorship of the writing phase (e.g., working with the field data, going through drafts before submission to committee, when professional editing is sought, intellectual property rights and plagiarism, developing the culture of crediting sources, setting examples through co-publishing, citing students' work) facilitates academic and social success for the community of learners. As part of the exemplary practices of academic community building, academic supervisors must maintain a database of students they are working with, keeping constant updates on their progress, contact information, etc. Faculty can bring students into joint publications, research, grants, conferences and other professional activities, and also encourage a buddy system that pairs up young and senior students as a mentorship practice in assisting with thesis work.

In advancing a way forward to [re]theorizing Blackness, a framework for analyzing power relations is crucial. The power of ethnographic authority lies in that ability to claim: I was there and therefore I must know. Clearly this is not always the case, especially when it negates those who have lived that experience, history, and place. Also, not everyone who is present is noticed, recognized, or validated. For racialized, oppressed, colonized, Indigenous body bodies, our power of knowing is diminished in our marginality, devaluation, and negation. In fact, when it comes to Black identities and our experiences, others claim to know us more than we know ourselves. The interpretive authority of the dominant is about interpreting our experiences. Such authority rests on how the dominant has succeeded in convincing everyone that their analyses or perspectives are more complete, objective, and in line with social reality. Counter or alternative perspectives and analyses are deemed subjective, politically motivated, and faulty (Wahab 2005; Borland 1991). Through the combination of ethnographic and interpretative control, a discursive authority (Clifford and Marcuse 1986) has been assigned on different bodies and, consequently, these bodies are accorded with power and knowledge.

Blackness is power. As an anti-colonial thinker, I work with an anti-colonial understanding of power. Achille Mbembe's theorization of necro-power offers useful insights in understanding anti-Black racism and the Black body in settler societies. According to Mbembe (2003), necropolitics is "the subjugation of life to the power of death," which "profoundly reconfigure[s] the relations among resistance, sacrifice and terror" (p. 39). In reflecting on Blackness, we must view Blackness "in terms of personal, social, cultural, political, and economic processes embedded in particular time-space contexts, which are constituted within local, regional, national and transnational dimensions" (Rahier 2014, p. 147 in Smith 2016). The Black body continues to be a site of the contestation of power as Blackness is regulated, knowledges and knowing of the self is devalued thus leading to marginality. We must acknowledge that Blackness in itself is a point of self-affirmation and reclaiming. Absolute claims of knowing the Other and the interpretation of the Black identity from the dominant are modernistic claims to understand the ultimate truth. Multicentric ways of knowing and reclaiming of Blackness are contestations, thus confronting dominant forms of power.

In his writings, Foucault (1978, 2002) does not specifically and forcefully identify colonialism or call attention to the devaluation of humanity for Black bodies. Specifically on the emergence of subjects and subjectivities, Foucault does take into account colonialism as central to the constitution of subjectivities. Instead, Foucault focuses on the concept biopolitics, "the power to let live or die," a kind of population control which entails two parts: first, discipline of the body (military, school, prison, medicine, health, sexuality through repression); and second, regulation of the population (security, management, and other forms of control—i.e., fertility, migration). Biopower is a political mission aimed at preserving what he calls the "White Nordic race" and used to justify death.

According to Mbembe (2003), the Foucauldian notion of biopolitics is insufficient to account for contemporary forms of subjugation of life to the power of death. Alternatively, Mbembe's conceptualization of necropolitics provides a fitting framework to understand the multiplicity of discourses and practices that exist alongside disciplinary and biopolitical forms of power. Necropower marks a form of social existence, "death-worlds," contemporary political spaces haunted by racial slavery in the Atlantic world and the ongoing colonial occupation of Palestine (Mbembe 2003, p. 40). The conceptualization of necropolitics, which Mbembe defines as a "work of death," in that it identifies "who matters and who does not, who is disposable and who is not" based on race and the logic of racism and colonial domination. Mbembe argues that the meaning of death in necropolitics emerges through interpretations of embodiment: of corpses, of who kills, and of who is targeted for death. In White settler societies like Canada, it is not difficult to argue that the most accomplished form of necropower is the ongoing colonial occupation of Indigenous Lands and bodies. Moreover, Smith (2016) argues that the gendered necropolitics of trans-American anti-Black violence is expansive and includes the direct, immediate death of Black people and the lingering, slow death experienced by those who live on (i.e., family members of victims of police brutality).

While biopolitical powers work to manage, order and foster life for citizens worthy of protection, such powers work in tandem with necropolitical powers that produce death for those destined for abandonment, violence, and neglect. Bureaucratic discourse and Western rationality show state-sanctioned killing as justified and something other than murder. The political ability to separate and kill populations with legal sanction leads Mbembe to interrogate the apparent contradiction between the sovereign's right over life and death: "Under what practical conditions is the right to kill, allow to live, or to expose to death exercised? Who is the subject of this right?" (2003, p. 12). While Mbembe's analysis focuses primarily on situations of military occupation, colonialism and war, we must expand our thinking to include the work of other institutions that subject bodies to regimes of slow death and dying. However, we must also not deny the resilience and agency of those who survive on a daily basis.

I have pursued this very brief analysis of power referencing Foucault and Mbembe's work to highlight an important reality for Black/African peoples. Our collective survival is always at stake. It is therefore imperative that we use ancestral knowledges about our cultures, histories, and identities to resist and forge new ways forward as a community. Such knowledge is our power. How is power exercised and enforced in the national state and elsewhere? We see examples through both material and non-material means such as violence, speech, economic disparity, systems of surveillance, laws, rules, and policies. In the articulation of Black Lives Matter, we see a contestation of power, not valuing one truth over the other, but a claim for humanity and the negation of anti-Black racism which perpetuates the systemic and cyclical instrumental modes of power. If power can be institutionalized, what then are the forms of institutionalization? How do hierarchical structures operate through traditional structures (legal, state, education systems, military) and matters of habit (family/personal relationships)? As highlighted, Blackness is managed and studied. Studies across institutions from education systems highlight the *push out* of Black bodies to the regulation of the Black body in police carding/police brutality practices. The extent to which power is institutionalized is seen in the contemporary and historical realities of the Black identity. There is a recognition that there are degrees of rationalization of power. So we must ask, how are power relations "more or less adjusted to the situation"? Examples can depend on the cost, on the "effectiveness" of the instrument, and on the results and implications. Understanding who benefits from such instruments of power and the system it upholds paints a reality about the rationalization and the cost. There comes a point though, as seen in other forms of modernity, when the rationalization and measures of effectiveness become tautological.

In rethinking power in relation to Blackness and Black identity however, I want us to be working with power as not necessarily repressive, but productive in terms of self-actualization, resistance, and coming to voice. Asserting a Blackness/Black identity that challenges conventional readings is about coming to voice. It is also about using a collective power to produce active and resistant subjects. Such assertion and insistence on Black power must not be feared, but be taken as economically beneficial and politically productive to the communities themselves. We use power to resist and to create and design our own futures. The question of power in resistance brings home the understanding of identity as political.

Although necropolitics is a useful framework for conceptualizing the state's repressive apparatus and its relationship with Blackness in the Americas, feminist scholars note that Mbembe's definition of necropolitics fails to critically engage with the question of gender (Ahmetbeyzade 2008; Wright 2011; Puar, 2007). Body politics is significant in putting on the table some questions of gender that will be helpful in re-theorizing Blackness. For example, what are practices that normalize gender and race? How is gender constituted in Black identity? How is gender conformity resisted in articulations of Blackness? What are the disciplines involved in not conforming to gender and gender expectations? And how are power relations embedded in gender practices? We need Black leadership in helping think through responses to these questions.

This book speaks to how leadership might be informed by an African Indigenous knowledges and a sense of community. I raise key issues and questions in imagining pan-African leadership in ways that have not been seriously theorized since the formal closure of "decolonization" and abolition of apartheid. Contestations of claims of "community," "Africanness," etc., while relevant and even fashionable, are not my intellectual concern. I do not dismiss such contestations however. My main reasoning is that there is a problem of Western conceptions of leadership, and leadership in our educational institutions. Counter definitions of leadership are necessary (see also Kitossa et al. 2017). The Western conception of leadership is about individual attributes, skills and capabilities and the manner these are marshaled in the service of a purpose or objective. While such an understanding of leadership is important and relevant, I argue that it is inadequate. I am proposing that leadership ought to be framed from an Indigenous sense of African awareness (see Dei 2017b). Clearly, in the Euro-American context, we cannot speak about leadership without also a recognition of migrations and Black presence and the effects on politics of place. We also need an "essential anti-essentialism" stance in articulating Indigenous Black leadership.

There is an urgent need to look back to African Indigenous knowledges, and engage in a community politics that eschews individualism and the sense that the community is simply a "sea of individuals." On the other hand, to the extent that individual freedoms and liberties are important, the idea of subordination to the dictates of the masses can be equally problematic and I do not want to downplay this fact.

Consequently, while we must be aware of critiques of a race-based or African-centered politics, we must also see when such criticism becomes a mere detraction from a collective politics as a guiding assumption of an Indigenous leadership project. My intellectual arguments are predicated on a clear philosophical premise that "Black lives matter" and should be lived to the fullest expression of that humanity. I reiterate here that the African diaspora can express a common African intellectual character rooted in a set of clear principles. In such a reading, shared physical space is not a required precondition. As with Rasta who took up slave chants of "back to Africa," the centering of Africa need not imply a physical return to the source. There is saying that we bloom on the fertile Lands on where we sow our seeds. It is about a shared history and affinity, however fictive.

This book provides dialogue about important conversations around Blackness and reiterates that "Black lives matter." By centering race, the body and my own situatedness in Blackness and anti-Blackness, I have set forth for a re-theorization of Blackness. There are clear calls to action and next steps for new imaginaries, new horizons and possibilities engulfed in hope as addressed earlier. In taking steps forward, I ask as Black and African communities, how do we ground our theorization in praxis? How do we theorize our own lived realities? How do we create new imaginaries entrenched in resistance and intentional political intellectualism? How do we understand our implications and collective responsibility toward First Nations, Me'tis and Inuit (FNMI) communities? In which ways, can we further the re-theorization of Blackness through the raced and gendered experience of the Black woman? The embodied experience of Blackness, our locatedness, histories, and connecting to Land are all relevant to conversations today. For me the idea of Indigeneity as an international category has been a manifestation of a need to re-write hegemonic visions of history position Black bodies as complicit in colonial and imperial project of nation states.

References

Ahmetbeyzade, C. (2008). Gendering necropolitics: The juridical-political sociality of honor killings in Turkey. *Journal of Human Rights, 7*(3), 187–206.

Borland, K. (1991). 'That's not what I said': Interpretive conflict in oral narrative research. In S. B. Gluck & D. Patai (Eds.), *Women's words* (pp. 63–75). New York, NY: Routledge.

Clifford, J., & Marcus, G. E. (Eds.). (1986). *Writing culture: The poetics and politics of ethnography*. Berkley: University of California Press.

Dei, G. J. S. (2017a). New framings of collective futures: African diasporan reflections on the possibilities and challenges of an Internal Association of African Educators. In O. Ukpokodu (Ed.), *African education*. Newcastle upon Tyne: Cambridge Scholars.

Dei, G. J. S. (2017b). An indigenous Africentric perspective on black leadership: The African scholar today. In T. Kitossa, P. Howard, & E. Lawson (Eds.), *Re/visioning African leadership: Perspectives on change, continuity and transformation*. Toronto: University of Toronto Press [in press].

Foucault, M. (1978). *The history of sexuality: Vol. 1. An introduction*. New York: Random House.

Foucault, M. (2002) .The subject and power. In J. D. Faubion (Ed.). Essential works of Foucault Power (R. Hurley et al., Trans.) (Vol. 3, pp. 326–48). London: Penguin.

hooks, b. (2001). *Salvation: Black people and love*. New York: William Morrow.

Jesso, J. (2014). *Kibera's dragon—Environmental racism*. Unpublished course paper, SES 1922H: Sociology of race and ethnicity. Department of Sociology and Equity Studies, Ontario Institute for Studies in Education, University of Toronto, Canada.

Kitossa, T., Howard, P., & Lawson, E. (Eds.). (2017). *Re/visioning African leadership: Perspectives on change, continuity and transformation*. Toronto, Canada: University of Toronto Press [in press].

Mbembé, J.-A. (2003). Necropolitics (L. Meintjes, Trans.) *Public Culture, 15*(1), 11–40.

Newson, J., & Polster, C. (Eds.). (2010). *Academic callings*. Toronto, Canada: Canadian Scholars' Press.

Puar, J. K. (2007). *Terrorist assemblages: Homonationalism in Queer Times*. Durham: Duke University Press.

Smith, C. A. (2016). Facing the dragon: Black mothering, sequelae, and gendered necropolitics in the Americas. *Journal of the Association of Black Anthropologists, 24*(1), 31–48.

Wahab, A. (2005). Consuming narratives: Questioning authority and the politics of representation in social science research. In G. J. S. Dei & G. Johal (Eds.), *Critical issues in anti-racist research methodology* (pp. 29–52). New York, NY: Peter Lang.

Walcott, R. (2003). *Black like who? Writing black Canada* (2nd ed.). Toronto, ON: Insomniac Press.

Wright, M. (2011). Necropolitics, narcopolitics, and femicide: Gendered violence on the Mexico--U.S. border. *Signs, 36*(3), 707–731.

Index

A

Academic freedom, 208

Africa, 2–4, 8, 9, 21, 22, 33, 34, 46, 48, 73, 102, 107, 122–128, 135, 136, 139, 140, 144, 152, 153, 156, 167, 178, 181–187, 189, 190, 192–195, 198–201, 214

African, 2–4, 8, 14, 17–24, 28, 31–38, 40, 43–45, 47, 49, 50, 52, 53, 56, 59, 67–70, 72, 73, 75–77, 81–83, 85, 89, 98, 100, 101, 114, 122–124, 126, 131, 135–148, 152, 154–157, 160, 169, 172, 173, 178–201, 206, 208, 213, 214

African body/experience, 190

African-Canadians, 15, 95, 96, 98–100, 104, 109, 111–113, 115, 139–142, 144, 146, 154–156, 163

African-centered perspectives, 32, 36

African Diaspora, 32, 34, 53, 58, 59, 67, 89, 141, 144, 152, 153, 192, 194, 206, 214

Africanness, 2, 17, 19, 20, 28, 32, 33, 49, 50, 53, 76, 122, 136, 146, 154, 173, 193, 195, 198, 206, 213

African temporality/historical solidarity, 194

Africentric schooling, 193

Africentric schools, 155, 156, 193

Agency, 4, 17, 32, 34, 45, 48, 53, 55, 60, 65–67, 71, 76, 78, 85, 93, 152, 166, 180, 200, 206, 212

Alignment, 14, 86, 124, 125, 146, 199

Alterity, 121, 157

Amputations, 36

Ancestral memories, 142

Ancestral remains, 36

Animality, 68, 126, 128, 138

Annihilation, 36

Antagonisms, 81

Anti-blackness, 15, 31–60, 65–78, 81, 84, 85, 88, 105, 121, 123, 127, 154, 214

Anti-colonial, 1–28, 32–34, 45, 55–60, 66, 69, 72, 74–78, 83, 85, 98, 100, 102, 103, 120, 136, 138, 139, 178, 183, 185, 188, 190–192, 197, 211

Anti-colonial intellectualism, 183

Anti-colonial solidarities, 26, 77, 83–85

Anti-essentialist, 16, 69

Anti-intellectual, 11, 14, 19, 49, 82, 181, 199

Anti-racism, 13, 43, 45, 52, 55, 60, 67, 85–88, 98, 100, 102, 110, 112, 123, 155, 161, 178, 180, 185

Appropriation, 8, 34, 43–45, 78, 85, 86, 88, 89

Arbitrariness, 5, 69, 106, 159

Attractive allegory, 73

Authenticity, 3, 20, 35, 51–52, 83, 85

Authentic selves, 82

B

Becoming Black, 48–50

Belonging, 12, 33, 40, 41, 82, 102, 129, 130, 140, 141, 143, 159, 169, 170, 172, 178, 194, 195, 209

Biological mechanism, 206

Biopolitics, 26, 75, 127, 128, 212

Biopower, 127, 128, 212

G.J.S. Dei, *Reframing Blackness and Black Solidarities through Anti-colonial and Decolonial Prisms*, Critical Studies of Education 4, DOI 10.1007/978-3-319-53079-6